Another America

Another America

THE STORY OF LIBERIA
AND THE FORMER SLAVES
WHO RULED IT

★

James Ciment

 Hill and Wang

A division of Farrar, Straus and Giroux

New York

Hill and Wang
A division of Farrar, Straus and Giroux
18 West 18th Street, New York 10011

Copyright © 2013 by James Ciment
All rights reserved
Published in 2013 by Hill and Wang
First paperback edition, 2014

The Library of Congress has cataloged the hardcover edition as follows:
Ciment, James.
    Another America : the story of Liberia and the former slaves who
ruled it / James Ciment. — 1st ed.
        p.   cm.
    Includes index.
    ISBN 978-0-8090-9542-1   ISBN 978-0-8090-2695-1
    1. Liberia—History.   2. African Americans—Colonization—
Liberia.   3. Liberia—Relations—United States.   4. United
States—Relations—Liberia.   I. Title.

DT631. C56 2013
966.62—dc23
                                                        2012051089

Paperback ISBN: 978-0-8090-2695-1

Designed by Jonathan D. Lippincott

Our books may be purchased in bulk for promotional, educational, or business use.
Please contact your local bookseller or the Macmillan Corporate and Premium
Sales Department at 1-800-221-7945, extension 5442, or by e-mail at
MacmillanSpecialMarkets@macmillan.com.

www.fsgbooks.com
www.twitter.com/fsgbooks • www.facebook.com/fsgbooks

P1

For Gloria

In coming to the shores of Africa, we indulged the pleasing hope that we would be permitted to exercise and improve those faculties which impart to man his dignity; to nourish in our hearts the flame of honorable ambition; to cherish and indulge these aspirations which a beneficent Creator had implanted in every human heart, and to evince to all who despise, ridicule, and oppress our race that we possess with them a common nature; are with them susceptible of equal refinement, and capable to equal advancement in all that adorns and dignifies man.　　　　　—Liberian Declaration of Independence, 1847

Blessed are the meek: for they shall inherit the earth.
　　　　　　　　　　　　　　　　　　　—Matthew 5:5

CONTENTS

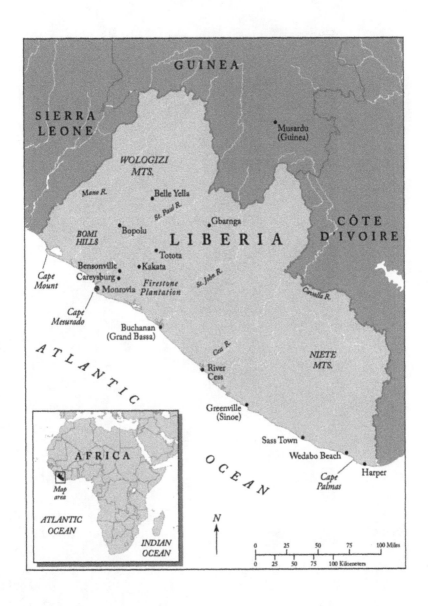

PREFACE

On the afternoon of April 22, 1980, Gabriel Nimely, the Republic of Liberia's newly installed information minister, summoned forty or so foreign reporters to the pressroom of the Executive Mansion, which overlooked the Atlantic from its perch in Monrovia, the Liberian capital. "Gentlemen," he announced, "you are all invited to some executions at Barclay Beach."[1] Ten days before and seven floors above, soldiers under the command of Nimely's new boss, Master Sergeant Samuel Doe, had burst into the presidential bedroom and gunned down William Tolbert, the last in an unbroken, 133-year line of improbable rulers—freed slaves and free blacks who had fled America, established black Africa's first republic, and passed it on to their descendants.

The reporters raced to the nearby oceanfront in taxis. When they arrived, they found hundreds of soldiers and thousands of civilians milling about excitedly, the focus of their attention nine telephone poles hastily erected atop a gently sloping dune. After a short while, a white Volkswagen bus pulled up. Soldiers pulled thirteen men from it, all condemned officials from the previous administration. They included, among others, Richard Henries, the former Speaker of the House; Joseph Chesson, the much-hated justice minister; and Frank Tolbert, president pro-tem of the Senate and older brother of the recently murdered president. All had endured ten days of confinement and humiliation in front of kangaroo court tribunals, and looked the part. They were unshaven and their clothes were torn. Some appeared to have been beaten. The soldiers stripped them to their waists and then grabbed nine and tied them to the poles with a single long strand of green rope.

It took half an hour for the noncommissioned officers in charge to clear the line of fire, as many of the soldiers were drunk and shouting epithets at the men. Two of the older prisoners passed out; the cloudless sky, so typical of late dry-season weather in Monrovia, offered no protection from the equatorial sun. Finally, nine rifle-wielding soldiers opened fire. Several missed their targets. Other soldiers, armed with machine guns, ran up and poured bullets into the now slumped-over bodies. The dead were untied and left lying at the base of the poles as the four remaining prisoners were lined up. This time, there was no pretense of order. When the shooting stopped, there was a brief silence and then cheering, first from the soldiers and then from the crowd. As one enlisted man told a reporter, the men had "no right to live" after all those years "killing our people and stealing our money."[2]

It was a rage generations in the making.

Like many American high school students, I first learned of Liberia in passing—a brief aside from the heroic story of abolitionism and the headlong rush to civil war. That tiny colorless patch surrounded by British pink and French blue on colonial maps of Africa intrigued me. What happened to those freed slaves who had gone back to Africa? An answer of sorts came from the photos of the 1980 executions that appeared on the front pages of newspapers across the world. I began to think of Liberia as a noble experiment that had ended awfully. Freed slaves, given the chance to govern themselves, had turned out to be no better than the white imperialists who had descended upon Africa around the same time. If there was any lesson to be taken from Liberian history, it was a general one about human nature: an oppressed people could readily become oppressors.

Events after 1980, especially the civil war that began on Christmas Eve, 1989—it would prove to be one of the most brutal in postcolonial Africa's bloodstained history, shocking the world with images of drugged child soldiers, costumed as if for Halloween, AK-47s hanging loosely from their skinny brown shoulders—led to a new round of questions. What could possibly have led to this? What role did that century and a half of Americo-Liberian rule play in the terror that followed? And, again, what had happened to the descendants of the former American slaves who founded the nation? When a temporary peace came in the late 1990s, I traveled to Liberia to find out.

It was not easy to get to then, not even from Abidjan, the commercial capital of neighboring Ivory Coast. There were no regular flights to Liberia—the country's international airport had been destroyed—but there was an expat Ukrainian operation running Soviet-era turboprops into the country. From the air, I saw that Liberia began where the roads ended. For the next two hundred miles, there was nothing but endless forest and the occasional village of conical-roofed huts. Liberia appeared unchanged from Graham Greene's descriptions of the country sixty years earlier, in his travelogue *Journey Without Maps*.

On the ground, however, recent history was all too evident. Monrovia was in ruins, having been the objective, in 1996, of the last great offensive of the civil war, a battle residents referred to with the shorthand "April 6." Few buildings had windows; many bore the distinctive gaping holes that rocket-propelled grenades left behind. Still, there were people everywhere—along the streets, in the rubble, on the beaches. When Doe took power in 1980, Monrovia was home to 100,000 residents. Now it had a million, mostly refugees from the war-torn countryside.

My residence was a large, well-appointed house on the heights of Mamba Point, once Monrovia's ritziest oceanfront address. With its manicured tropical gardens and solid Mediterranean furniture, the house could have been in Florida. It appeared untouched by the war. And, indeed, it hadn't been. Its owner, a scion of one of the wealthiest

and most powerful America-Liberian families, had been the country's sports minister before the war and had recruited a score of burly
soccer players to stand guard on his property.

Getting into town every day proved difficult. Monrovia's fleet of
taxis, many in no better shape than its buildings, did not cruise the
district where I was staying. So each morning, before the sun got too
hot, I would climb the small hill that separated Mamba Point from
downtown. Above and to my left stood the Ducor Hotel, where the
America elite had once danced through the night at weddings and
debutante balls. To the right loomed the gray stone, fortress-like Masonic Temple, the largest in Africa, where America politicians met in
conclaves to decide the fate of the nation they still ran. Both buildings were derelict now, each occupied by hundreds of refugees.

During my trips into Monrovia proper and up-country, when I
would hitch a ride with aid workers, I interviewed everyone I could:
politicians, military men, church leaders, journalists, human rights
activists, businessmen, ex–child soldiers, ordinary citizens. These
were Americoes (many of whom still occupied high places in Liberian society), natives, and people of mixed heritage. Almost to a person,
I was greeted warmly. Having never been the subjects of Western
imperialists, Liberians evince little animus toward white people.
They also genuinely like Americans. In the interviews, I sensed that
many felt we were practically kin, though the sentiment always
seemed tinged with disappointment. As one refugee recalled won-
dering as he watched helicopters rescue American personnel from
the embassy during "April 6," "We think America is a big brother.
What do they think of us now? They all want us to die here?"

I tried to examine the nation's archives, but they had been destroyed in the fighting. Fortunately, I found when I returned home
that substantial records had been preserved in this country: Liberian
and foreign newspapers, official and personal papers, travel accounts,
memoirs, and thousands of letters the America settlers wrote home
to their families and their former masters. First impressions confirmed suspicions. The America-Liberian ruling class had been cor-

rupt, callow, and callous, at one time even being accused by an international tribunal of running a slave ring.

But as I progressed through the literature, the story acquired nuance and specificity. The kinship contemporary Liberians of all backgrounds felt with Americans had deeper and more meaningful roots than I—and perhaps even my interviewees—had ever imagined. The early settlers of Liberia brought the mores of their homeland with them. They arrived in West Africa full of entrepreneurial energy but also with a propensity to settle disputes with violence. Their benevolence was inseparable from their firm conviction that theirs was a superior civilization. In Africa, they endeavored to re-create the only social and political order they knew, that of the antebellum South—with themselves as the master class. They erected buildings in the style of plantation mansions and dressed in formal nineteenth-century clothes, despite the equatorial climate. They adopted the symbols of home, evident in the red-white-and-blue lone-star flag and the Liberian dollar. They established familiar institutions: one-room schoolhouses, fraternal organizations, and evangelical churches. A few of the more well-to-do settlers carved plantations out of the jungle and, from columned porches, sent orders to the natives tilling their cotton, tobacco, and coffee crops. The Americoes by and large equated liberty with the pursuit of money, and venerated the merchants among them who made small fortunes trading with Westerners. Most telling, they established a republic but kept it for themselves. The Liberian Declaration of Independence began, "We, the people of the Republic of Liberia were originally the inhabitants of the United States of North America." The Liberian constitution largely ignored the natives, except as objects of paternalist protection—much like the slaves the Americoes had once been, at least in the minds of the planters who owned them.

But Liberia occupies a mere slice of land, and the Americo population never topped 20,000. Just as the history of the United States is inseparable from the vastness of the North American continent, the history of Liberia is inseparable from its geographic and demographic smallness. The Americoes, especially the Monrovia elite, intermarried so often that a few generations into their history many of them were related in one way or another. As in America, the elite had a dynastic quality: politicians begat politicians, and the right last name could mean everything. But in Liberia the circle was a fraction of the size. The Americoes' history can be seen as a family saga, spanning generations and rife with profligate sons and malcontent daughters, strivers and schemers, scandal and achievement. It has the feel, the richness, of a novel. Viewing the Americoes in this light leads one to see tragedy, not justice, in their violent demise at the hands of a people they by and large oppressed. Hidebound by their Americanness and surrounded and outnumbered by natives, they could never reconcile their idealism with their pursuit of power and wealth, and with their very survival.

This book is about how that tension between idealism and survival defined a nation. The freed slaves and free blacks who first colonized the Windward Coast, and the whites who sent them, disagreed on many things, including who should run the colony. They did agree that, if nothing else, Liberia should be a black man's place. They meant different things by this, of course. Liberia was born of a white idea: that the burgeoning and unwanted population of free blacks and emancipated slaves in post-Revolutionary America could be sent to Africa. The early nineteenth-century politicians who devised this idea considered it an inspired one. America could rid itself of its most "useless and pernicious" class of people while simultaneously establishing a beachhead from which Africa could be civilized and Christianized.

The settlers who eventually signed up to be a part of the experiment, meanwhile, dreamed only of a free haven for all persons of African descent. But their idealism was hard to sustain on the Windward Coast. To the natives, the settlers, though they looked uncannily like themselves, were just another group of outsiders with hostile intentions. They called the newcomers the "black white men" and attacked their settlements. As one early settler explained in a letter to his former master in America, you can try to help the natives but "they still will be your enemy."[3] This was not entirely fair. The settlers did plenty of their own provoking. But the remark was revealing, as it was a sign that the erosion of the settlers' idealism started almost concurrently with the experiment itself. The settlers, and later the Americoes, could never really decide whether the Africans were their long-lost brethren, heathens to be redeemed, or savages to be conquered. And in almost every instance, they put their survival over their ideals.

Not that every Liberian was determined to keep the native in his place, beyond the frontier or laboring for a pittance in settler households and on settler farms. Edward Blyden, Liberia's greatest intellectual and one of the progenitors of black nationalism, condemned his countrymen for their reluctance to truly integrate with the natives. He thought that the Americoes were uniquely positioned to create a new kind of civilization, part African communalist traditions and part progressive Western thought. He even got one of his allies, Edmund Roye, elected president in 1870, though this had less to do with African solidarity than it did with the resentment the dark-skinned majority of poor Americoes, many of them fresh from slavery, had for the mulatto elite.

The ideal of Liberia as a haven for blacks endured after Blyden's time, though the welcome was now a more conditional one. Liberia did everything it could to lure new immigrants from America, offering them farm lots or town plots, immediate citizenship, and racial supremacy: Nobody except persons of African descent could be citizens, the Constitution declared. But in the 1920s when Marcus Garvey promised to send tens of thousands of American blacks to Liberia in the largest back-to-Africa effort in history, the Liberian elite demurred, worried that his provocative anticolonialist rhetoric would hurt its relations with the West.

This kind of survival had its perks. The Americoes, strengthening

their ties to the West in the aftermath of World War II, began to prosper. Tire and steel manufacturers across the world came to Liberia
for its rubber and iron ore, making possible the rise of an Americo
middle class. Many Liberians saw their influence and wealth peak in
the 1950s and 1960s. This was the era of those fancy-dress balls at
the Ducor Hotel; of Americoes going on shopping trips to the White
Rose Supermarket in their American sedans; and of vacations in
Europe.

But even as they thrived, their world was coming undone. The
liberation of much of the rest of the continent from European rule
turned Liberia, with its slavishly American culture and pro-Western
foreign policy, into an anachronism. At home, concubinage, intermarriage, and the ward system—through which Americo families adopted
native children, inculcating them with civilization and Christianity—
were slowly blurring the line between the Americoes and the more
educated classes of natives. Many of the radical leaders whose ideas
inspired Doe in the spring of 1980 were the half-breed products of
these institutions.

There was a profound irony to all of this. One hundred and thirty-
three years of putting survival ahead of idealism, a tenable strategy
for its time, was what ultimately led to the demise of Americo-
Liberian rule and the Americo-Liberian way of life. Anxious that the
African masses would overwhelm them politically, they gave them
little say in the republic; fearing the idea of going native, they clung
to their Western culture and forced the Africans they admitted into
their ranks to give up theirs. Finally, the very people the Americoes
had done so much to co-opt or keep down had had enough and rose
up against them. For the Americoes, being in Africa but not of it
proved an impossible proposition in the end.

Yet if irony pervades Liberian history, so do hope and courage.
They have from the very beginning, when the first settlers left this
country with dreams of a better one, in a land that, despite their ancestry, they knew almost nothing about.

Another America

ONE

The Black *Mayflower*

Even to the casual waterfront visitor, there would have been something unusual about the departure preparations of the *Elizabeth*, an otherwise ordinary-looking three-masted ship berthed on New York City's North River. The goods being loaded onto it—farm equipment, artisan tools, the materials to build a gristmill, enough weaponry to arm a company of troops—were neither the bulk freight of commerce nor the baggage of travelers planning on a return voyage. The appearance of the *Elizabeth*'s passengers would have likewise caught the eye: they were all either black or mulatto. Most had their families with them, including a couple of dozen children, though there were a few single men and women, too. And on this last day in January 1820, they were about the only people in motion on the normally bustling waterfront.

New York City was then on the cusp of greatness, primed to become the young and unnaturally restless nation's gateway to the world. The change was most noticeable in the speed and scale of things. Just two years earlier, a transplanted English merchant named Jeremiah Thompson—having made an unparalleled fortune in cotton—launched his Black Ball Line, which offered the first regularly scheduled voyages in modern maritime history. At first devoted to freight, the packet ships were quickly adapted to passenger traffic by former merchants in the now-illegal slave trade eager to wring a profit from the business of moving impoverished immigrants across the Atlantic.

But on that bitterly cold day in early 1820, nature intervened. Global temperatures at the tail end of the "little ice age," as historians call the three centuries between the early 1500s and 1800s, were on average only about a degree colder than normal, but that was enough for the North River to routinely freeze over. Commerce slowed down but New Yorkers did not. So popular were winter promenades across the ice that vendors, many of them former slave women (New York's last slave would not be freed until 1827), set up stands to sell smoked oysters, roasted corn, and baked sweet potatoes from the Manhattan docks to the Jersey Palisades.

For the ninety-odd passengers and crew aboard the *Elizabeth*, however, the ice was no playground. For six days, they struggled with pikes and shovels to break the ship free. As they did so, the passenger list shrank. The Joshua Moses family of Philadelphia, laid low by illness, returned to shore with "seeming reluctance."[1] The body of a two-year-old was carried off the ship to be interred, without fee, in the vault of the African Methodist Episcopal Zion Church, the city's oldest black congregation.

Then came a thaw and, on Sunday, February 6, the ship weighed anchor off White Hall Street, near Battery Park, the naval escort *Cyane* by its side. "We left standing on the wharves, I believe some thousands of people, both white and coloured," recorded one passenger.[2] But even though contemporaries likened the sailing of the *Elizabeth* to that of the *Mayflower* from England exactly two centuries before, the mood was not celebratory. For the "coloured" people in the crowd, it was a solemn occasion; some were there to bid farewell to friends and loved ones, others to witness a bittersweet moment in the history of their people. For the whites in attendance, there was satisfaction of various sorts. A few saw a group of despised and degraded people at long last set free. Many others simply subtracted ninety or so "niggers" from a population that darkened the soil of a white man's republic.

For the *Elizabeth*'s passengers, the first of thousands of black

Americans who would eventually settle in what would come to be known as Liberia, it was surely a moment of great, and conflicting, emotion: They would have felt sadness over leaving loved ones behind, fear of what awaited them on a continent none of them knew much about, and relief about leaving the burden of race behind. They watched the harbor come alive to enterprise and opportunity as the ice melted, and beyond the harbor they saw a city and a nation with a limitless future—a nation, they had been told since birth in ways both subtle and crude, that did not belong to them.

Little is known of most of these emigrants. They were a mixed lot. Just over half were male, about one-third were children, and roughly two-thirds were residents of either New York or Pennsylvania. About half had a notation in the ship's registry indicating if they were literate or not. (Roughly three-quarters of the respondents were.) Twenty or so had their occupations listed. Of these, about a third were farmers and the rest artisans of various kinds, carpenters constituting the largest group. Just two of the passengers, a nurse from New York City and a popular minister from Baltimore, would qualify as professionals. There was, however, one aspect of their lives that unified them and, at the same time, distinguished them from the vast majority of their fellow African Americans: They were not slaves.

The 1820 census revealed that of the roughly 9.6 million persons, other than nontaxed Indians, living in the twenty-four states and various territories between the Atlantic Ocean and the Missouri River, some 1.75 million were nonwhites, all but a handful of them of African or mixed-African origin. And of these people, just 229,620—or 13 percent—were free, all of them exceptions to two of the oldest rules of antebellum American life: race is destiny and blackness equals slavery.

Daniel Coker and Lott Carey were exceptional men within this exceptional minority. Each had, through hard work and by taking great risks, escaped from bondage and made as much of themselves as early nineteenth-century America allowed a black man to make. And each, as he pushed up against the limits of freedom, would relinquish one struggle only to take up another, abandoning the only country that he knew for a continent that, by all contemporary accounts, was a land of "burning sun and tortuous [*sic*] insects—poisonous exhalations, corrupted water . . . unwholesome food,"[3] and savage men, a "graveyard" for civilized persons. Coker sailed on the *Elizabeth*, while Lott would leave a year later on the ship that followed. Each, in turn, would lead the first emigrants as they struggled to survive in West Africa. Beyond these similarities, though, their lives and fates could not have been more different.

Coker was a child of relative privilege, if that word can be applied to a black man of his race and time. He was born in Frederick, Maryland, around 1780, the son of a slave and an Irish indentured servant who worked on a neighboring plantation. While his parentage represented that rarer and more scandalous of interracial liaisons—black man, white woman—mixed-race persons were often the rule rather than the exception in free black communities throughout the South. Mulattoes were typically the first to be manumitted, and they often exited bondage with a trade or a rudimentary education, skills that helped them better navigate freedom. But they also lived in racial limbo, not always trusted by their darker free black neighbors and viewed by many whites as an affront to the God-given racial order. Coker himself would take up such attitudes, later declaring racial amalgamation "truly disgraceful to both colours."[4]

Coker was not born free, odd given the laws and customs of the South, where the mother's status usually passed to the child. But he became a favorite around the plantation and the inseparable companion of one of his master's sons, who refused to go to school without him. The "peculiar institution," of course, made no room for the education of slaves, and for good reason. A literate slave often meant a discontented slave, and one with the ability to make his way in the wider world. Coker's life offered all the evidence slave owners would have needed for the proscription. He escaped to New York City in his teens, joining one of the largest free black communities in the country, and by twenty was a lay minister. In 1801, he returned to his home state and became the first black teacher at the African Academy, a school for free blacks, and the first licensed black minister in Baltimore, even though technically he remained a slave until he was purchased and freed by a Quaker abolitionist five years later.

The ambitious Coker went on to found his own school and, in 1810, blazed yet another trail by writing *A Dialogue Between a Virginian and an African Minister*, the first abolitionist tract published by an African American. Frustrated at the reluctance of white church officials to let black members run their own affairs, he set up his own Methodist congregation in 1814 and raised the money to buy a building to preach in. Two years later, he joined with the pioneering churchman Richard Allen of Philadelphia to found the African Methodist Episcopal Church, the first national black church. But Coker soon had a falling-out with Allen and the congregation, though over what is not exactly clear. It may have had to do with color, as many members objected to a mixed-race person—contemporary accounts and portraits reveal Coker as extremely light-skinned, with pronounced Caucasian features—becoming bishop. Ultimately, the dark-skinned Allen was chosen. Or it may have had to do with his views on African colonization.

In the first decades of the nineteenth century, free blacks represented the fastest-growing segment of the American population. Many of them had run away during the revolution, while others had been freed by slave owners who took the rhetoric of the struggle against Britain—"*all* men are created equal"—to heart. Since even these enlightened masters—George Washington, most notably— usually stipulated that freedom would be granted upon their deaths, manumissions surged after 1800. Nowhere was this population explosion more evident than in the three-state region (Delaware, Maryland, and Virginia) surrounding the Chesapeake, a region that was home to a majority of immigrants to Liberia and to the white men who sent them there.

The idea of colonization was not new in 1820. Thomas Jefferson, for one, had broached it in his *Notes on the State of Virginia*, written just five years after the Declaration of Independence. "Among the Romans emancipation required but one effort," Jefferson wrote. "The slave [usually of the same race], when made free, might mix with, without staining the blood of his master. But with us a second is necessary, unknown to history. When freed, he is to be removed beyond the reach of mixture."[5] Like most other people of his era, Jefferson loathed the idea of racial amalgamation, but there was also a degree of patronizing charity in his conclusion—being the inferior race, free blacks could never possibly compete with whites and so would become a permanent, and permanently oppressed, underclass.

The burgeoning free black population of the early 1800s added a new element to the equation: fear. In the paranoid depths of the white imagination, free blacks represented a threat to order: they loitered, they stole, they fenced goods pilfered by slaves, they hid runaway slaves or shepherded them to freedom, and, worst of all, in the dark of night, they gathered with their still-enslaved friends and family in dirt-floored plantation cabins, infecting them with tales of an idle and carefree life on the other side. Their very presence lowered property values.

It was with these fears in mind that a group of men met on the evening of the winter solstice of 1816, in the tavern of the Davis Hotel in Washington, a smoky, shabby brick affair that was nevertheless a favorite haunt of the district's power brokers. Attending this initial plenary session of what would come to be called the American Colonization Society was a veritable who's who of early nineteenth-century movers and shakers: Congressman John Randolph of Virginia, Representative Robert Wright of Maryland, several members of the prestigious Lee clan, the lobbyist (and part-time lyricist) Francis Scott Key, the aging "lion of New Hampshire," Senator Daniel Webster, as well as key members of the clergy, the business community, and the law profession.* Although not in attendance, Bushrod Washington— Supreme Court justice and closest living link to his demigod uncle— agreed to serve as the new society's president, though in what all viewed as a figurehead capacity.

No attendee commanded more respect than the man presiding over the meeting. Henry Clay, "Star of the West" and the Speaker of the House of Representatives, was the second most powerful individual in America. Later known as "the great compromiser" for his attempts to forge a North-South consensus on slavery, no one represented the conventional wisdom of Washington better than Clay. His opening remarks set the tone of the meeting and the course of the organization: "Can there be a nobler cause," he asked, "than that which, whilst it proposed to rid our country of a useless and pernicious, if not dangerous portion of its population, contemplates the spreading of the arts of civilized life, and the possible redemption from ignorance and barbarism of a benighted quarter of the globe!"[6] The benighted quarter Clay and his audience had in mind was Africa.

Clay's words were inspiring, even if they amounted to a call for what later generations would have called ethnic cleansing. But what magical transformation did he expect to occur during the crossing that would turn a "useless and pernicious" people into heralds of "civilized life"? And who had the money or ships to send the hundreds of thousands of free blacks to Africa anyway? Ultimately, the society would extract a risibly inadequate $100,000 from Congress, under the guise of establishing a haven for recaptives—Africans rescued by the U.S. Navy from the recently banned international slave trade—and raise modest sums from supporters, mostly through appeals

---

*The appeal of colonization persisted for decades, especially among moderates on both sides of the slavery question. Abraham Lincoln, for one, was an advocate up through the early years of his presidency, though he preferred the more accessible Central America or Haiti as destinations.

to evangelical congregations in the North and Upper South.* Still, as overblown as Clay's rhetoric now seems, and as daunting the logistical obstacles to the goal he set for the ACS were, his plan had an even more fundamental flaw—as events one hundred miles to the north would soon reveal.

It did not take long for word of the ACS's founding to spread to Philadelphia's free black community, the nation's largest and most influential. Its leading members—including Allen, Coker, and one of America's richest black men, the sail manufacturer James Forten— supported the ACS's plan on first hearing it, until they presented it to the men and women whose interests they purported to represent. A public meeting convened in mid-January to calmly discuss the merits and defects of colonization quickly turned into something else entirely, as speaker after speaker blasted the motives, methods, and aims of the ACS. Then Forten put the question to the three thousand attendees at the Bethel Church. The "aye" vote was met by a resounding hush while the "nay," he reported, "seemed as it would bring down the walls of the building."[7]

The community's uniform response startled its leadership. After all, the very first effort at colonization, an expedition of thirty-eight led by the wealthy whaling merchant Paul Cuffe the year before, had spurred vigorous debate in the free black community, not outright condemnation. But then Cuffe was black. Whereas Philadelphia's black leadership frequently met with well-meaning white reformers and evangelicals as near equals, ordinary free blacks knew only fear in their encounters with whites. As Forten's own granddaughter later wrote, "there was no Northern city in which colored people were so badly treated as in that 'City of Brotherly Love.'"[8] So when whites started making plans to remove free blacks, it sounded awfully like a

---

*President James Monroe's crucial role in securing the $100,000 led to the first Liberian settlement being named after him. Today, Monrovia has the distinction of being the only capital in the world named for the elected leader of another country.

sophisticated form of kidnapping, a phenomenon so rife in Philadelphia that Allen himself was once captured by a kidnapper who claimed with straight face to have recently purchased America's most prominent black ecclesiastic.

But now that the people had spoken, the leadership responded. The official declaration of the meeting questioned everything the colonization society stood for—from its "unmerited stigma . . . upon the reputation of the free people of color" to its assumption that blacks should and would return to Africa. The United States was just as much their home as any white person's, while colonization was but a "circuitous route" back to slavery.[9] Most ominously for those ACS members who saw in colonization a means to protect slavery, the Philadelphia blacks resolved that they would "never separate [themselves] voluntarily from the slave population of the country."[10] Later meetings even targeted cooperative blacks as "a few obscure and dissatisfied strangers among us . . . in favor of being made presidents, governors and principals, in Africa."[11] This last comment may explain why Coker, a man conflicted over his racial identity and possibly rejected for leadership of the African Methodist Episcopal by darker-skinned parishioners, decided to cast his lot with the ACS.

Despite the suspicions and misgivings of lower-class blacks, Coker and the ACS eventually attracted eighty-two willing emigrants. History is silent as to what exactly motivated them, what made them different from the hundreds of thousands of their fellow free blacks who opted not to go, but the letters and writings of later emigrants offer some suggestions. Beyond escaping the indignities, inequities, and outright dangers free black men and women faced in a white's man's country, there were more proactive reasons for going. The more evangelical of the emigrants no doubt bought into the ACS's rhetoric about delivering the light of the Gospel to a benighted continent. Others certainly sensed economic opportunities that had been largely denied them in their native country—land to farm, trade to pursue, businesses to start. And, of course, there was the simple hope that they would be able to determine their own fate, make their own laws, and elect their own leaders. They were Americans, after all. Even if they had not enjoyed such freedoms yet, they knew what these freedoms were worth and wanted them for themselves.

To that end, the settlers drew up a compact, its contents sadly lost to history. Whether they did so before their departure or mid-voyage is also not known. But contemporaries who were familiar with it say it was modeled after the Mayflower Compact, drawn up by the Pilgrims two centuries earlier. If so, it was a brief document, pledging the settlers to the service of God in their new home and proposing a civil government, under their own leadership and with the power to make laws for the community.

But it was not to be. Unbeknownst to the *Elizabeth*'s passengers, the ACS and the federal government, which helped fund the expedition, had something very different in mind. In their view, free blacks—not to mention the freed slaves who were expected to follow in their wake—were not ready for meaningful self-government. Just look at the squalor of their communities in America, the sponsors insisted, and their licentiousness, though this latter conclusion was less the product of observation than the prurient musings of white minds. No, these people needed guidance, with a firm hand and for a long time to come, before they might be able to run their own affairs.

In the meantime, those affairs would remain the responsibility of the three white agents aboard the *Elizabeth*, one from the ACS and two dispatched by the government to run the recaptive program, including that program's leader, the evangelical minister and former U.S. marine Samuel Bacon. Unsurprisingly, the dictatorial powers the ACS placed in the hands of its agents did not sit well with the colonists, who only learned of them during the voyage. Jehudi Ashmun, Bacon's contemporary biographer and a future ACS agent himself, noted that "it was but too apparent that a mutinous spirit was secretly working in the minds of some of the people on board."[12]

Bacon did not respond to the grumblings himself, asking the colonists' unofficial leader to do so instead. But Coker, for all his antislavery credentials, rubbed the hotheads among the colonists the wrong way. He not only refused to stand up to the agents, he sided with them. At one point, Coker lined the men up on deck and ordered them to sign a petition expressing "full confidence in the judgment and sincere friendship of the agents."[13] In his journal that night, he vented, "It appears to me the height of ingratitude to manifest any distrust . . . of the agents, after such proof as they have given, not to say any thing of their having left friends and the comforts of civilized life."[14] Fair enough, but the next day's entry found him lavishing praise on a far less worthy candidate. "May these children [of the colonists] ever cherish a grateful remembrance of this benevolent and humane act [i.e., sponsoring colonization] of the country that gave them birth . . ."[15]

How much of this diary talk came out in Coker's shipboard sermons is not known, but there would soon be revealed another reason for the colonists' distrust of him: Coker would help draw up the plan giving life-and-death power over provisions to the ACS agent, a decision that would nearly undo the great experiment when it was just getting started and was at its most vulnerable.

It took the *Elizabeth* just over a month to reach Africa. The crossing was not without its moments of drama. The colonists endured storms, "a dangerous leak . . . providentially discovered," and witnessed a vicious fight between two dogs that nearly triggered a brawl between the black passengers and white sailors.[16] Finally, on March 9, 1820, the disgruntled and seasick colonists arrived at Freetown. They were greeted by a haunting sight: a ghost armada bobbing and creaking in the green waters of one of West Africa's most magnificent natural harbors. Framed by verdant hills and the stone walls of Fort Thornton, these dozens of captured slave ships rotted in the tropical humidity of the wettest colonial outpost in the British Empire.

Liberia, then simply known to sailors as the Windward Coast, did not yet exist, of course, and would not for another two years. Sierra

Leone, the colony Britain had founded as a refuge for its own free blacks and recaptives, was the obvious destination for the ACS, especially now that the United States and Britain were no longer at war. Several years before, the society had sent two agents to evaluate Sherbro, a large, coast-hugging island about sixty miles south of Freetown. Despite the evident hostility of the island's eponymous native tribe and the many shortcomings of the miasmic spot their chiefs were willing to cede, the agents wrote a glowing report, largely based on the sales pitch made by one John Kizell.

An island native who had been captured as a boy, shipped to South Carolina, and then freed by the British during the Revolution, Kizell had returned to Sherbro, where he became a local trader and intermediary between natives and British officials. At once charming and unctuous, the former slave genuinely seemed to believe in the colonization idea, having befriended the whaler Cuffe a few years earlier. But then, as a merchant, he had a clear pecuniary interest in seeing a shipload of well-provisioned African Americans settle down in the vicinity of his trading post, a site known as Campelair. Hawking Sherbro's advantages, he failed to inform the two ACS agents that the local water supply was so foul that he had barrels of clean water shipped in. He showed them miles of forest and savannah, confidently predicting that the chiefs would gladly sell what appeared to be empty wilderness but was, in fact, the fallow component of the local slash-and-burn agricultural system. He also insisted the natives would welcome both the trade and the civilizing influence the colonists would bring. What Kizell left out of his pitch was as important as what he included. Despite his local upbringing, he had little influence with the island's chiefs, who were wary of him for his connections with the British and looked down on him for his westernized ways. And these same chiefs, who had no concept of owning land, were never going to sell the soil of their ancestors to the newcomers, even if they shared the same skin color.

British colonial officials and merchants were equally unwelcoming, as the experiences of the Cuffe expedition survivors encountered by Coker in Freetown made clear. Fearing an influx of independent-minded New World blacks, apprenticed in American democracy and likely to establish competitive trading relations with the United States, a recent enemy in the War of 1812, they had tried to thwart colonization efforts from the beginning, leaving Cuffe's settlers impoverished and isolated. Those fresh off the *Elizabeth* encountered the same ill feelings. The British authorities told the ACS agents in no uncertain terms that they could remain in port for no more than fifteen days. The latter remained undeterred, though, since Sherbro, not Freetown, was their ultimate destination and because they had to move quickly in order to start building the colony before the rainy season set in. But the captain of the *Elizabeth* balked when he was asked to steer his ship across the notorious sandbars around Sherbro.

John Bankson, Bacon's assistant, looked out at the vessel-strewn Freetown harbor and came up with the obvious solution. With a huge cauldron for boiling rations of rice still bolted to its deck, the shallow-drafted Spanish schooner *Augusta*, only a few months removed from hauling slaves across the Atlantic, could be used to haul the colonists. To Coker, this development was another sign of Providence's mysterious ways.

"Dear Mother," the colonist Nathaniel Peck wrote on March 27, 1820, a week after his arrival at Campelair, Kizell's post on Sherbro Island. "It is with pleasure I take up my pen to tell you that I am well . . . I am now treading the soil of my mother country—thanks be to God! and find that it is good . . . The natives receive us with joy and gladness. The climate is very mild and good."[17] A twenty-two-year-old miller from Maryland, Peck had every reason to be hopeful. The weather was indeed fine, the natives did celebrate the colonists' arrival, and Kizell, who had built a dozen houses in preparation for the new arrivals, appeared to be the ideal host. "Get ready to go," he told his mother in closing.[18] In fact, Mrs. Peck would never follow her son to Africa and Nathaniel would soon be fleeing for his life.

It did not take long for Peck and the others to learn that things were not as they seemed at Campelair. The natives' apparent joy at their arrival had less to do with the return of Africa's lost sons and daughters than with the wealth of cargo they unloaded from the *Augusta*. As for the settlement, it was surrounded by mosquito-infested swamps and barely above the level of the bay itself—the chiefs had been happy to unload the land on Kizell. Still, it was only supposed to be temporary, as negotiations for a better site were to commence immediately. Gazing from the beach, Coker remarked, "the land we hope to get on the main [part of the island], is much higher. We can see from here high ridges of mountains, covered with tall trees; it is said that the water there is very good and plenty."[19]

Soon, though, it became clear that the locals were not keen on African American colonization and Kizell was not the influential broker he claimed to be. Within days of arriving, Bacon began pushing Kizell to set up a general council of the chiefs in order to negotiate for a tract of land in the island's interior. But Kizell procrastinated, so Bacon took the lead, setting out for the village of King Fara, the local headman, with Kizell, reduced to a translator, in tow. "We were received and seated in the *palaver* or *council house*, on native mats . . . and after our presents had been produced and accepted, the palaver began," Bacon wrote. "I stated through Mr. Kizell, the objects of our visit to Africa, and the benefits likely to accrue to the native tribes, from our religion, agriculture, and the mechanic arts."[20] Fara smiled and nodded and then said there was nothing he could do. Authority lay with King Sherbro. Bacon ventured on, visiting village after village, but everywhere was told the same thing: talk to the king. As for Kizell, Bacon began to sense that he was not just unable, but unwilling, to set up a meeting with Sherbro. There was no time to lose.

From the time it starts in April through its end in November, the rainy season, inaugurated by howling windstorms that mariners of the day called "tornadoes," brings torrential downpours to Sherbro that can last for days on end. Farming is impossible, life is miserable and, in an age before mosquito netting and chloroquine, very tenuous.

The settlers began to sicken even before the first drops fell. By April 6, twenty-one of them were incapacitated. Two days later, the number had risen to thirty-five, two-thirds of whom "exhibited symptoms of a dangerous character; and all, appeared to be hourly getting worse," Bacon recounted. "There are eight entire families sick, amongst whom there is not one able to cook his own food, or wait upon a child."[21] The former marine captain turned evangelical preacher—who combined physical stamina with a zeal for benevolence—ran himself ragged tending to them, and hazarded some guesses as to the causes of the epidemic. "I reckon the following as the principal:—a too free use of the country fruits—the neglect of personal cleanliness—alternative exposure to the sun, and the dampness of the night—the want of flooring in the huts."[22] Fruit consumption aside, none of this could have helped but it did not matter in the end. The settlers were dying of malaria and the vector was the mosquito—specifically, the female anopheline mosquito—endemic to the region and especially prevalent in swampy, low-lying spots like Campelair.

Days went by and more new arrivals fell ill. "I passed the day," Bacon wrote in his journal, "in visiting the sick, inquiring into their wants, and administering medicines. Wherever I move, I meet little besides groans and tears."[23] The symptoms were excruciating. "These consisted," he noted, "of pains in the head, back, limbs, attended with inflammation of the eyes, lassitude, and depression of spirits . . . The fever is bilious, and in many cases attended with delirium."[24] The sick were suffering from diarrhea and high fever and were extremely dehydrated. But the expedition had brought little potable water and the local supply was undrinkable. Bacon was all but alone, as Crozer, the ACS agent-physician, had gone with the schooner to fetch more supplies from the *Elizabeth*.

The colonists, at least those with any energy left, grew angry. Absent from the ACS's plans was any sense of the dangers awaiting them or advice on how to survive in their new home. At Sherbro, the colonists drew up a petition demanding that they be moved and, if their request be denied by the agents, that they take direction of their own affairs, including the immediate distribution of the remaining provisions. According to John Dix, surgeon aboard the *Cyane*, which had escorted the *Elizabeth* across the Atlantic, "[the colonists] consider the Agents as sent out to take care of the goods, and to deliver them as the colonists choose."[25] The opinion of the colonists, Dix noted in his report to Navy Secretary Smith Thompson, was that their days of being ordered around by white men ended once they left the white man's country.

Bacon would have none of it. As long as he was in charge, he told an assembly of colonists, he would decide who got how much and when. "I have heard the complaints of the people," Bacon noted in his diary. Bent over a crude table, straining against the dim lantern light of his hut, he gave vent to a rare instance of self-doubt. Were these people he had given up so much for—family, friends, career, and potentially his life—worthy of the sacrifice? They complain "because there is no good water . . . because they were brought to this place—because I did not take possession of the land by force—because the people are visited by sickness—because there is no fresh meat, sugar, molasses, flour, and other luxuries . . . because I cannot give them better tobacco—because the *'palaver'* is not over . . . because the houses are not better . . . They complain of every thing they have; and are clamorous for every thing they have not."[26]

He did not seem to understand that the colonists felt betrayed. While Bacon and Coker insisted a few "mutinous spirits" were responsible for the trouble, the dissatisfaction seems to have been more widespread.[27] Among the many faults in the ACS's plan was the notion that the colonists, as descendants of Africa, enjoyed a special immunity to the "seasoning" fever that afflicted newcomers to the Windward Coast. They did not. And from its advance scouts the society must have known the danger of sending anyone, immune or not, to Africa at the commencement of the rainy season. But in its eagerness to grab government money and launch its first expedition, the ACS ignored the risks involved. Its agents suffered along with the colonists. Bankson fell ill early on, briefly convalesced, then died in May, while Crozer, the only trained physician in the colony but sick almost from the moment the expedition arrived in Campelair, succumbed on April 15. Bacon fell sick that same day.

Despair set in. Not only were the colonists' bodies racked by pain and their minds by delirium—in the end, a quarter of them, mostly women, would die—but they were marooned. If the natives visited their fetid encampment, it was only to steal unguarded supplies, especially rum, which the teetotaling ACS had reluctantly stocked as a necessary commodity to trade with the natives until the day they could be weaned from this "nasty habit" introduced by slavers.[28] According to Dix's report, the natives' actions were yet another source of colonist complaint. "They [the colonists] consider themselves also as citizens of the United States," he wrote, oblivious to the irony, "and entitled to support and protection as such and threaten the natives with our vengeance for every wrong done them."[29] This was only the beginning of the mutual distrust and animosity between the colonists—soon to be Liberians—and the natives they would, over the next century and a half, seek by turns to mollify, trade with, make war on, dispossess, and rule.

As for the British, they were not so much hostile as unconcerned, although given the dire circumstances facing the colonists, there was not much difference between the two. Informed of the epidemic raging at Campelair, the authorities did worse than nothing. While Bacon and dozens of others lay dying, a British schooner arrived and sent two men ashore, including a physician. But according to an embittered Coker, "no entreaties of the dying, suffering people, could prevail with them to remain, or to administer any medicine to the sick . . . Indeed, they manifested a most unfeeling indifference."[30] They did, however, agree with much reluctance to carry Bacon back to Freetown. Yet when the rowboat carrying him came in sight of the British schooner, the latter weighed anchor and sailed off, or so claimed eyewitnesses on shore. For six hours, the oarsmen labored to catch the ship, the ailing Bacon lying between them, unprotected from the sun. Finally, giving up, he directed them to head for a nearby island, where he died on May 2.

The sixty or so remaining settlers huddled in their huts against the onslaught of the rainy season. The healthy and the ailing alike turned to bitter arguing over who was in charge and what was to be done. As he lay dying back in April, Crozer had done the necessary but once unthinkable thing: he transferred his authority to one of the colonists— Coker, of course. Many of the colonists, however, had long since lost faith in a man they considered the society's lackey. Nor did the Reverend help his cause. Why had he left his wife and children behind in America, some colonists wanted to know. Why, amid the suffering, had he devoted himself to a Bible school for native children? And why did his faith in the ACS not waver? "My confidence is strong . . . in the honour of your society and the [American] government," he wrote the ACS's board during the crisis. "Tell my brethren to come— not to fear—this land is good—it only wants men to possess it."[31]

Dissent quickly emerged after Bacon's death. According to Coker, the colonists immediately declared themselves "under no man's authority" and refused to obey his orders. They took from the store of provisions as they pleased and threatened him when he tried to stop them. But it was Kizell, the Reverend decided, who was the real source of trouble. To Coker, the man who once welcomed the colonists with open arms was a huckster, a price gouger, and, worst of all, a usurper. Kizell was stirring up the survivors in an effort to take charge of the colony, poisoning the locals' view of Coker—"white blood is good, and black blood is good but . . . mulattoes are bastards," he allegedly told them—and pilfering the lion's share of provisions, distributing them among chiefs to win their allegiance.[32]

Whether Coker panicked at this point is open to interpretation, but he did flee to Freetown soon after Bacon's death and once again put his faith in the counsel of white men. "I found Mr. Coker, on whom all the affairs of the settlement had devolved . . . in a state of the greatest despondency, and on the point of abandoning the settlement," wrote Captain Alexander Wadsworth, a U.S. naval officer on anti-slave-trade patrol, to the ACS secretary, Elias Caldwell. "I advised him to sustain himself in his present situation, till he should receive instructions from the United States, as the ultimate success of the colony depended so materially on such a course."[33] Coker did as he was told, returning to Sherbro with the remaining supplies from the *Elizabeth*. It would be one of his last official duties. Physically exhausted and thoroughly alienated from his fellow colonists, he would elect to settle permanently outside Freetown, where he would sire an influential clan of Krios, the non-native black and mulatto elite who would rule Sierra Leone for its British masters until independence in the 1960s.

In the meantime, however, the new provisions Coker brought from Freetown allowed the surviving settlers to survive the wet months at Campelair. But, as they all agreed, Sherbro was no place to settle. By November, and the end of the rains, the last of the surviving colonists had relocated to the elevated and dry Freetown suburb of Fourah Bay, a desperately needed refuge granted, reluctantly, by the British governor. As news of the Sherbro disaster made its way back to America, the ACS remained committed to the experiment, perhaps, given the catastrophe at Sherbro, even criminally so. The next year, once again backed by federal funds, it launched another expedition destined to arrive in West Africa at the start of the rainy season.

The *Nautilus* dropped anchor in Freetown Harbour almost a year to a day after the *Elizabeth*, bringing with it thirty-four more colonists, including a forty-year-old ne'er-do-well-turned-missionary named Lott Carey. All we know about Carey's life before Africa comes from his own postconversion writings and the accounts of his fellow Baptists, who preferred and needed—for fund-raising purposes—the predictable trajectory from sinner to saint. Still, his backstory is revealing, both in explaining the importance of religion in Carey's decision to cross the Atlantic and in the Liberian story as a whole.

Like Coker, the Virginia-born Carey's early life was as fortunate as a slave could hope for. His family was intact, his father a respected "plantation preacher," and his grandmother Mihala, an African-born healer, still alive.[34] According to Carey, she taught him about his African family, who thirsted for the gospel of Jesus Christ, and related the story of her Middle Passage so that one day he might return to spread the gospel in the land of his ancestors. She had suffered, he believed, so he could save souls.

But Carey, according to his own words, must have been a disappointment to her. On the plantation, he was a hell-raiser, a profane youth given to drinking, gambling, and cursing—habits he indulged in all the more after his master rented him out to a nearby tobacco warehouse owner. But in the fleshpot that was Richmond, Carey eventually found God one Sunday morning in 1807 in the blacks-only gallery of the First Baptist Church. From that day on, he claims, he was a new man—pious, hardworking, determined to better himself. He learned to read and write. On one occasion, according to an oft-repeated story, a white "gentleman" came to the warehouse and interrupted his reading to send him on an errand.[35] While Carey was off attending to the task, the man picked up the book Carey had laid down and saw that it was Adam Smith's *The Wealth of Nations*.

Indeed, Carey applied himself to secular and spiritual pursuits with equal discipline. He rose up the ranks at the warehouse, diligently saving the earnings he was not required to turn over to his owner until, six years after his conversion, he presented his master with a check for $850 to purchase freedom for himself and his two children, his wife having died some time before. His was a rare but not impossible path to freedom for urban slaves in antebellum America. Now a free man, Carey eventually became the supervisor of the warehouse, which came with the solid middle-class salary of $800 per annum. He remarried, had several more children, and settled them on a farm in the suburbs. Carey also took up his father's vocation, becoming an itinerant preacher, respected by his colleagues, even white ones. His sermons, J. B. Taylor, pastor of Richmond's Second Baptist Church noted respectfully, though with some condescension, were "clear of the senseless rant too common among uneducated colored preachers."[36]

Sometime around 1812, Carey caught the missionary bug, a common ailment in early nineteenth-century America. As did other evangelical denominations, the national Baptist leadership tried to harness the newfound fervor among its congregants through institutionalization and fund-raising. It also concluded that Africa offered some of the most fertile ground for proselytizing, and that black Christians from America were the ideal candidates for spreading the good word among their benighted brethren.* For the worshippers at Richmond's First Baptist Church, the newly founded ACS and its report on Sherbro seemed like a God-given opportunity that could not be passed up. The First Baptist Church was a very different institution than Philadelphia's African Methodist Episcopal Church—a mixed-race congregation with a white clergy and far less politicized black parishioners. All of which led to Carey finding himself at Fourah Bay, Sierra Leone, in March 1821, hopeful but heartsick. Within weeks of arrival, his beloved second wife—never well to begin with—succumbed to the fever. "The greatest loss I can sustain in this world," he whispered to her as she died, "except my own soul."[37]

If he thought he might bury his grief in missionary work, he was quickly disabused of the idea by J. B. Winn, the newly arrived replacement for Bacon. Winn's highest priority was building and provisioning a "receptacle," or settlement camp, for recaptives the U.S. Navy was expected to deposit at the already strained colony. "He [Winn] has rented a farm, and put us [Carey and his co-missionary Colin Teague] on it, and we must cultivate it for our support, and for

---

*They were also cheaper, the Baptists reckoned, their upkeep costing just one-fourth that of a white missionary, though what this calculation was based on is not clear.

the support of these Africans; and pay as much of the rent as we can," he reported to the Baptist Board of Foreign Missions.[38] Ever the faithful servant, Carey tried to put a positive spin on things. "Jesus Christ our Savior when he came on his mission into this world, was often found with a broad axe in his hand; and I believe a good many corn field missionaries would be a great blessing to this country." But, he added in an uncharacteristic display of contrariness, only if "they were not confined to the field by the law and by necessity. We are bound by both." Still, the indefatigable and indestructible Carey—he did not catch the "seasoning fever"—managed both to learn a new craft, cooperage, and establish a mission among the local Mandingoes in Fourah Bay.[39]

The latter accomplishment was especially poignant, since it fulfilled his grandmother's prophecy that he would slake the spiritual thirst of his African brethren. Soon, out of necessity, he would drift away from missionary work. His highest priority became the survival of his fellow colonists, even when that survival required making war on the natives he had come to save. In doing so, Carey would bend his noble intentions to the exigencies of survival, which those who followed him would do time and again throughout Liberia's history. The compromises would not always be about religion. Later in the century, after Liberians declared their independence from the ACS, they would establish a republic but keep it for themselves, for fear of being overwhelmed by masses of native voters. And when forced to choose between African liberation and national survival in the early twentieth century, they would opt for the latter. All of it was not so much a reflection on their characters as it was on their immediate circumstances. Carey was one of the first colonists to recognize that the colonists, soon to be Liberians, were a tiny and largely friendless people in a big and hostile world.

The first episode in Liberia's history—or rather, prehistory—came to a close as the oblivious ACS leadership recognized that things were going terribly awry in Sierra Leone. The Sherbro fiasco and the continuing obstructionism of British authorities led the ACS to conclude that a new and independent colony, in a more salubrious setting, was necessary if the great experiment—Clay's "nobler cause"—was to succeed. And so, in November 1821, agents for the federal government and the ACS—Robert Stockton and Eli Ayres, respectively—sailed southeastward to find a more suitable place to settle the colonists. Stockton headed the expedition. A former student of the Reverend Robert Finley, the pious New Jersey schoolmaster and a key inspiration behind the ACS, he was also an ambitious naval officer, an opponent of the slave trade on religious grounds, and a proto-imperialist who would go on to serve in the U.S. Senate. In short, he believed in African colonization for every possible reason: Christian benevolence, opposition to slavery, and the extension of American influence abroad.

Stockton and Ayres did not discover many viable options for the colony, as the Windward Coast offered precious few safe anchorages. The obvious destination, Cape Mesurado, a rocky headland and lagoon two hundred miles from Fourah Bay, presented a major obstacle: a native leadership notoriously suspicious of outsiders, especially those claiming to come in the name of civilization. The chiefs correctly interpreted such sentiments as a threat to their status as middlemen in the now illegal transatlantic slave trade. This reputation for intransigence had frightened off an earlier team of ACS agents sent to secure land for a settlement, and that had then promptly succumbed to fever. But Lieutenant Stockton—young, righteous, and impatient—was not so easily intimidated.

TWO

Original Sin

Inbound from the northern savannah, the original home of the Mel- and Mande-speaking peoples who migrated in the fifteenth century, or from the western sea, as the first Americo settlers encountered it in the nineteenth—or from above, as the modern-day visitor approaches—nothing grabs the attention of the newcomer to Liberia quite like the trees. The dabema (*Piptadeniastrum africanum*), with its tapering reddish brown trunk, is the most common species; there are thousands of them, each a foot or two across and fifty to one hundred feet high, per acre. But the dabema is far from the most striking example. Grander and more verdant are the tigerwood, the aptly named ironwood, and mahoganies of bewildering variety, all vying for sky beneath the king of the forest, the makoré, or African black cherry, eight feet in diameter and two hundred feet tall.

To J. W. Lugenbeel, physician and U.S. government agent to Monrovia in the 1840s, Liberia was a vision of fecundity itself. "Far as the eye can reach," he wrote, "from the highest points of land in the vicinity of the ocean, the whole country presents the appearance of a deep, unbroken forest with hill-top rising above hill-top toward the vast interior . . . hills and valleys covered with the verdure of perpetual spring."[1] Others were reminded of a boundless garden. The Reverend Samuel Williams, a missionary in the 1850s, wrote of a cornucopia of wild-growing tropical fruit—"the orange, lemon, lime, soursop, guava, pawpaw, mango, plum, pine apple, and many others of less importance."[2]

Not every visitor was so impressed, however. William Nesbit, a free black reconnoitering the country for possible emigration, had a different take, as the title of his 1855 travelogue—*Four Months in Liberia: Or African Colonization Exposed*—leads the reader to suspect. "No man there has now or ever had, five acres of land cleared and in cultivation, and I am one of those who believe that it is impossible to clear the land, owing to the dense and rapid growth of the bush. The nearest description that I can give this bush is to call it a bramble . . . nothing can exceed the density and rapidity of its growth. Everything grows crooked and thorny . . ."[3]

The rain makes for the lushness. Mile for mile, Liberia gets about as much of it as any country on earth. The northwest coast, where the Americoes first settled, receives 200 inches in an average year. And it falls biblically, in great torrents. On a March day in 1954, the University of Liberia weather station in Monrovia recorded an inch in less than eight minutes. At the height of the summer rainy season, the downpours are relentless. Again, a disapproving Nesbit described the worst of it. "The rainy season is awful . . . it rained without ceasing for three weeks so hard, that we could not see outside the house; and, for the last four months, we have not had ten dry days. I thought I had seen it rain in the States, but find I was mistaken."[4]

In the winter months, when high-pressure systems above the Sahara and the Harmattan winds drop a million tons of desert grit on the forest canopy, weeks can go by without a drop, the season defined by the scorching equatorial sun. While some settlers highlighted in their letters home the ocean breezes that kept evenings cooler than might be expected—the origin of the name the "Windward Coast"—no one could ignore the midday onslaught. Even the Reverend Williams, who wrote his 1857 book, *Four Years in Liberia*, as a riposte to the querulous Nesbit, admitted that the heat was brutal. After pointing out that the thermometer rarely topped 90 degrees, he added "[b]ut this was always in the shade; to go into the sun there was a great difference . . . it was imprudent to be out from 10 a.m. to 3 p.m."[5] Yet there were those who called this land of extremes home.

Some archaeologists theorize that humans have inhabited the rain forests of Liberia for at least 50,000 years, but the region's unforgiving climate washed away the evidence long ago. Of the native inhabitants when the first colonists arrived, the oldest were the Mel- and Kwa-speaking peoples. Both were part of the Niger-Congo family of Africans; the main distinction between the two was in their social organization. Mel-speaking peoples, who inhabited a broad swath of territory from the Niger Delta in the east to the interior of Sierra Leone in the west, developed more-structured societies. It was they who developed the rituals of Poro and Sandé, initiation associations for males and females respectively, which created a rigid, age-based social hierarchy. The chiefs of the Mel-speakers derived authority from their lineage. Kwa societies, by contrast, were more anarchic. Villages largely governed themselves while the local headmen were usually chosen by councils of elders, to whom they were answerable. It was a Kwa people—the Dey—that Ayres and Stockton sat down to negotiate with at Cape Mesurado in December 1821.

Two events in the middle part of the last millennium had a dramatic impact on the human geography of the Windward Coast. One was the collapse of Songhai—and of its legendary metropolis, Timbuktu—the last great indigenous trading empire of the Western Sudan. Its demise sent large numbers of Mel- and the related Mande-speaking peoples southward into the interior of what is now Liberia. The migration pushed the existing Kwa, Mel, and Mande inhabitants into the coastal rain forest, though a number of anthropologists conjecture that members of the two former groups were there to begin with. In either case, these tribes were farmers, not hunters and gatherers like the Kwi (Pygmy) of the Congo. They laboriously hacked away clearings in the jungle and planted their crops of cassava and rice in the depleted red laterite soil. Meanwhile the Kru, another

Kwa-speaking people, took to the sea, as fishermen and eventually crewmen on European ships.

The second major event was the arrival of Portuguese traders in the fifteenth century, though they were not the first visitors from the sea. That distinction belongs to Hanno of Carthage, whose crew, according to the Greeks, sailed to the region in 550 B.C. and bagged hairy creatures they called "gorillas" but which were probably chimpanzees. The Romans also made tentative forays into the Atlantic but otherwise no ships plied the seas off the Windward Coast until the Portuguese explorations of the fifteenth century. In 1461, the mariner Pedro de Cintra left the first permanent European mark on the region, naming Cape Mesurado (Portuguese for "moderated," probably for the gentler surf on the headland's leeward side) and transporting the first native of the land to Europe. The man would return two years later with a pile of gifts, a working knowledge of Portuguese, and many marvelous tales. Other mariners followed, as the stretch of coast between Cape Mount and Cape Palmas (at roughly the present-day borders of Liberia) became a profitable trading run. The quarry was pepper, specifically *Aframomum melegueta*, better known as grains of paradise. Until the Portuguese opened up the spice trade with the East Indies in the early sixteenth century, the piquant *melegueta* was Europe's favorite source of gastronomic heat. For four hundred years, maps of the littoral bore the name the Grain Coast.

Still, despite the demand for *melegueta*, trade with the coast remained slight through the early nineteenth century. The shoreline offered no natural harbors, at least none free of treacherous sandbars, and the steady winds produced heavy surf. Not surprisingly, as the Portuguese—and then the Spanish, Danish, Dutch, Swedish, French, English, and Americans—turned from trade in peppers to trade in people, the Grain Coast was bypassed for more accessible points north (notably, the Gambia and Senegal Rivers), east (the Slave Coast, or Nigeria), and south (Angola). While slave trading was not entirely unknown along this stretch of coast, the land that would be named for liberty did not have large slave factories like those at

Gorée Island, Elmina, and Luanda. Still, local tribes engaged in the practice and were violently jealous of any interference. There were small barracoons up and down the coast, including at Cape Mesurado, that were visited from time to time by legitimate slave traders before the 1807 British ban, and by smugglers thereafter. Slave dealing was the locals' best source of the hard currency needed to buy the coveted goods—rum, tobacco, guns—brought by white traders.

Stockton and Ayres were well aware of what went on along the Windward Coast. "By the purchase you have made," Stockton later communicated in his first official letter to the ACS board, "a fatal blow" has been struck against the local slave trade, "under which it may indeed linger some time, but must eventually expire."[6] Knowing that their cause was not welcome among the Kru, the agents demonstrated their "pacific" intent by displaying no weapons, though Stockton hid a brace of pistols on his person, a risk that would prove decisive. They brought casks of rum and hogsheads of tobacco as gifts, though Ayres soon began to question whether these would be enough to ensure their safety. "While sitting and waiting for the king, under the shed of a Crooman, the people kept collecting, most of them with knives hanging at their sides," he recalled. "I began to think there might be some truth in the reports" that the locals were not friendly.[7]

Message after message was sent to King Peter, the local Dey chief, without bringing a reply. Finally, one of the natives spoke up. "The king be fool—he no talk English—I his mouth, what I say, king say—What you want?"[8] Whether or not Ayres was taken aback by such typical Kwa disrespect for authority, he launched, in his high-pitched voice, into the ACS talking points: we come in peace, we come to trade, we come to offer you civilization. "This," Ayres admitted, "immediately excited their suspicions that we were going to break in upon the customs of their forefathers."[9]

When King Peter showed up later that day, an aide with an English umbrella protecting him from the sun, the two agents began to compliment him shamelessly, though in a thoroughly Protestant sort of way. "We did not fail to let him know the high estimation in which we held him for veracity and punctuality," Ayres reported, "and that this had induced us to prefer him to some other chiefs." Peter was duly flattered but unmoved. He could offer the two islands at the mouth of the Mesurado river, small muddy flats barely above the high-tide mark, but not the headland. "If any white man was to settle on it," he explained through his interpreter, a local mulatto trader named John Mills, "then King Peter would die . . . and his women would cry a plenty."[10]

The agents pressed their case, emphasizing the trade the colony would bring and keeping the Christianity-and-civilization part to themselves. "[We] took great care, after our former experience . . . [not] to offer to their consideration any views which they could not fully comprehend," Ayres remembered, condescendingly. Finally, Peter relented. He would talk to his headman and return the next day "to make book," local pidgin for the peculiar white man's practice of consummating deals on paper. He then left with his entourage and the tobacco and rum. The next day, the agents found themselves waiting once again, and begged the local headmen to send for Peter. When he showed up three hours late—so much for the agents' praise—there was little talk of land. Instead, Ayres noted, "the unfortunate subject of the slave-trade was broached, and we again broke up the palaver. Our prospect at this time was very dull."[11]

Despite Ayres and Stockton's avoidance of the topic, Peter and the other chiefs understood that these men and their plans presented a grave threat to the local business. Stockton in his naval uniform could only have reminded them of the British officers who had fought slave smugglers in the region for the previous fifteen years, while Ayres's religious talk was a sign that the interlopers were not interested in a slice of the slave trade. As for the former slaves from across the ocean the two white men spoke of, the chiefs were not so sure what their intentions were but probably surmised that they, too, would cause problems and disruptions that could cost the natives access to their most readily available supply of foreign trade goods.

When Peter failed to show on the third day, the agents decided that if the king would not come to them, they would go to the king. But, the anxious Ayres noted, "[t]o go to the town was to place ourselves entirely in the power of a nation who had always been represented to us so savage as to render it unsafe to land on their shore without being completely armed." With a Kru man in the lead, the two made their way—"wallowing through the mud; passing through thick and dark swamps"—to King Peter's Town, some six miles into the interior of what the settlers would later call Bushrod Island.[12]

The trek, it turned out, was the least of the agents' difficulties. While Dey custom demanded the two agents be treated as guests, their hosts made it clear they were not welcome. When Peter finally made his appearance in the palaver hut he shook their hands but dispensed with the diplomatic approach. "What you want that land for?" he barked.[13] Ayres made his well-worn pitch once more. The room began to fill with men and murmuring. One Kru man said loudly that he had seen the new colonists on Sherbro, and that all they did was quarrel among themselves. Another man pointed at Stockton and claimed to have seen him seizing a French slave ship. The room rose to its feet, Ayres recalled, as the murmuring turned into "horrid war shouting."[14] Stockton, who had sidled his way to the king's side, drew his pistols and pointed one at the head of the king. He then handed the other to Ayres and told him to shoot anyone who threatened them.

The crowd, Ayres recalled later, prostrated itself and Stockton began to lecture them; Mills interpreted. It was a theatrical performance. With his free hand raised to heaven, the navy lieutenant swore he would not be made a fool of. For three days, he said, Peter's people had drunk the rum and smoked the tobacco he and Ayres had brought, with no intention of dealing with them honorably. At this point, according to Ayres, the sun broke through the clouds, bathing Stockton in ethereal light. It would become one of the iconic moments in Liberian lore.

The threat worked. Ayres wrote, "I believe the old king was afraid of being served as the French vessel was, for he soon came to, and promised to call some more kings, and meet us on the shore next morning, and make a book, which was to give us the land."[15] On December 15, King Peter and five other chiefs put their mark to the first treaty ever reached between the ACS and the natives. Three casks of tobacco, five casks of beef, one barrel of rum, six muskets, twelve guns, three barrels of gunpowder, twenty looking glasses, four umbrellas, one box of the proverbial beads—these were among the three hundred dollars' worth of goods Ayres and Stockton exchanged with Peter and the local chiefs for a forty-mile stretch of territory with the several-hundred-foot-high Cape Mesurado, future site of the Liberian capital, Monrovia, at its center.

For generations, Liberian schoolchildren—both the descendants of the settlers and the "civilized" natives they shared their classrooms with—would memorize the terms of the trade as shorthand for the ignorance of the natives and the cleverness of the colonists. It was a myth not unlike that of the twenty-four-dollar Dutch payment to the Lenape people for the island of Manhattan, and indeed, taking two hundred years of inflation into account, it amounted to about the same deal. By the 1970s, however, revisionist historians would turn the myth inside out. Emphasizing Stockton's gun at Peter's head, they would condemn the deal as Liberia's original sin, the first of many acts of duplicity and arrogance perpetrated by the colonists.

Neither version of events does justice to the facts of the deal, though. Peter and the other chiefs signed it the day after Stockton drew his pistol on the king, when they could have brought plenty of their own guns to bear on the two agents. But the real problem with each version is that there was no deal, in the agents' sense of the term, to begin with. As with their counterparts in the New World, the natives of the Grain Coast knew nothing of fee-simple land ownership. Though they were surely aware that white men had a different take on the subject—a glance at the British takeover of Sierra Leone would have told them as much—as far as they were concerned, the "black white men," as they came to call the settlers, might live at Mesurado as guests or sojourners, but it was not theirs. And even if they did accept the concept of land ownership, no king of the proudly anarchic Dey would ever have the authority to make such a deal. Peter, much to his regret, would very soon learn this lesson. And so, to theirs, would the colonists.

Lott Carey's first glimpse of Cape Mesurado came a few weeks after the treaty's signing, from the deck of the *Augusta*, in the company of Ayres and a dozen of the haler male colonists. Though lacking the drama of Freetown's mountainous backdrop, the colonists' new home was not without its charms: a calm bay and dense mangrove swamps, all bathed in the pink of an equatorial dawn. By squinting, to blur the distinctive shape of palm fronds, some of the colonists might have been reminded of a summer's morning on the lower Chesapeake, from which Carey had sailed the year before. "If you think of coming out, you need not fear," he wrote to a friend back in Virginia, "for you will find as fine a spot as ever your eyes beheld."[16]

But the irenic scene concealed a region in turmoil. As the *Augusta* carefully made its way over the sandbar at the bay's mouth, the local Dey emerged from their huts on the banks, making unwelcoming gestures. The tattooed Kru man who rowed out to the schooner to offer his lightering services briefed Carey and the others: King Peter had been arrested and was now the prisoner of neighboring chiefs. What the local monarch had warned Ayres and Stockton might come to pass had come to pass. For selling the cape, Peter was to have his head chopped off.

The richly forested cape rising gradually from gentle leeward waters to cliffs several hundred feet above the crashing surf of the Atlantic was now off limits. Instead, the colonists would have to settle on tiny Dozoa (later Providence) Island in the bay. The thought must have made Carey shudder; the low-lying spit of land bore a close resemblance to fatal Campelair. But if Ayres was shaking, it was in anger; a deal was a deal. As he told Carey, he would explain to the headman exactly what it meant to scratch their Xs on a white man's contract.

Ten days later, the agent, once again seated in the palaver hut at King Peter's Town, with the local headmen and a handful of armed colonists also in attendance, attempted to do just that. But the Africans were in no mood to haggle. "Their answer was they were not willing we should have the land," Ayres later wrote to the ACS secretary, Elias Caldwell, "that I now take back the money [sic] which we had paid King Peter, and leave the country." After the legalistic agent pointed out that the natives had drunk the rum and smoked the tobacco, a headman named King Willey turned to him and patiently explained what he thought a white man's contract was really worth: "he would eat all our tobacco and drink all our rum," Ayres quoted him saying, "and then he would drive us away." The headmen picked themselves up and walked off—all but Peter, that is. He was desperate. "Big tears rolling down his furrowed cheek," he pleaded with Ayres. "They will kill we, and we no want to die."[17] The colonists had to leave.

A 1962 Liberian reader for elementary school students written by A. Doris Henries, wife of the Speaker of the Liberian House of Representatives, described Chief Boatswain in terms that would not have been unfamiliar to American schoolchildren learning about Squanto and the Pilgrims.* According to Henries, Boatswain was the proverbial good native. "He was a friend . . . Boatswain helped the pioneers . . ."[18] Once again, however, a Liberian myth, like all myths, diverges from history.

Boatswain's real name was Sao Boso, a half-Portuguese moniker. The odd English spelling derived from his youthful stint as a petty officer aboard British ships. Like his better-known and more ruthless South African contemporary, Shaka Zulu, Boatswain—a member of the trade-oriented Mandingo nation, though lacking a chiefly lineage of his own—had forged through will, physical strength, and statecraft a broad confederation of tribes, an unusual accomplishment in the

*The book did not go through its last printing until 1972.

fractious political environment of the Windward Coast. From his capital at Bopulu, several days' caravan from Mesurado, he made his influence felt far and wide. Ayres's successor, Jehudi Ashmun, later captured, in a Rousseauian portrait of the "noble savage," some of the attributes that had permitted Boatswain to rise above his station: "To a stature approaching seven feet in height, perfectly erect, muscular, and finely proportioned—a countenance noble, intelligent, and full of animation—he unites great comprehension and acuity of mind."[19] In other words, Boatswain was perceptive enough to see in the settlers a potential trading partner, and therefore to side with them in their moment of peril.

Several months after the settlers' arrival, Boatswain descended on the cape with his entourage, including no fewer than twenty of his wives, to indulge his curiosity about the strange newcomers—African in mien but European in dress—and resolve the discord between them and his vassals with a traditional palaver. With great satisfaction Ayres noted the locals' discomfort. "They were equally afraid of our guns and of Boson."*[20] Ayres's testimony, here as elsewhere, is self-aggrandizing and untrustworthy; the natives were surely more afraid of Boatswain, for camped several miles away were two hundred of his well-armed soldiers.

Boatswain chose for his court a palaver hut set at the center of one of the native towns near Mesurado, a twenty-five-foot-long structure of grass and wood resting on a raised earthen floor. Ayres waited as Boatswain ruled on a docket of cases unrelated to the settlers. Finally, his turn came to make his case. "I had not made war yet," he wrote in a summary of his address for the ACS board, "but if they attempted to drive us from this land, I would show them what fighting was." The local chiefs, he wrote, "appeared uneasy and said one to another, Oh, look, white man getting mad." But Boatswain apparently just laughed. And "by this, I found I had touched the right chord, and did not spare the invectives."[21]

---

*Ayres employed one of the many variations in the spelling of the Mandingo leader's name.

Ayres had read the situation correctly this time. When Boatswain finally rose to speak, it was to dress down his vassals. He affirmed that a deal was a deal. He noted that while the headmen said one thing and Ayres and the colonists said another, "It was useless to multiply words about it, but he should like to see the man who would attempt to drive [them] away." The headmen then retired for several minutes. Upon their return, Ayres recalled, they were sheepish. "If [the settlers] liked the cape, [they] might have it; [the chiefs] would not receive anything for it." The tension lifted. "[The chiefs] said during the remembrance of the oldest of their kings there had been no such thing known as war between black man and white man."[22]

The official ceremony came the next day. With hundreds of locals looking on, Ayres, Carey, and the colonists took formal possession of the cape, hoisting the American flag for the first time in sub-Saharan Africa and firing a salute with their one working cannon. When it was over, the colonists watched as Boatswain and the chiefs took their leave while dark gray clouds rolled in from the Atlantic.

But the cape was theirs in name only. They had no shelter, not even a clearing in the forest, and the rainy season was beginning to set in. Despite the vows of friendship, no natives would work for the settlers, no matter how many iron bars—the currency of the coast—were offered. The burly Carey led a detachment upriver to hack palm fronds for roofing. After an exhausting day's labor, dripping sweat and bitten raw by insects, they returned with barely enough materials to build a single hut. The recently confident Ayres gathered the colonists together to tell them that the muddy island was a death sentence. Let us return to Sierra Leone, he suggested, wait out the season, and come back after the rains to start anew. Some of the colonists agreed. Carey's missionary partner Colin Teague, for one, was ready to abandon the entire endeavor.

But most settlers, including Carey, remained determined. "They had rather risk their lives," Ayres quoted him saying, "than to run the least hazard of losing a place possessing so many advantages."[23] But it was the settler Elijah Johnson, a New Jersey–born son of slaves who would become the father of Liberia's eleventh president, whose words would echo in a hundred Pioneer Day speeches down the years: "I have been two years searching a home in Africa and I have found it; and here I remain."[24] With Johnson in charge—the ailing Ayres sailed back to America by way of Sierra Leone—the settlers set out to build their village on the cape.

As was their time at Campelair, the early months on Providence Island would be remembered as a time of want and fever. The storms and downpours came especially hard that year, keeping ships away while supplies dwindled. There were skirmishes with the Dey as the settlers hammered and sawed and laid stone. These encounters consisted of a shot or two fired from or into the curtain of dense green beyond the clearing, but that was surely as unnerving to the colonists as the sudden aches and chills that signaled another bout of fever.

For all their kowtowing to Boatswain, the headmen were divided over what was to be done about the colonists. That was the word brought back by King Bob Gray, a minor chief recruited by the colonists that summer to spy on the conclaves held in the villages around Cape Mesurado. The elders, Gray said, were debating furiously among themselves: Who exactly were these interlopers? And what were they after?

Peter, his head saved from the chopping block by Boatswain's intervention, argued for inclusion, according to Gray's account of the debates. "They were not a settlement of foreigners, but of their countrymen and friends, as was proved by the identity of their colour . . . they had a right to reside in their country."[25]

King George, whose ancestral lands included the contested cape, remained unconvinced. "The Americans were strangers who had forgotten their attachment to the land of their fathers," he insisted.[26]

Maybe so, Peter allowed, but they "might be expected to turn all the civilization which they had learnt abroad to the improvement of their common country."[27]

The only thing they brought, George countered, was a predilection for meddling in the affairs of others. We have "already found to [our] cost that these new people were hostile to the slave trade," he proclaimed to the increasingly receptive chiefs, "what was to be expected from them when they should have grown into a powerful nation[?]" Now was the best chance they would have to get rid of them. "[The colonists] were weak and few in number . . . Many of the newly arrived"—another boatload of settlers had landed in August—"were sick and . . . could be easily overcome." The only question was the means: "sudden surprise or . . . a wasting and harassing blockade."[28]

While concerned enough to strengthen their defenses—refitting cannons, erecting a palisade, and widening the clearing around the settlement—the colonists and Ashmun, a former seminary teacher and their new agent, treated Gray's reports skeptically. "There is not a headman within fifty miles of us, who can arm properly fifty men. They are cowardly in the extreme, and have little control over their men," Ashmun noted in his journal. "It is morally certain, we shall not be taken by surprise."[29] Yet Gray offered ever more worrisome reports. Messengers, he said, were being sent far and wide to recruit the tribes in the area with promises of loot and slaves, which must have been chilling to the colonists. If the colonists believed that the chiefs would not dare challenge Boatswain's ruling, Gray was not so sure.

Then the reports stopped. As Gray explained to Ashmun, "the plan of attack being left to the lead warriors, whose trade it is to concert and conduct it, was not to be learnt." This ominous sign was compounded by the unexplained departure, one by one, of the native youths at the cape, who had been placed there by their elders to learn of "civilized ways" and to assure peace with the settlers. They were receiving, Ashmun suspected, "secret intelligence conveyed them by their friends."[30]

•

The native canoes crossing and recrossing the Mesurado River on November 10, 1822, made it evident that Ashmun had been wrong; the chiefs had the will and the men for an attack. By evening, there were hundreds of native warriors camped a half mile from the settlement's flimsy palisade and its few dozen defenders. At dawn, under "dusky" skies, they attacked, some firing muskets, most charging with spears. The settlers, several falling to gunfire, were quickly driven back inside the palisade. "Had the enemy at this instant, pressed their advantage," Ashmun wrote later, "it is hardly conceivable that they should have failed of entire success."[31]

But as Carey, who was overseeing the settlement's defenses, witnessed, the natives stopped to loot the settler huts they had overrun. The settlers fired their guns, forcing the natives' front lines to retreat headlong into the oncoming rush of their second wave. The result was pure chaos. "Imagination can scarcely figure to itself a throng of human beings in a more capital state of exposure to the destructive power of the machinery of modern warfare!" Ashmun wrote years later, still breathless at the victory. "Eight hundred men were here pressed shoulder to shoulder . . . and all exposed to a gun of great power . . . Every shot literally spent its force in a solid mass of living human flesh!" By eight o'clock that night, the fighting was over. "A savage yell was raised, which filled the dismal forest with a momentary horror. It gradually died away; and the whole host disappeared."[32] The colonists continued their cannon fire at the retreating canoes. Over the following several days, the natives returned for their dead.

The colonists had suffered just eight casualties, four killed and four injured. An equal number of children had been seized by the attackers, though, and their fate was unknown. Moreover, the battle had left the colonists low on food, medicine, and ammunition, the latter "insufficient for a single hour's defence of the place if hotly attacked."[33] And while the natives had retreated from the cape, their army remained camped nearby.

The colonists dispatched a messenger. They wanted peace but were "prepared to carry on the war; and can render it immensely more bloody and destructive than you felt it before." This was a bluff. A sally of familiar replies came back. The settlers deceived us. They paid for the island and took the cape. Native traders had been "cheated and roughly abused by the [settlers'] store-keeper." The colonists "had not fulfilled their promise of instructing the people." Remedy these injuries, the headmen said, and we will "gladly make peace."[34]

But as Boatswain had pointed out in a different context, this was just more idle talk. What really pitted settler against native again went unspoken: the slave trade, a business for the natives, was an abomination to the settlers, who were determined to wipe it out as soon as they had the means to do so. That was the implication of the ACS's mission to spread the benefits of legitimate commerce to Africa. For those who had escaped slavery in America, it was something more; it was a responsibility and a duty to the millions of their brethren in slavery back home. They would prefer to do it by persuasion but the natives' resistance made it appear that it would be achieved only by force. Meanwhile, having witnessed the settlers' arms in action, the chiefs must have understood that the settlers' ability to carry out that mission would only grow once they had firmly established themselves at the cape. And so there was nothing to negotiate and everything to fight for. Within a few weeks, the two sides would be at it again.

For more than a hundred years, from the mid-nineteenth century through the mid-twentieth, the people of Liberia, descendants of both settlers and "civilized" natives, would celebrate December 1 as the nation's second national holiday, after Independence Day. They called it Matilda Newport Day. Government offices and schools closed. Barefoot children paraded the streets and politicians made patriotic speeches. The centerpiece of the celebrations was a reenactment of the day in 1822 when a lonely band of settlers defended itself against the native hordes bent on their destruction.

Groups of citizens dressed up, some donning the frock coats and stovepipe hats of the settlers, others the pelts and face paint that passed for African warrior garb. The "natives" would grab their spears, begin to shriek, and charge the "settlers," who braced in formation beyond makeshift wooden palisades, muskets at the ready. The dramatic climax of the reenactment occurred when the eponymous elder made her appearance and put an ember to the fire hole of a cannon. If the timing was right, the blank discharge would catch the "natives" as they were about to storm the barricades. Newport would once again turn the tide of battle, saving the settlers in their moment of greatest peril and assuring Liberia's survival.

This version of events, Molly Pitcher at the Alamo, as it were, is more national myth than history. Colonial records show there was in fact a Matilda Newport in Mesurado in 1822 and, given the settlers' precarious position, woman colonists did participate in the colony's defense. But there is no contemporary account of a pipe-smoking woman in the thick of the fighting. The holiday would fall into disrepute and eventually be abandoned in the 1970s, when Liberians, including, for the first time, radical young native intellectuals, began to contest national identity. The ritual humiliation inherent in the reenactments was a not-so-subtle reminder that some Liberians were more Liberian than others.

The second battle for the cape went down much like the first. Hundreds of natives, in greater numbers than before, were again driven back by the outnumbered settlers. While Ashmun, Carey, and the others knelt in prayer and attributed their victory to the "special guardianship of Divine Providence," the records show it was their artillery—whether fired by a pipe-smoking Newport or not—that carried the day. "None of the kings of this part of the coast are without cannon," Ashmun noted. "But to load a great gun, is with them the business of half an hour; and they were seriously disposed to attribute to sorcery the art of charging and firing these destructive machines from 4 to 6 times in the minute."[35]

After the battle, when a British captain passing through—the celebrated Alexander Gordon Laing, the first European to reach Timbuktu—offered to mediate between the colonists and the chiefs, he found the latter "entirely exhausted, and . . . overwhelmed with vexation and shame," their warriors dispersed far and wide and their "resources . . . entirely exhausted."[36] The chiefs agreed to a truce with the settlers, though it remained an uneasy one. Captain Robert Spence of the U.S. Navy found the headmen "in no manner inclined to be appeased" during a visit in March 1823, four months after the fighting had ceased. They continued to claim that they had never intended to sell the cape to the Americans, and once again raised the issue "which doubtless formed the true, and only cause of hostilities . . . the embarrassments thrown in the way of the slave traffick, by a contiguous active check, restraining by its presence, a trade they never can willingly forego."[37]

Around the same time as Laing's visit, a native messenger appeared outside the palisades of the settlement on Mesurado. The chiefs, in their wisdom and mercy, had agreed to drop their demands for the last of the eight children abducted during the battle of November 11, "extravagant" demands that, Ashmun had insisted, the colonists were "steadily resolved not to pay."[38] The parents, the messenger said, were welcome to come and retrieve their children.

The scene was a heartbreaking one. "If any redeeming trait had at this period appeared to soften and atone for the moral deformity of the native character," Ashmun grudgingly wrote, "it certainly was perceived in their treatment of these helpless and tender captives." The children had been turned over to elderly ladies who had been "proverbially tender and indulgent"; they had sent messengers to the colony to inquire "the proper kinds of foods" to which the children were "accustomed."[39] More than any treaty, the transfer of the children signaled a reconciliation of sorts, even if it was founded in the natives' fear of settler arms.

After this temporary resolution of the conflict between native and settler, a new challenge arose, perhaps inevitably. For suppressed in the struggle against the enemy from without, the unresolved ten-

sions within—between white paternalism and black autonomy—
would soon snap the bonds between the settlers and their agent.

These tensions had been gestating for years. They had first
arisen in America, of course, when the vast majority of free blacks
voiced their anger at both the assumptions of the ACS—free blacks as
a "useless and pernicious" people, in Clay's words—and its conclusion that they must therefore vacate their homes for the "burning
sun" of Africa. Then, even the more amenable settlers, who had
taken up the ACS's offer rather than rejecting it out of hand, rose up
aboard the *Elizabeth*, as the white agents of the federal government
and the ACS declared their intention to establish near dictatorial authority over the settlers. These tensions would also serve as a harbin-
ger of the future, as Liberians struggled first to gain their independence
from the ACS and thereafter resisted attempt after attempt by white
Americans and Europeans to assert their paternalistic authority over
the black republic.

The most consequential dispute between white agents and black
colonists in Liberia's early history began in July 1823, when Ayres,
having recuperated back in the United States, returned to reassume
his former position. He did not like what he found at Mesurado. Ashmun, his temporary and unofficial replacement, was in over his head;
the colonists were running the show. Ayres exhibited the contradic-
tory thinking that had characterized the ACS from the start: He could
grow contemptuous of the black colonists for failing to live up to their
duty as civilizers of the dark continent while at the same time condescendingly treat them as inferiors incapable of addressing even the
most mundane demands of survival. To him, the confusion at Mesurado was a manifestation of the lack of white authority.

With instructions from Washington in hand, Ayres gathered the
settlers together shortly before Christmas and imperiously informed
them that the current haphazard arrangement of houses, clustered
near the water's edge for protection and convenience, would not do.
New lots would be distributed at the agent's discretion. And so they
were, except to those who complained.

Food was of more immediate concern than real estate, however. The settlers had lost their gardens to the battles with the natives and, with the return of the rains, they had had no chance to plant anew. Yet Ayres lectured them on the merits of self-sufficiency, telling them that they had become too dependent on supplies from home and so rations would cease the following June. Then, for reasons unexplained in the historical record, he opted to return to America. Before he departed near the end of December 1823, the colonists presented him with a petition of grievances, mostly aimed at his mandates, that they insisted he take back to the ACS board. The agent was not amused, and as he took his leave at the Waterside dock, he warned that anyone who refused to work on their newly assigned lots would be expelled from the settlement. It had little effect. A week later, Carey led a dozen of the colonists on a raid of the settlement's storehouse; they carefully doled out provisions as needed. Ashmun, now the lone white man in the settlement, could do little but threaten to report them to the board.

Yet the food shortage only worsened. On February 13, 1824, the *Cyrus*, carrying 105 men, women, and children from Petersburg, Virginia, arrived at Mesurado. When it was learned, however, that the ACS had failed to stock the ship with enough provisions for the emigrants, let alone those already in Africa, the colonists directed their growing anger at Ashmun, who had tried to reassert his authority by imposing a 50 percent cut in rations. According to the agent, whose account of the incident is the only one extant, Carey confronted him in his residence, the only completed stone building in the settlement, about five weeks after the arrival of the *Cyrus*. We, Carey said, gesturing at his fellow mutineers, will decide who gets what and how much, not you. He then charged Ashmun with secretly stocking his own larder and selling supplies to the natives to pay debts he had accrued back in the States in a failed publishing venture.

That evening, March 22, Ashmun called the healthier colonists to the half-finished Providence Baptist meetinghouse, which survives to this day, the oldest standing building in Monrovia. He denied the charges of profiteering and made several of his own. "The evil remains," he recounts telling the gathering in his journal, "that instead of labouring, as you ought to raise food, you would obtain it by plunder."[40] He then pointed at Carey and accused him of mutiny. Though it should have been apparent for some time, Ashmun was perhaps finally beginning to understand the reality his predecessor Ayres described in his resignation letter to the ACS board: "The principle which really actuated [the colonists] from the first . . . [is] that the Society had deceived them; that they went out expecting to govern themselves, and had no idea of having white agents."[41]

Everything was falling apart at once for Ashmun. Despite constant pleas, he had failed to win new provisions or funds from the cash-strapped ACS board, making it impossible to buy provisions from the few natives who offered to trade with them or the occasional ship anchoring at the cape. The only news coming from the States, in fact, were press accounts lambasting the agent, based on settler complaints to U.S. naval personnel passing through the colony. Ashmun had had enough. Bleeding and in pain from a botched tooth extraction, he boarded a schooner in April for the more salubrious environs of the Cape Verde Islands, before heading back to Washington to defend himself to the board and to the American public.

Yet only four months after what he thought would be his last glimpse of the tiny settlement on forested Cape Mesurado, Ashmun returned, in good health and in the company of the ACS representative Ralph Gurley. The two had met, quite by accident, in the sleepy Cape Verdean port of Praia, a resupply stop on the six-week voyage between the States and the West African coast. Gurley was on his way to Mesurado to relieve the allegedly incompetent and corrupt Ashmun of his duties and to restore order to the settlement. But Gurley took an immediate liking to the onetime seminary teacher—he would later write Ashmun's biography—and was convinced that he had the best interests of the colony and its inhabitants at heart, as well as good ideas about how to govern the place. Gurley asked Ashmun to return with him to the coast and, on the weeklong voyage, the two devised a more equitable division of ACS authority. The board in Washington, which consisted of some of the more active members, as well as its paid secretary and treasurer, would set general policy and the agent would have ultimate authority in the settlement. But the daily affairs of the colony would be handled by the settlers themselves or, rather, by their elected representatives. This was a radical step, and when it finally heard of the plan months later, the ACS board rejected it out of hand and then, for lack of an alternative, grudgingly relented.

Meanwhile, Ashmun had a pleasant surprise as he disembarked at Mesurado, and before he could announce the new dispensation. The settlers were actually grateful to see him. Sick, hungry, and isolated, they understood their survival depended upon the lifeline offered by the ACS board and secured by the presence of a white agent. And so they made their amends. Gurley called a meeting at which he informed the colonists of the outlines of a new constitution. He probably also told them then of the board's decision to give the colony and settlement their first formal names—Liberia, from the Latin *liber*, or "free"—and Monrovia, after President James Monroe, the ACS member who had done so much to pry the necessary funds from Congress that made Liberia possible.

When the meeting was over, Carey stepped forward, a picture, in Ashmun's words, of Christian humility. "He deplored the part he had taken [in the mutiny] . . . and acknowledged frankly that his influence had seduced others," the agent wrote. "[He] professed his willingness to be useful in the way the Agent thought fit to propose."[42] At first, Ashmun attributed the colonists' new docility to a wave of revivalism that swept over the settlement in his absence and climaxed in fervent services in the weeks and months following his return. "Some of our most turbulent subjects have assumed an entirely different character," he noted in a letter to the board, "which I am persuaded, nothing but the renovating power of the Word and Spirit of God can account for."[43]

Perhaps. The colonists were certainly a pious lot; every early visitor to Monrovia attested to that. But writing to the board at the end of 1824, Ashmun hinted at another cause. "The participation of the magistrates and council (according to the new form of government) in the deliberations of the Agent, and the administration of justice," the agent wrote, "has tended chiefly to form the officers themselves to a modesty of deportment and opinion, which they never manifested before, and to secure to the government the united support of the people."[44] Governing their own affairs with as little white interference as possible—that's what the colonists had risked fever and famine for.

All except Carey, who had come to Africa only to convert the natives. So when a native man calling himself John appeared in Monrovia one day in early March 1825, Carey treated it as a sign from the Almighty Himself. The man said he had walked eighty miles from Cape Mount for one reason: to be baptized. In pidgin English, he recounted to the parishioners of the Providence Baptist Church a redemption story to warm their Christian hearts: "Me be very bad man . . . Suppose a man can cus (curse) me—me can cus 'im too . . . Well, me go to church house—the man speak, and one word catch my heart." John paused, and placed his hand upon his breast. "[S]omething tell me, go, pray to God . . . [but] I can't pray . . . all day, all night—me can't sleep—by and by, my heart grow too big—me fall down this time—now me can pray—me say, Lord, have massy (mercy)—then light come in my heart—make me love the Son of God—make me love everybody."[45] Carey granted the man his wish and, with new clothes befitting a Christian and a small stack of Bibles and hymnals, sent him on his way.

But it seemed that every circumstance had conspired against Carey's mission: the fatal sojourn at Campelair, the native wars, the necessary mutiny against the ACS, and, through it all, the business of healing—not native souls but the broken, sickly bodies of settlers. Gathering what knowledge and technique he could from the physicians on visiting ships, Carey treated the fevers, the injuries, and the infections that killed anywhere from a handful to a full third of each shipload of new emigrants. "Although one of the most diligent and active men," Ashmun summed up to the board a year after the rebellion, "[Carey] has never had the command of leisure or strength to engage in any Missionary duties, besides the weekly and occasional services of the congregation."[46] Indeed, his only real accomplishment in the fields of the Lord was a missionary school at Cape Mount that the local Muslims—mostly Mandingo traders—had forced to close.*

In March 1828, Carey acquired a new set of responsibilities. Ashmun, now seriously ailing and determined to recuperate or die among family and friends in his native New Haven, made the man who had once challenged his authority his replacement. "I have the greatest confidence that his administration will prove satisfactory in a high degree to the board, and advantageous to the colony."[47] But the board appointed yet another white agent, an army surgeon named Richard Randall, to succeed Ashmun.

It didn't matter, in the end. Carey would be dead before his replacement could cross the Atlantic. At the end of the rainy season of 1828, natives robbed the colonists' trading post at Digby, a few miles north of Monrovia, an incident that normally could have been settled in a palaver with the chief who was responsible. But when the natives turned the outpost over to a local European slaver, Carey, as head of the colonial militia, had no choice. A slave factory an hour's walk from Monrovia demanded action.

On the evening of November 8, Carey and several others gathered in the old agent's residence, now the colony's armory, to pack cartridges for the march on Digby. A candle tipped over and the gunpowder lit. The massive explosion killed eight settlers. Carey was

---

*While Carey met with little success as a missionary during his lifetime, his story proved inspiring, especially to family members he left behind in America, who, in 1897, founded the Lott Carey Foreign Mission Convention. The oldest and largest African American missionary society, it remains active on every continent.

among them, though the sturdy former warehouseman lingered on in bloody rags, no one trained to attend to him, for two days.

In the final tribute to its founder, the Richmond African Missionary Society conveyed a hint of the disappointment that marked Carey's life and death. "We were looking with confidence to the more perfect consummation of our wishes, when that moral desert [Africa] should rejoice and blossom as the rose," the memorial read, "but God has seen fit to cross our expectations."[48]

THREE

First Families and Fresh Graves

Peyton Skipwith was born along with the nineteenth century in Virginia's Fluvanna County, on a tobacco plantation known as Bremo. The year 1800 was a momentous one. Just down the road, at his hilltop estate of Monticello, Thomas Jefferson contemplated his vision of a continental empire of white, freehold farmers in the wake of his electoral triumph over the forces of a recrudescent aristocracy. A day's ride in the other direction would have brought Skipwith to Richmond, a city still recovering from Gabriel Prosser's Rebellion, a slave uprising of hundreds that had been thwarted at the last moment by a fortuitous thunderstorm washing out a bridge. Skipwith's fate would reveal that the timing and place of his birth were not without their measure of meaning.

Little is known of his upbringing except that he, like Coker and Carey, was born into what were, for a slave, fortunate circumstances. Skipwith's mother was both plantation nurse and mammy to the planter's children. So rather than toiling in the tobacco fields and drying sheds, the boy was trained as an artisan, a stonemason in particular. More exceptional still, Skipwith, his siblings, and many of his fellow slaves were taught to read, write, and know their Bible in a schoolhouse built by his master—in defiance of state law and Southern custom—and run by Bremo's mistress and a white schoolteacher from the North.

Skipwith was part of a grand experiment. Like his neighbor Jefferson, John Hartwell Cocke was the liberal and educated scion of plantation privilege who questioned the solidity of the foundation upon which that privilege rested. Unlike Jefferson, however, Cocke had a plan as well as the means—a better businessman than the president, he did not mortgage his slaves—to put his ideals into action. But one obstacle stood in his way: what to do with the men and women whose freedom papers he planned to sign. Virginia law required that manumitted slaves leave the state, and few jurisdictions, in the North or the South, welcomed them. So a year after the American Colonization Society formed in 1816, Cocke joined its local auxiliary.

The experiment incubated for a generation. Then, one summer's day in 1833, Cocke summoned Skipwith and told the thirty-three-year-old father of six that he was granting the mason his freedom, on the condition that he immigrate to Liberia. Skipwith demurred for several months. He may have heard of the appalling mortality rate among the colonists, even if he had not read the abolitionist literature that relentlessly played up this terrible fact. What he was certain of was that going to Liberia meant leaving his family behind—not his immediate one, for Cocke planned to send them with him—but his siblings and his cousins and all the other kin that, as on plantations across the South, did so much to nurture and sustain body and soul against the brutality and capriciousness of the slave's life. But, in the end, the lure of freedom won out. On November 5, 1833, Peyton and his family set sail aboard the *Jupiter*, out of Norfolk, in the company of several white missionaries and two dozen fellow emigrants.

Skipwith and his family were part of a major shift in the demographics of immigrants to Liberia. During the first decade, free blacks—mostly out of the Upper South, but also from the North—made up the majority of the people dispatched by the ACS. Of the 3,160 colonists who set sail for Africa between 1820 and 1833, more than 1,700 were already free; just over 1,100 had been manumitted for the purposes of emigration. The remaining few hundred were Africans seized by federal authorities in their crackdown on international slave trafficking. Over the next fourteen years, from 1833 through Liberia's independence from the ACS in 1847, 200 free blacks and 1,500 man-umitted slaves, again mostly from the Upper South, left for Liberia. The shift was a product of the dying-off of liberal planters who freed their slaves in their wills for the specific purpose of emigration, and of free blacks being swayed by the news of disease and death in Liberia as well as by abolitionist attacks on emigration as the humbuggery of the age. Thus more self-sufficient and, in some cases, financially secure free blacks and mulattoes were supplanted by largely impoverished, illiterate, and often dependent former slaves (few planters put up a schoolhouse among the slave cabins, as Cocke did). The impact on the society emerging at Mesurado, as Peyton Skipwith was to discouragingly learn, was dramatic.

By December 1833, when the Skipwith family arrived in Liberia and made their way up the stone wharf on the Mesurado River side of the cape, Monrovia, or the "America place," as the natives referred to it, was a town on the make. But for the tropical foliage and the Atlantic Ocean, it might have struck a well-traveled American visitor as not unlike a promising new river town on the Mississippi. A few half-finished government buildings indicated the seriousness of the colonization endeavor, while large stone warehouses hinted at the mercantile cast of the local economy. Indeed, money was already leaving its imprint; the few large shingled houses of the merchant elite stood out amid a scattering of smaller dwellings barely more substantial than shacks. The populace, however, gave Monrovia an exoticism few American settlements could match, as half-naked Dey tribesmen, robed Mandingo traders, suited mulatto merchants, leather-aproned black American workers, and the occasional uniformed white U.S. Navy man mingled on the grid of broad grassy streets. These were part of the settlers' cultural baggage from America; such streets allowed wagons to turn around, except that there were no wagons in Liberia because draft animals kept dying from a host of deadly tropical parasites.

The Skipwiths, like other impoverished newcomers, were initially supported by the ACS with a guarantee of six months of provisions and housing in what officials called "receptacles," communal housing for the newly arrived. The African American missionary Augustus Washington offered a near-contemporary description of one of these places. "It is an old shabby, rickety building . . . one story high, with a garret, and is built of brick. It contains twelve pens below and four garret apartments . . . about six feet by nine, having one small windows without glass . . . Within these rooms, I have seen nothing but an excuse for a bedstead made out of rough saplings lashed together with bark or rope . . . Some of these stalls contained each whole families of six to ten and fourteen, . . . [many] passing through the raw ordeal of acclimation."[1] Indeed, every night a cacophony of coughs and moans and the stench of dysentery sufferers filled the receptacles. Even colonial officials admitted it was best for the bodily and mental health of the emigrants, as well as for the ACS's fiduciary responsibility, to get them into homes of their own as quickly as possible.

Like many other emigrants, Skipwith was thoroughly discouraged by his initial impression of Liberia. But it was not so much the housing that left him and his wife, Lydia, "dis sates fide" as the larger social ills he diagnosed, of which his poor accommodations were a symptom. Less than six weeks after his arrival, Peyton wrote back to his former master of the divisions he had discerned in Monrovian society between those who had emigrated early and with resources and men like himself. "There is Some that hav come to this place that have got rich and a number that are Sufering," he noted to Cocke. Opportunities were scarce. "Their is no chance for farming in monrovia for it is a Solid body of Stones." Of course, those stones could be put to good purposes by Skipwith, who had a highly useful skill in a place where wood quickly rotted and any building intended to last had to be built with stone. He admitted that his skills would be well compensated in Monrovia, but indicated that another obstacle might hold him back. "The Sun is So hot that people from America can not stand it in the dry Season and in the wet it rains to much," he wrote, though he had yet to experience the latter. At the close of his first letter home, Skipwith implored his former master to let him return. "I want you if you please to write to me by the first opportunity and let me no [know] on what terms I can come back for I intend coming back as Soon as I can."[2]

There was one consolation to starting a difficult new life in Liberia that Skipwith failed to mention but that many other recent arrivals noted: a sense of relief at being their own masters, an existential release from the burden of bondage. After his visit with the local white physician in Monrovia, Abraham Blackford, who emigrated a decade after Skipwith, wrote to his former mistress back in Fredericksburg, Virginia, "My conversation is to him when I call him is Dr. Luvenhal [U.S. agent Lugenbeel] and his to me in a Repli [is] Mr. Blackford. It is much Bether [better] than to be in the state [where the practice is] for them to call you Boy."[3] Young Burwell Minor, who arrived in Monrovia around the same time as Skipwith, viscerally experienced his liberation. An older relation, James Minor, who had migrated shortly before him, described Burwell in a letter to his former master. "When he [Burwell] first arrived, he acted like a young horse just out of the stable—he tested freedom."[4]

For Skipwith, by contrast, early disappointment became unremitting despair. The acclimating "African fever" (i.e., malaria) laid every member of his family low, and his five-year-old daughter Felicia died from it soon after their arrival. Skipwith, because his eyes were fixed all day on rocks that reflected the blazing equatorial light of Africa, was afflicted with the "blindness of nights," to the point where colonial doctors insisted he "stop laying stone."[5] But the worst of it came in July, when Lydia, his wife of more than ten years, died of unknown causes. A jobless widower with four children to care for, Skipwith contemplated leaving for Sierra Leone and, if his health did not improve there, leaving Sierra Leone and returning to Virginia.

•

Many emigrants suffered similar travails and setbacks. Early nineteenth-century medical thinking attributed the source of the tropical diseases that felled so many newcomers to Africa—black Americans and white Europeans alike—to the "nightly clouds of deadly miasma," smells and mists emanating from the decay of the region's abundant vegetative matter.[6] Disease and death were as rife at Mesurado as they had been at Campelair. According to a Dr. Henderson, in a report to the ACS board in 1832, roughly one in six emigrants were dying of "fever" (that is, malaria) alone. The historian Eric Burin has described early Liberia as a "charnel house." Gathering data from a host of ACS and other sources, he calculates that of the 2,887 African Americans who went to Liberia between 1831 and 1843, fully 42 percent died of disease, war with the natives, accidents, and "the sundry dangers of settler life." As the colonist Thomas Brown wrote in 1834, Liberian graveyards "always look fresh."[7]

The ACS and other colonization supporters in the United States responded to what one modern demographer has labeled "the highest rate of mortality ever reliably recorded" with cover-ups and excuses.[8] At first, they denied that fever itself was harmful, repeatedly quoting a letter from Ashmun stating that malaria was "less . . . a disease, than a salutary effect of nature to accommodate the physical system of its subjects, by a safe and gentle process of attenuation, to the new influences of a tropical climate."[9] When this reasoning no longer convinced anyone, they began to cite the equally appalling death rate in seventeenth-century Jamestown, writing Liberian deaths off as the price of pioneering a new land. Or they blamed the victims themselves. "Many of those who arrived in the *Harriet* [an emigrant ship of 1829] owe their death to imprudent exposure during convalescence and a free indulgence in the fruits of the place, particularly the pine-apple," noted the colonial agent Joseph Mechlin in a letter to the ACS board that was reprinted in the organization's newspaper, the *African Repository*.[10]

As Skipwith's experience revealed, however, disease was part of a cycle of poverty and poor health that crippled initiative among new emigrants. Rather than finding their feet during the six months they were housed and fed by the ACS, recently arrived colonists spent much of the time in bed or wandering the streets in a fever-induced daze. By the end of the half-year, they had often failed to become self-sufficient. Many remained too ill to work, and unable to buy food, they starved, which triggered relapses of malaria. Writing from the settlement at Grand Bassa (now Buchanan), Virgil McParrhan, who had taught himself medicine by treating fellow slaves on a North Carolina plantation, noted in an 1848 letter to his former master, "Every Boddy wants Drs But non Can pay Them. I have at this Time 5 pathints [patients] and The five is not worth $5."[11]

The ACS did gradually make adjustments. Recognizing the deadly conditions caused by summer rains, the ACS and its auxiliaries moved embarkation dates to ensure that colonists arrived during the dry, though hotter, winter months. The society also discovered that Southerners, particularly those from U.S. coastal areas (where a milder form of malaria existed), survived a little better than blacks from the North, though they still regularly came down with, and died from, the more severe African variety. Thus mortality rates ebbed a bit with the shift in emigrants from free blacks to former slaves. The colonists also developed their own countermeasures. Whether brought from America or picked up from the natives, herbal remedies the colonists experimented with, including so-called fever tea, helped allay the fatal dehydration accompanying high fever and dysentery.

But even though mortality rates dropped, poverty persisted. "The people in the colony are generally poor," reported Captain J. I. Nicholson of the U.S. Navy after a visit to Monrovia in 1837. "Many of them were sent without anything of consequence; and others who had a little property have been obliged to expend it in consequence of sickness after the expiration of the six month[s] in which they drew rations from the Society."[12] The poorest of the poor ended up on public farms, where, noted the colony's black lieutenant governor,

A. D. Williams, "the poor, such of them at least as require charitable assistance, from [the Society's] store . . . with the exception of one or two who are incapacitated by age or infirmities, are made to work."[13]

The selfless and energetic William Burke, manumitted and sent to Liberia by the future Civil War general Robert E. Lee, established an almshouse for the colony's many orphans and widows in the up-river settlement of Clay-Ashland. "You are aware," he wrote the ACS secretary Ralph Gurley in the 1850s, "that in many of the expeditions from the U.S. to this Country there are old mothers & fathers at the head of Large famileys of Children and those aged persons' Constitution generly broken down. After arriveing they Like a butterfly flap about for a few days and then pass away leaveing there Children to the mercy and Cold Chariety of the Country and particular that Kind of Chariety which might be expected in a new Cuntry where things are hard and inconvenient to come at and where every one feels that he has as much as he can do to Look out for himself & family."[14] But penury was not confined to newcomers alone. In an 1836 letter to the ACS, Jane Hawkins, who survived a stabbing during the battles of 1822, wrote that "[o]ur house scarcely shelters us from the torrents of rain which fall during the wet season & but for the occasional help of those who remember the poor among us, we should not have so much of the common necessaries of life as to sustain nature!"[15]

Visitors, officials, the ACS, and the colonists themselves disagreed as to the causes of the pervasive poverty. The ACS and its agents, as usual, blamed the settlers. Responding to tales of poverty in the abolitionist press, Mechlin, whose penchant for authoritarian dictates underscored his low estimation of the colonists, filed a report with the board of settler "indolence and stupidity . . . [T]hey have never when in the U. States voluntarily laboured for their own support, and now, when the stimulus of the overseer's lash is removed, cannot be induced to exert themselves sufficiently to procure even a scanty subsistence."[16] Surprisingly, some of the colonists agreed. "It is true that it is very hot here," wrote Washington McDonough in 1842 of the settlement at Setter Kroo, about 120 miles down the coast from

Mesurado, "but if a man is industrious after he becomes acclimated [he may] get along very well but the most of the people that comes out here by the time they get over the fever they becomes some thing like the natives and wont work if they find that they can get along by stealing."[17]

Not everyone associated with the ACS believed that the settlers were entirely at fault. The agent Ezekiel Skinner understood that ACS policy and practice bore at least some responsibility. "The people in the colony are generally poor," he wrote in an 1837 letter to the board. "Being acclimated in Receptacles, they were prevented from cultivating any ground. When Emigrants are at once placed on their land, this disadvantage is obviated. Owing either to the sickness or negligence of my predecessors in the Agency, a large proportion of the Emigrants entitled to land, had not drawn it."[18] The last part of his assessment was not fair, however. As early as the mid-1820s, the board and its agents, as well as many colonists, had pushed for settlements along the St. Paul's River, whose rich bottomland was far more conducive to farming than the stone and sand at Mesurado. And away from the swamps along the coast, the region was also more salubrious. The first new settlement was Caldwell, founded by Ashmun, about twenty miles from Monrovia. Lott Carey established Millsburg, another twenty miles upriver from Caldwell, in one of the last acts of his life. By the 1840s, there were settlements up and down the St. Paul and the nearby Junk and St. John's Rivers, though well over half of all settlers still lived in Monrovia and its environs. But expansion did not solve the problem of how to turn bedridden emigrants into productive members of Liberian society.

Nor could it resolve a related problem the settlers faced. As the ACS archives reveal, letters emigrants sent home to their masters often included pleas for provisions. "Anything You may Choose to send will be acceptable wheither dry goods or Provision," George McDonough wrote his former master in 1847 with a directness that bespoke his desperation. "[T]he amount of three or five hundred Dollars would be of no consequence to a man of Your wealth and as I find myself so much in need in this hard Country and feeling assured that while I was with You I acted upright and just toward You."[19] Even the proud Skipwiths were forced to beg. "Pleas to Send us out Some flower or anything that yo awl hav to Spar for we Stand in neede of Somthin verry much . . ." wrote Peyton's oldest daughter, Diana, to Cocke's wife, Sally, in 1837, "for we awl Like to Starv this Season."[20] For all their wants, though, McDonough and the Skipwiths were luckier than most—the masters who sent them to Liberia were still alive. Emigrants who had been freed in testamentary wills could only plead with the often unsympathetic heirs of their masters. "My Dear Bro.," wrote Peter Ross to the ACS secretary Ralph Gurley in 1857, "[O]ld Captain Ross leaves one hundred thousand dollars for his people . . . and then we cannot Get Twenty five Dollars of that money, after he placeing the Money in the Bank . . . we ask you to Be so kind as to intersede for that money four us . . . Isaac Wade [Ross's grandson and heir] is and was a meane man."[21]

The ACS could prove equally stingy, as Henry Stewart, an emigrant from 1849, attested. The six months of provisions he had been provided with lasted barely three; adults got just six pounds of food a week and children only half that; and, "from the Looks of things it will have to be a greadill [great deal] less." This shortfall, he concluded, "has Bin the generl complant in most all the Emigrant privus [previous] to ous."[22] Joseph Corker, part of an 1840s contingent out of Greenville, Mississippi, learned that complaining to the ACS was fruitless. "I observed the list of goods that you desire me to send you," the ACS official William McLain wrote to Corker in 1849. "But you are very much mistaken if you think *I am made out of money*."[23] A year earlier, in a communiqué with the ACS agent in Monrovia, McLain had vented his spleen at the presumptuousness of the Greenville settlers who refused to remain on the land allotted them by the society. "Those who went to Monrovia sent me a beautiful little piece of *personal abuse* which I trust they may live to become ashamed of," he wrote, before adding, "I entirely approve of the policy . . . of withholding their provisions from them. If emigrants refuse to stay for six mos. after we place them, they must take the responsibility of their own support."[24]

There were plenty of reasons why the Greenville emigrants refused to stay in the settlement they had named after their hometown in America. While the ACS promoted Liberia as a land of perpetual summer and fecundity, and in spite of the fact that many of the former slaves had a lifetime of fieldwork behind them, farming did not prove easy. Clearing the land of thick jungle was laborious and, until agricultural practices could be adjusted, the torrential rains wreaked havoc on even the most well-tended settler farm. The lack of draft animals and tools didn't help. "I am still trying to farm," wrote James Skipwith, two years after his arrival, "[b]ut cannot see But little means and cannot get surfision tools."[25]

The difficulties of farming in the unfamiliar tropical climate, as well as the sheer isolation and monotony of life in the upriver settlements, led many emigrants to choose the city, which baffled some white observers. "It is really astonishing that newcomers should prefer to remain in [Monrovia] with one fourth of an acre of rocky land . . . when they might have ten acres of as good land as any other in the world, in a much more healthy location," wrote the physician J. W. Lugenbeel, a choice he attributed to "ignorance" and "fanciful notions excited by seeing some fine looking houses, occupied by well dressed persons, who live in pretty handsome style."[26]

Emigrant fantasies notwithstanding, the capital had its share of problems beyond poverty and ever-present disease. As Lugenbeel noted, Monrovia bred "drones [loafers] in the community and obstacles to the prosperity of Liberia."[27] Even worse, at least as far as the ACS and its agents were concerned, was that many settlers saw the lure of the fast buck and easy living as synonymous with commerce. Despite Monrovia's marginality to the transatlantic trading network—it would wait until after World War II, and a U.S. aid project, for a deep-water port—the Liberian littoral offered opportunities for entrepreneurial middlemen. Products of the forest, such as palm oil and camwood, a source of red dye, could be bartered for manufactures and crops, tobacco especially, from the Americas and Europe. Coastal tribes had long engaged in such trade, along with that in slaves, but now found themselves being muscled aside by the colonists.

Indeed, nothing aggravated the colony's white overseers more than settlers abandoning the hoe for the ledger. Most white Americans believed that blacks were best suited for agriculture and manifestly unfit for commerce. But there was more to the ACS officials' hostility to colonial trade than racist assumptions. From its beginning, the society had been dominated by Southern planters and politicians like Cocke, most of whom subscribed to the Jeffersonian ideal of a free-holding republic of small farmers. In debt to merchants themselves, many held the profession in contempt as a parasitical one that created nothing. As country farmers, they also remained suspicious of cities, an attitude reinforced by the tendency of free blacks to gravitate to urban areas where, in the imaginations of white Southerners, they indulged their instincts for immorality, criminality, and indolence. The ACS thus saw the growth of Monrovia and Liberian trade as obstacles to the colony's long-term prospects and even its survival. "Some of the [naval] officers who have been here [Monrovia] before," Nicholson wrote in his 1837 report, "tell me that it is evidently not so prosperous as it was at their former visit, which I would ascribe to the neglect of agriculture for the pursuit of trade."[28]

Some colonists had similar reservations about their society and economy. "The present states of affairs here is not very flattering," wrote Moses Jackson from the settlement of Kentucky, like many, named for the place where its inhabitants hailed from. "The people here from all that I have seen and heard take but little interest in the improvement of the country. They Generaly engage in trading with the Natives for Camwood and Pam [palm] Oil which they barter agane for such things as they need with merchant vessels and neglect almost entirely the Cultivation of the ground."[29]

But for many former slaves who had endured years of backbreaking plantation labor, trade, like Liberia itself, meant freedom. Not to mention that it could mean wealth, too. Augustus Adee, a U.S. Navy surgeon, described one merchant's table as positively groaning beneath a display of delicacies. "We were greatly astonished to find a large table richly furnished for 30 or more persons . . . ragouts, roast beef, muscovy ducks . . . porter, spirituous liquors, Madeira, were freely circulated. Paupau [pawpaw], pies, African cherry tarts, pineapples, bananas, coffee and segars finished the repast."[30] With the exception of the tropical products, all of these items had been imported at great cost, and at a time when there was genuine hunger in the colony. Little wonder that so many settlers aspired to the life of the merchant.

One dire effect of a largely urban population obsessed with trade was a greater reliance on purchased foodstuffs, which inflated their cost. High prices were the most frequent source of complaint among settlers in their letters home. "The things heare Sell verry dear," Diana Skipwith notified her former mistress in 1837. "Yo cannot get So much as one fould [fowl] without giving twenty five cents for it."[31] And when fighting broke out with and among the natives, goods could not be had for any price, resulting in shortages and even starvation. Native leaders understood this and at times enforced embargoes as a means of negotiation. In the early 1840s, one embargo nearly plunged the colonists at Maryland, Liberia's southernmost settlement, into war with the local Grebo people, a conflict narrowly avoided by the arrival of a U.S. naval squadron and a timely cannon salute by a young Commodore Matthew Perry, who would use a similar ploy to force open the ports of Japan a decade later.

In an 1843 letter to her former mistress, Diana Skipwith, Peyton's daughter, noted how the Africans "call us [the settlers] all white man."[32] In fact, most used "Mericans" or "kwi," a Kru term that meant essentially the same thing. And from their perspective, it made sense; the settlers lived, talked, and acted like white men, from their climate-inappropriate woolens and the pungent odor it lent them to the strange courtesies they paid their womenfolk.

They caused trouble like white men, too. Their very presence led to violence that would have not have been out of place on the contemporary U.S. frontier. In the middle years of the nineteenth century, thanks in part to the settlers themselves, the Liberian hinterland was riven by fighting. The colonists' expansion into the interior displaced villages and even whole tribes, setting off internecine warfare among the natives. At the same time, their efforts to combat the slave trade provoked chiefs into attacking outlying colonial settlements. In his plea to the ACS chief, Ralph Gurley, for help in getting some of the Ross inheritance, George Jones, another of Ross's manumitted slaves, wrote, from the coastal settlement of Louisiana, "[t]he native hav Burn our houses and Destroy our farm and all the produce and we Got no help at all."[33] It was stories like this that drove the emigrant George McDonough to ignore his former master's explicit instructions to bypass Monrovia and take up farming at Sinoe, a coastal settlement about one hundred miles southeast of the colonial capital. McDonough was convinced by family members already settled in the colonial capital that should he go to Sinoe, "the natives would take up arms again[st] them."[34]

Yet settler-native relations were not always so bellicose. The two sides traded with each other, often to the advantage of the colonists. The settlers endured periods of famine with the help of native produce; though settler agriculture gradually improved, it was never quite adequate to feed the growing settler community. "[T]he colony has made some effort to exonerate herself from hunger by a few of our ablest men turning thire attentions to agriculture," Skipwith wrote to Cocke in 1839, "but before that we could have hardly thought that we could have existed for our dependence was mostly on the tribes of the country."[35] Apart from the trade for food, some Monrovia merchants made small fortunes trading goods from Europe and America for forest products gathered by the natives.

Many Africans also came to live and work in Monrovia and the other colonial settlements. "The streets are full of these fellows, who walk about in their native costume—and native dignity—exhibiting the most perfect proportions of body and limbs," the navy surgeon Adee admiringly wrote after an 1827 visit. "[S]ome wear a few yards of cloth thrown over their shoulders in the manner of the Roman toga. Their bodies and faces are marked with various figures according to the customs of their respective tribes. Around their necks, wrists and ankles they wear ornaments of different kind, as leopards or tigers' [*sic*] teeth, rings of iron or brass, rams' horns, compositions of clay &c. sewn in a small bag," which the perceptive Adee called their "deities, or rather substances in which their Guardian spirit resides."[36]

Native children lived among the settlers as well. Raised in the enforced ignorance of slavery, the settlers valued education and established schools in new settlements as quickly as they could. Native chiefs and parents, recognizing that the colonists—some literate, many of them technically proficient and knowledgeable about the encroaching outside world—had much to offer, sent their most talented children to these schools. The chiefs and parents may have gotten more than they bargained for. "I have 16 promising [native and settler] students whom I have been teaching since 1st January 1849," H. W. Ellis reported to the ACS secretary William McLain of the high school he taught at in Monrovia. "The greater part of them have read through the Historia Sacrae, and are making rapid progress in Greek, besides other sciences . . . The minds of youth in Africa are, if possible, more susceptible of literary and scientific improvement, than any other part of the world," though he lamented the fact that his pupils "cannot study intensely . . . no more than 7 or 8 hours in 24."[37]

A few native children and adults were also educated in Christianity. But the proselytizing results in those early years of settlement were surely disappointing to both the ACS and the more evangelical settlers. Converting Africans to Christianity had, after all, been one of the two missions—along with the moral regeneration of free blacks and freed slaves—motivating the Liberian experiment. Like Lott

Carey, most settlers were simply so busy trying to survive that they had little time or energy to devote to saving native souls. The preachers among the emigrants were forced to focus more on the settlers; with the death rate so high and the lures of freedom so enticing, they had their hands full comforting the bereft and keeping the wayward out of trouble.

That left the task of conversion to visiting missionaries, both white and black. But their task was not an easy one. Traveling to the interior was an ordeal full of danger; the hinterland tribes did not appreciate interlopers who might disturb long-standing trade, both of the legitimate and illegitimate kinds. Bishop Scott, sent by American Methodists to report on the church's missionary efforts in Liberia, found that few natives were open to conversion, though he was quick to add that this was "not due to any want of faithfulness on the part of the missionaries." The missionaries also had to compete with another aggressive, evangelizing religion. For centuries, Mandingo traders, like their counterparts throughout the Muslim world, spread the faith along with their goods as they traveled the footpaths of West Africa. Among their converts was nearly the entire Vai tribe, which inhabited much of the hinterland just north of Monrovia.

Conversions that did occur were usually the result of a peculiar aspect of settler-native contact known as the ward system, which arose in the early years of colonization and persisted well into the twentieth century. Wedding African custom, Anglo-Saxon jurisprudence, and the survival strategies African Americans had forged across generations of slavery, the ward system saw native parents and communities send their sons and daughters to live with settler families. The complex political geography of West Africa had long made alliances necessary, as the Liberians quickly came to understand. These often involved the exchange of children, with chiefly sons and daughters sent to rival tribes and clans to secure peace, trade, and general goodwill. The "ward" aspect came from English and American legal traditions for dealing with the orphans when death was such a common occurrence. Slavery, particularly in North America, where the law granted masters the right to break up "marriages" and families at will, led adults to informally adopt children who were not blood relations.

So common was adoption of natives that the colonial council drew up rules in 1838 to regulate the practice. The adopters had to get prior consent, provide their wards with "suitable clothing," and make sure they were "instructed in some day school at least three months in each year." The adopted, in turn, were expected to obey their guardians, perform chores in return for food and lodging, and behave like "civilized" Christians. To ensure that its regulations were followed, the council appointed two "suitable persons" to keep an eye on the wards, while guardians were expected to have the wards "forthwith entered as free citizens in the Colonial Records."[38] This last stipulation would prove crucial to the course of Liberian history. Native children, legally absorbed into the settler community, augmented its ranks, which were constantly being depleted by disease. Over time and into the twentieth century, wards grew up identifying with the descendants of the settlers, helping the latter to maintain their rule over the natives even though they never exceeded a few percent of Liberia's population.

Were the ward rules of 1838 written to regulate existing practice or to rectify a widespread problem? Was abuse of wards rare or widespread? The historical record is mixed. In the close confines of a settler home, with natives and colonists interacting on a daily basis, adults could be tyrannical or tender. In an 1832 letter to her sister in the United States, Eliza Hatter wrote about her mutually beneficial relationship with her ward. "I keep a [native] girl ten years old, for her victuals and clothes, I have taught her to read and sew, and she assists me in cooking and cleaning."[39] But one white colonial physician abhorred the ward system. "These pawns," the doctor wrote, using another term for wards, "are as much slaves as their sable prototypes in the parent states of America."[40]

More troubling still was the treatment of native adults who came to Monrovia and other settlements to work. As Peyton Skipwith wrote in his first letter home, "Those [settlers] that are well off do hav the natives as Slavs and poor people that come from America hav no chance to make aliving for the natives do all the work."[41] Hostile observers, like the abolitionist William Nesbit, threw about the dreaded "s word" with abandon. "Every colonist keeps native slaves (or as they term them servants) about him, varying in number from one to fifteen, according to the circumstances of the master. These poor souls they beat unmercifully, and more than half starve them, and all the labor that is done at all, is done by these poor wretches."[42]

The possibility that former slaves subjected their African brethren to servitude and the lash remains a disturbing one almost two centuries later. Again, the circumstantial evidence offers a mixed picture. On the one hand, the colonists did not have a powerful state behind them to enforce the harsher aspects of a slave regime. African natives in Liberia were not isolated an ocean away from their homeland; they could and did readily pack up and leave the settlements if conditions became intolerable. On the other hand, natives displaced by war or famine often had no alternative but to work in the colony. And there is little question that native labor was cheap and readily available. "Labourers can be hired in Liberia for 25 cents per day and the outside from 3 to 4$ per month," Mathilda Skipwith Lomax, another of Peyton's daughters, happily wrote to her former master.[43] One thing we do know: natives were never legally recognized as slaves, as that would have been a violation of every constitution written by and for the colony.

"It is something strange to think that these people of Africa are calld our ancestors," Skipwith wrote to Cocke in a contemplative letter some half dozen years after his arrival. "In my present thinking if we have any ancestors they could not have been like these hostile tribes in this part of Africa for you may try and distill that principle and belief in them and do all you can for them and they still will be your enemy."[44] The Skipwith who wrote this disillusioned letter had only recently returned from a military campaign against King Gatumbe, one of the more hostile chieftains of the Monrovian hinterland.

Like many settlers, Skipwith's attitude toward the natives consisted of equal parts fear, anger, contempt, and paternalistic concern. He looked down on the Africans as lazy and duplicitous. When put to work, they had to be watched or they would slack off. They had no respect for property. In one letter, Skipwith lumped the natives together with monkeys as crop thieves.

Skipwith's attitude sounds all too familiar, to us if not to the former slaves and freedmen who embodied it. Yet the settlers' racial outlook could be more nuanced than it at first appears. Skipwith may have been unable to overcome the prejudices his homeland had imbued in him, but his daughter Diana, just twelve years old when she first landed in Monrovia, could, to a degree. "In conversing with one of [the natives]," she wrote her mistress in 1843, "I ask him how was it that the[y] could not read & write like white man . . . & he said it was thire own fault; that God give them the Choice either to learn book proper as they says or make Rice & they told god they had rather make rice. I labored with him & told him that it was a misstaken Idear altogether. God had bless them with as many Sences as the white man and if they ware to only put them in exercise that would be the same as white man." Diana reported that she had won the native to her side and then voiced the same paternalist sentiments that had inspired her former master and mistress two generations earlier. "I think by theas means we will be able to get them out of their Supisticious Idears & at last they will become Siverlise [civilized]."[45]

The Africans, too, had their hopes and doubts. The coastal people resented the settlers' encroachment on their land and their middleman position between European traders and the interior tribes. Nor did they enjoy being bossed around by the newcomers. "One fact is this," the Cape Palmas settler Alexander Hance wrote to the head of the Maryland Colonization Society, in a letter that demonstrates that Diana Skipwith's experience with the natives was not entirely representative, "the natives do not like to be governed by a colored Man and they do just as they please almost."*[46] But the settlements did offer certain advantages. Natives could trade with settlers for tobacco, machine-woven cloth, mirrors, and other coveted goods from across the sea. And because the colonists manifested a degree of military discipline, a number of villages and a few of the weaker tribes sought "refuge under the guns of the Cape."[47]

By the time James Skipwith, Peyton's nephew, migrated to Liberia in the late 1850s, a modus vivendi had emerged between settler and native. There would still be many misunderstandings and conflicts in the future, but most of the neighboring tribes had come to recognize that the colonists could not be driven out by force. Relations improved as a result of the decline of slave smuggling, a result of increased British patrols as well as the military campaigns undertaken by the colonists themselves. But James insisted the new comity rested on a more benevolent foundation. "The natives are more & more friendly," he wrote to Cocke in 1859. "Their confidence begins to awaken. They see that it is our wish to do them good & hostilities have ceased with them. We have daily applications to receive their children in to our church & Sabath school. 4 of the converts are natives of this country and are fil[le]d with the holy Goast."[48]

It was a hopeful assessment but not a very convincing or farseeing one. The conversion statistic he cited hardly made his case, not to mention that those wards who came to live among the settlers and adopt their religion represented a tiny sliver of the overall African population of the hinterland. As for the wars between natives and settlers, far from having "ceased," they would continue well into the twentieth century, and over much the same things that had always sparked them—trade, land, and settler arrogance.

*Founded in 1827, the MCS had a similar mission to the ACS but was independent of it. Maryland, the colony it founded at Cape Palmas, near the present-day border with Ivory Coast, was annexed by Liberia in 1857.

•

Over time, Peyton slowly came to terms with life in Africa, though it took all of his willpower. "The idea of being in a new country with a large family of helpless childrine, who could depend only on me for support, & I being so indisposed as to be of no use to them nor myself having no means and the prospect of their suffering made me feel distressed and greatly so," he wrote to Cocke two years after his arrival. "[B]ut thanks be to God my health and sight is recovered and that day of awful gloom is gone and I feel satisfied with my present home and desire no other."[49]

Although he and his family continued to be plagued with health problems—"such are the diseases of a tropical climate"—they began to prosper as the colony grew.[50] Because the mercantile elite preferred to build their homes and warehouses of stone, Peyton's skills as a mason made possible his ascent up the social ladder. He sent his children to school, some in buildings he himself had helped construct. His son Nash followed him into the masonry business, though he died in his twentieth year. Sometime around 1840, Peyton remarried, this time to a devout Methodist woman twenty years his junior named Margaret Skinner.

Still, the sense of isolation and separation persisted. Peyton, and particularly his daughters, missed friends and family back home. Diana had been especially close to her master's daughter. "I cannot take rest of nights Dreaming About you," she wrote to Sally Cocke in 1838. "Some times I think I am thire and when I awake I am hear in Liberia & and how that dos greave me but I cannot healp my Self. I am verry fraid I shal never See your faice again but if I never Do I hope I shal meat [you] in the kingdom."[51] Diana's letters, like those of many of the settlers, particularly the women, were filled with appeals for news about loved ones and requests that her tender wishes be passed on to others.

Inevitably, the homesickness faded with time. Diana and her sister Mathilda married and started families of their own, though not until they had found appropriate partners in their social class. Diana, for all her political correctness, refused to marry an African. Peyton's consolation for the difficulties of his life in Liberia came in part from his rising status in the colony. As more and more of Cocke's slaves were manumitted and sent to Liberia, he took on the role of paterfamilias. His modest financial success allowed the family to "live comfortably . . . [in] a fine house," on a town lot he had purchased with his own earnings. He developed friendships with some of the eminent individuals of Monrovian society and was appointed an officer in the colonial militia, a highly coveted post that marked him as a man of note in the tiny settler community.

But not everyone in the Skipwith family found a similar measure of contentment. "I am sorry to say that Erasmus [Skipwith, Peyton's younger brother] is displeased with the Country because he is of no trade, & therefore he sees no way to make a living," Peyton wrote to Cocke in 1846. "I wanted him to come in and learn the Mason's trade, but I could not prevale on him enough to get his consent."[52] When the son of one of Cocke's planter neighbors, an officer aboard the U.S. Navy brig *Porpoise*, offered the young man a steward's position, Erasmus took it. James Nicholas, a former slave of Cocke's deceased sister Sally Faulcon, left the colony for Jamaica in 1844, just two years after his arrival in Monrovia. "Brother James could not Contente himself here," a sibling explained to Cocke.[53] James was never heard from again, which was not unusual. According to the ACS's own records, more than five hundred colonists—or roughly one in nine emigrants—left Liberia for other destinations between 1821 and the first colony-wide census in 1843. Most went to the West Indies or joined the ranks of African American seamen, or "black jacks." A few ended up in other parts of Africa, usually Sierra Leone or the Maryland Colonization Society's independent settlement at Cape Palmas. Some even returned to the United States.

All who left were lamented both by family members and by a community concerned for its own survival, except for this last group. These failed emigrants drew the ire of those who remained in Africa because they appeared to undermine Liberia's very reason for existence, as a refuge for the persecuted free man of color. When two brothers returned to the United States in the late 1850s, complaining of Liberia as a hell of high prices and broken promises, the Reverend James Wilson fired back: "As for my part I do not know What William & James Watson return for unlest it Was for the Whipe [whip]," the minister wrote to the ACS secretary William McLain. "It cannot be for som thing to Eate, for We have . . . a variety of [foods] . . . too tedus to menthion. I can not see What a man of Coller Want to go Back to the united States to Live for un Lest he has no Sol in him, for Whare thire is a sine of a sole With in a man it Panc [pants] for freedom in this Life & the Life to come."[54]

As the years passed and the colony grew, the settlers began to test that freedom. White men still ran Liberia. Many of the more successful residents, while appreciative of the ACS's efforts on their behalf, chafed under its authority, even after the colony became a semi-autonomous "commonwealth" in 1838 and one of their own was appointed governor three years later. A Liberian national identity began to emerge, a pride in what black men and women had achieved in the land of their forefathers despite the intolerable harshness and deprivation of their upbringing. Writing to his former mistress in 1846, Abraham Blackford bespoke a fierce patriotism. "People speaking about this country tell them to hush their mouths if they are speaking anything disrespectful of it . . . Africa is the very country for the colored man."[55]

A year later, Blackford, Skipwith, and several thousand of their fellow colonists announced to the world their freedom from the ACS, an act that had been in the making since the agent Samuel Bacon had informed the first colonists during the voyage of the *Elizabeth* that the white agents, not the colonists, were in charge. "In coming to the shores of Africa," their Declaration of Independence read, "we indulged the pleasing hope that we would be permitted to exercise and improve those faculties which impart to man his dignity; to nourish in our hearts the flame of honorable ambition; to cherish and indulge these aspirations which a beneficent Creator had implanted in every human heart, and to evince to all who despise, ridicule, and oppress our race that we possess with them a common nature; are with them susceptible of equal refinement, and capable to equal advancement in all that adorns and dignifies man."[56]

The high ideals and soaring prose masked the underlying reason for the split, which was not so different from the cause of the American Revolution seventy years before. Liberia's struggle for independence had as much to do with taxes, and who paid them, as it did with freedom.

FOUR

Africa's Lone Star

What is Liberia? For the American Colonization Society board, the 2,000-plus settlers, and, most pressingly, for the officials at Government House in Monrovia, that was the question of the 1840s. Every group agreed on what it was not—a Western-style nation-state or a tribal entity in the African tradition. And it was not a colony. The U.S. Congress had made certain of that. From the moment they first contributed money in 1819 for the resettlement of African slaves seized from smugglers, Washington policymakers insisted that the United States had no territorial ambitions in Africa. Moreover, no federal money was ever explicitly set aside for the emigration of free blacks or emancipated slaves from America.

In the 1820s and 1830s, Liberia was still firmly under ACS control, even after 1825, when, toward the end of Jehudi Ashmun's time as agent, the board had reluctantly agreed to a new political dispensation: executive power would still rest exclusively in the agent's hands but the colonists would elect a council to advise him. Settler discontent did not abate, however, as evidenced by Joseph Mechlin's tenure as the ACS agent in Liberia from 1829 to 1833.

A May 13, 1835, letter from the settler Joseph Blake to the ACS corresponding secretary Ralph Gurley in Washington alleged that Mechlin, who had disappeared from Liberia, had slept with Blake's wife. "Dr. Joseph Mechlin Jr. during his residency here committed a most heinous depredation on the peace of [my] family. He, by criminal conversation decoyed my wife away, and debauched her. He has left here for me to maintain a mulatto child." The telling passage in the letter followed this initial lament: "Permit me to ask your wisdom," Blake wrote, "if this is a proper course for one to pursue who was placed at the head of any community. He was put here to be our father and our guide."[1]

Blake's letter is an anomaly—there is no other evidence of sexual predation by ACS agents—but there are voluminous records of settler dissatisfaction with the virtual dictatorial powers the board in Washington granted its agents in Monrovia and the high-handedness with which the agents wielded them. The compromise of 1825—giving settlers a voice, if not a vote, in their own affairs—meant little if the agent remained convinced that his settler charges still needed the firm hand of the plantation overseers they had left behind.

Apart from the fact that he was a doctor, little is known of Mechlin's life before he became a colonial agent in 1829. The normally judicious Charles Huberich, author of the exhaustive two-volume *Political and Legislative History of Liberia*, called Mechlin "a reactionary of the worst type."[2] He acted like a petty Caesar in his dealings with neighboring African chiefs. When a local Dey headman, besieged by other tribes, begged for the colony's protection, Mechlin made him a vassal and insisted his people "consider themselves Americans," that is, subject to colonial law.[3] This meant that they had to surrender to Liberian merchants their middleman status in the trade between the hinterland and the coast. When the Dey rose up against this dictate and against encroachments on their lands, Mechlin organized a militia that proceeded to torch the chief's home village; the agent then forced upon him a humiliating treaty that annexed vast new tracts of territory.

For this, Mechlin was praised by the settler-run *Liberia Herald*. His efforts to impose a similar authoritarianism at home did not sit as well with the colonists, however. In his first months on the job, his heavy-handed rule sparked protest and a petition to the ACS board in Washington, demanding Mechlin respect the decisions of the settler council. The agent, the petition claimed, had violated the 1825 constitution by ignoring settler input on official appointments. And his triple role as ACS agent, U.S. government representative, and commander of the colonial militia gave him near absolute power. In their complaint, the petitioners cited the laws upon which the colony had been founded: "All persons born within the limits of the territory held by the American Colonization Society . . . or removing there to reside, shall be free, and entitled to all the rights and privileges of the free people of the United States."[4]

The board was not persuaded. Ignoring the irony that the colonists had never enjoyed the "rights and privileges of free people" when in the United States, Gurley denied each of the petitioners' demands for redress. To their rights-of-free-men appeal, the ACS official responded with the paternalist thinking that had informed the Liberian experiment from the very start. With thinly veiled impatience, Gurley explained that the colonists were not ready to exercise such rights and that the society, through its representative in Monrovia, knew what was best for them: "your committee [i.e., the ACS board] are of opinion that the time has not yet arrived when the powers and duties of the colonist Agent can be properly relaxed."[5]

Over the next several years, Mechlin further consolidated his power, granting lands and provisions to supporters, forcing natives to trade with the agency rather than with local merchants, and repeatedly vetoing acts of the colonial council until he finally dismissed it altogether. The agent did little to hide his contempt for the settlers, especially those who challenged him. In an 1832 letter to the board, Mechlin even questioned the fitness of newly freed slaves to come to Liberia. Of a recent contingent out of Norfolk, he wrote, "I regret to be compelled to state that they are . . . the lowest and most abandoned of their class. From such materials it is vain to expect that an industrious, intelligent and enterprising community can possibly be formed; the thing is utterly impracticable, and they cannot but retard, instead of advancing the prosperity of the Colony."[6]

Mechlin might have heeded the example Carey and the settlers had made of Ashmun. Though backed by the board and surrounded by hand-picked settler officials, he was, in the end, a solitary white man in Africa. By early 1833, most of the colonists were in open rebellion, forcing Mechlin to resign and return stateside. It was not the "lowest and most abandoned" colonists who spearheaded the demand for self-government, but the colonial elite. Although deaf to the political yearnings of the settlers, Mechlin recognized easily enough the self-interest of others. Facing rising demands for constitutional "amendment or alteration" during his last months in office, Mechlin hinted to Gurley that his enemies in Monrovia's merchant community had ulterior motives. "I mean such [amendments] . . . would give into their hands the power of making such port regulations [that is, tariffs and other duties] as would affect the intercourse of foreigners with the colony[;] should this be committed to their hands we have no guaranty that they would not on the one hand so stretch their prerogative as to enact laws vexatious and oppressive in their bearing on foreign traders and destructive of our [i.e., the ACS's] commercial interests."[7]

Mechlin's assessment is borne out by what followed. The nation's founding fathers were not so different from their American counterparts, who had once enslaved them and their parents and grandparents. The Liberian elite spoke sincerely of liberty and the rights of man, but political freedom, to them and to their descendants, was inseparable from the freedom to make money.

To all but the practiced eye of a nineteenth-century Southerner, keen to the nuances of racial feature and coloration, the Virginia-born Joseph Jenkins Roberts—Liberia's first president—was a white man. Photographs capture his distinctively Caucasian features. One 1844 oil portraitist even gave him wavy locks of auburn hair. "Roberts," a dark-skinned settler told a visitor to Monrovia in 1860, "is a very fine gentlemen, but he is more white than black."[8] In the legalistic but oddly lyrical language of race in antebellum America, Liberia's "George Washington" was an "octoroon," meaning just one of his eight great-grandparents was black. Under Virginia's "one drop of blood" rule, however, that was enough.

Disproportionately represented among the early settlers and among America's free persons of color, most mulattoes who went to Liberia not only went early, allowing them to acclimatize themselves to the new country and stake claims to its land and institutions, but went with all the advantages their caste had typically enjoyed over freed black slaves—education, training in a craft or profession, a habit of self-reliance, and capital. Roberts enjoyed every one of these advantages. He was born free, in Norfolk, in 1809, the second of seven children of Amelia Roberts and a father who died when Joseph was young and whose identity is lost to history. His mother was pious and hardworking, attributes that earned her the protection and patronage of influential whites, critical to any free black family's survival and success in the slave South. No less important to Joseph's privileged upbringing was his mother's second marriage, to an ambitious entrepreneur from Petersburg. James Roberts made his small fortune operating flatboats up and down Virginia's riverine tidewater, one of the few businesses open to African Americans of the Chesapeake. When he died, he left his family an estate unusually large for a free black man: two houses, several boats, and scattered parcels of land.

Joseph and his siblings were undoubtedly influenced by their stepfather's ambition and industriousness. His brother Henry would study at the Berkshire Medical School in Massachusetts and work as a doctor in Liberia, while his brother John would become bishop of Monrovia's Methodist Episcopal Church. Joseph, for his part, not only learned the elder Roberts's trade but apprenticed as a barber, among the most lucrative of free black professions. He met with luck again when he began working for a free black named William Colson, a man of many talents: entrepreneur, minister of the gospel, and self-educated scholar. Roberts, who received little formal education, was tutored by Colson and given access to his well-stocked private library.

Why Amelia and six of her seven offspring decided to emigrate in the winter of 1829 is not known. But the reasons can be guessed. Virginia's racial laws were harsh and getting harsher, even two years before the panic set off by Nat Turner's rebellion. Free blacks did not have the right to vote, no right to represent themselves in court, and whites could humiliate them with impunity. The restrictions and racism of Jacksonian-era Virginia were stifling for every free black person, but must have seemed especially galling to a man of means and nearly all-white ancestry.

Faith also played a part in the Robertses' decision. Amelia had tried to imbue her children with the piety that sustained her through impoverished widowhood, and it seemed to have taken root in her second son. Like the evangelical founders of the ACS, Joseph Roberts considered himself a subject of the "benevolent empire." Later, in his speeches as president of Liberia, he rarely missed an opportunity to invoke the settlers' providential mission. "[A]s the political happiness or wretchedness of ourselves and our children, and of generations yet unborn, is in our hands," he told the crowd assembled in front of Monrovia's Government House during his first inaugural address, "nay more, the redemption of Africa from the deep degradation, superstition, and idolatry in which she has so long been involved."[9]

As with most aspects of Liberian history, before Roberts and after, the prospect of making money was bound up in the more lofty missions of colonization. Roberts intended to turn his modest inheritance into great fortune in Liberia, but, like most pious Americans of his day, he saw holy writ in the commercial ledger, a convergence of impulses with special meaning for Liberia. According to the dogma of colonization, legitimate commerce would drive out illicit commerce—trade in commodities, in addition to providing the settlers with economic opportunities independent of whites, could offer African natives an alternative to the slave trade. In fact, the idea of an all-black trading network, anchored by colonies of enterprising and Christian African Americans, had been broached by the black whaling merchant Paul Cuffe at least a decade before the ACS's own colonization plans. And stripped of evangelism, the idea would outlast the ACS itself, informing Marcus Garvey's pan-African movement of the 1920s.

It was in this spirit of benevolence and business that Roberts and William Colson conceived their plans for a transatlantic company, with Roberts as factor in Liberia and Colson as Virginia broker, to deliver American emigrants to Africa and African products to America. Their timing could not have been better. In Liberia, under agent Joseph Mechlin's command, the settler militia was breaking the resistance of local tribes and opening up the lucrative trade with the tribes of the interior. Roberts's gift for winning business, honed on his stepfather's flatboats, was said to rival those of the legendary Mandingo traders now being pushed aside by colonists. Within a few years of his arrival in Liberia, Roberts was dispatching hides, ivory, camwood, and products derived from the ubiquitous areca palm to ports up and down America's Atlantic seaboard. He soon became a rich man, joining the tiny, moneyed elite who dominated Monrovia society and politics.

The members of this elite socialized and married among their own: one of Roberts's younger brothers wedded the daughter of the Liberia pioneer and declaration of independence signer Elijah Johnson; the *Liberia Herald* editor John Russwurm took Sarah McGill, the daughter of Vice Governor George McGill, as his bride; and Roberts himself married Jane Rose Waring, daughter of the colony's leading ecclesiastic and one of its most successful commercial farmers. They were a relatively homogeneous lot. Charles Thomas, a white visitor in the late 1850s, called Monrovia society "an aristocracy of means and education," dominated by the light-skinned, freeborn sons and daughters of the Chesapeake.[10]

Men like Roberts ran the colony's institutions, from the lay leadership of churches to the officer corps of the militia, and chaired the committees that arranged the frequent civic celebrations that played such a crucial part in Monrovian life in the nineteenth century. Charitable organizations, such as the Ladies Benevolent Society and the Ladies Liberia Literary Institute, were founded and led by the womenfolk of the leading families, while the men established branches of American fraternal organizations: the Odd Fellows, Good Templars, and, above all, the Masons, who elected Roberts as their first grand master and whose membership included virtually every leading merchant and member of the governing council.

The Liberian elite also lived well. "We found a degree of refinement and taste for which we were not prepared," Thomas wrote, though not without a hint of patronizing criticism. "The people desire to live in comfortable and pretty houses, the ladies and beaux dress in fashion . . . above their means, extravagantly so, and the quantity of kid gloves and umbrellas displayed on all occasions does not promise well for a nation whose hope rests on hard and well developed muscles."[11] The elite represented their own variant of colonials emulating the imperial metropolis. The Monrovian merchants and their wives were determined to refute racist assumptions that the colonization experiment would fail as the settlers atavistically descended into the savagery that surrounded them and in which they had originated. They endeavored to demonstrate their "civilized" status, as members of a transatlantic community of Anglo-Saxon refinement and morality. Parents chastised their children for adopting the pidgin "kwasai" or "waterside" talk of Monrovia's streets and docks, insisting they speak standard American English. And while many of Liberia's merchants and upriver sugar and coffee planters adopted African concubinage, taking on native "country wives," elite society was more Victorian than the Victorians. "[S]o far as outward behavior, law, and language, they are prudish to a truly American extent," noted the British historian Harry Johnston, during a stay in the 1880s. "Sparsest of clothing on the part of the natives is treated . . . as an offence . . . The Americo-Liberians still worship clothes as an outward and visible manifestation of Christianity and the best of civilization."[12]

Still, not all of Monrovia's "aristocracy of means and education" sought Christian refinement. For Edward Blyden, the West Indian–born black nationalist educator—who would become a kind of Monrovian Socrates, exiled for needling the powerful and radicalizing the young—the elite's "civilized" pretenses represented hypocrisy of the highest order. "[D]ishonesty stalks abroad under the semblance of piety; and impiety assumes the appearance of religion for the sake of gain," he lectured what must have been an uneasy Independence Day audience in 1857. "And . . . this extravagant manner of living . . . are made in the minds of many the standard of respectability . . . we attach more importance to *display* than to *reality*. There is very little that is substantial about us . . ."[13]

For the poor and middling black majority, however, the problem was less the pretenses of Liberia's ruling class than its power. Through connections with ACS officials and foreign traders, and ownership of the coasting vessels that plied Liberian waters, Monrovia's merchants controlled the flow of goods into and out of the colony, making it difficult for smaller operators—many Liberian farmers supplemented their meager incomes with petty trade—to compete. The operations of the merchant John Lewis, a brother-in-law of Roberts, were typical. As manager of the ACS warehouse, he controlled most of the colony's tobacco supply, the commodity most coveted by natives and hence most lucrative for settlers. To Sion Harris, a carpenter living in the upriver settlement of Caldwell, "Mr. Lewis [was] engage[d] in the menopolist [trade monopoly]." The whole tobacco business, Harris decided, was "only good for the merchant."[14] Predictably, the merchant elite's economic stranglehold extended to politics as well. Ever since the constitutional reforms of 1825, which had given the settlers a say in their own affairs, the merchants of Monrovia had been gradually taking control of Liberia's government as well as its economy, a trend the weakened ACS could do little about.

•

By the late 1830s, the society was under siege from all sides. In America, abolitionist and free black broadsides against the idea and practice of colonization had taken their toll, evidenced by declining donations from evangelical philanthropists, the lifeblood of such a capital-intensive enterprise. Relentless accounts in the press of Liberia as a disease-ridden swamp had dissuaded all but a few free blacks, who could pay their own way, from emigrating. And the growing conflict over the fate of slavery meant most members of Congress wanted little to do with colonization, a middle-of-the-road solution that was fast losing its political appeal. The ACS simply did not have the resources to support the colony nor the standing in international law to defend it. European interlopers, drawn by the lucrative trade opportunities and backed by their own governments, were refusing to recognize the sovereignty of what, from their perspective, seemed like a charitable foundation by another name.

For years, ACS board members operated under the assumption that they knew what was best for their black charges. But in a paternalistic situation, if the "parent" cannot provide, the "child" need not obey. More to the point, paternalism rests on the premise that adults will accept being treated as children. Time and again, history has demonstrated this premise to be unsustainable, and so it proved for the overburdened ACS and the increasingly restive Liberian colonists. In 1838, the board issued instructions to its agent Anthony Williams: assemble delegates from all the major settlements other than the independently run settlement called Maryland and have them draw up a constitution for a more autonomous government.

The delegates, unsurprisingly, virtually wrote the ACS out of the decision-making process, but the board summarily dismissed the idea that its agent would no longer have veto power over the decisions of the local legislature. As long as it was, figuratively speaking, putting a roof, however leaky, over the colonists' head, the ACS intended to have the final say. But the constitution the ACS offered in 1839 granted broad powers to the colonial legislature, including the right to declare war, issue currency, and collect tariffs and taxes. It also provided for the creation of an independent judiciary, and included something that benefited the merchant elite in Monrovia: a property requirement to vote. While not an inordinate sum, the minimum $25 in real estate eliminated the poorest and the landless citizens—who represented the majority of the 2,000-plus settlers—from the electoral rolls of what would now be known as the Commonwealth of Liberia.

Although Liberia's elite was not altogether pleased with the ACS retaining veto power, most members accepted the new constitution. As it turned out, the ACS appointee to the newly created post of governor, the young Thomas Buchanan, cousin of the last pre–Civil War president of the United States, rarely second-guessed the legislature, even as it passed new tariffs and restrictions on foreign traders. And when the legislature launched punitive expeditions against local tribes—often for failing to pay their debts to Monrovia merchants—Buchanan served as commander. The continuing presence of the ACS was not entirely unwanted. Roberts and other merchants had for years been more than happy to sell the society supplies when its warehouse for newly arrived emigrants ran low, and often did so, according to an ACS report, at "exorbitant prices." In 1834, the board had complained of the "ruinous practice of purchasing provisions from the merchants in Liberia on credit . . ."[15] The same businessmen also leased their coasting vessels to the society at high rates to transport emigrants and supplies to far-flung settlements.

In Monrovia, these merchant advantages did not go unnoticed. When the society ceased its retailing business in 1841, even Buchanan had to admit that the "poor people said it must be the result of a scheme of the merchants," though it had more to do with the ACS's strained finances.[16] Colonists in the outlying settlements along the coast and up the St. Paul's River valley were especially resentful, paying more for imported goods, getting less for their crops, and often being shut out of the lucrative native trade altogether.

The first signs of provincial unrest emerged in Grand Bassa, a tiny settlement fifty miles down the coast from Monrovia. John Seys, a white, West Indian–born, and entrepreneurial Methodist Episcopal minister, had first come to Liberia in 1834 to evangelize among the natives. The missions he founded served local settlers as well, many of whom earned money working for or selling to the church. Thus, when Buchanan and the legislature revoked the missionary's exemption from tariffs in 1840, Seys and many of the outlying settlers, already chafing under the political and economic hegemony of the Monrovia merchants, were outraged. The ambitious missionary—a demagogue according to Roberts and Buchanan—became the figure around which provincials and poor alike mobilized. "The citizens," one settler recalled Seys declaring, "ought to rise up and shake off this rotten system of tyranny and oppression."[17]

In the 1840 elections, the first under the commonwealth government and a portent of bitterly divided, postindependence contests, the Seys faction squared off against Monrovia's elite. Seys successfully rallied the people he represented, or at least appeared to. "At Millsburg [a farming settlement on the St. Paul's River], every voter was employed at unusually high wages on the [Seys-run] Saw Mill and sugar plantation," Buchanan complained, "and there *every vote* was polled for his friends." The other side had its own laments. As one financially struggling settler explained to the ACS board, "I am not influenced by Money, for I earn a living by the sweat of my brow . . . [S]till my situation is far more preferable than if I were placed in a condition where my 'salary' must govern the dictates of my conscience."[18]

In the end, the candidates of the government party, all of them businessmen, crushed the Seys faction. A year later, when Buchanan, Liberia's last white governor, died of fever and Roberts was appointed to replace him, the merchants' takeover of the government was complete. Roberts, a gifted politician, was a source of calm, at least for a time. But as the head of an impoverished outpost of exiled black Americans, he was less effective in disputes with outsiders. While commonwealth status, constitutional reforms, and a governor from the settlers' own ranks helped to satisfy settler demands for greater autonomy, it meant nothing to the foreign traders or their governments, which insisted on unfettered access to the territory and native trade the Monrovia authorities claimed as their own.

By any mid-nineteenth-century measure, Great Britain was the best friend the black man generally—and the Liberian people, in particular—had in the Western world. It was the British who, in Sierra Leone, first experimented with the idea of a refuge for former and recaptured slaves. It was the British who first abolished the transatlantic slave trade, in 1807, and enforced the ban with naval patrols. It was the British who, in 1833, became the first European nation to permanently ban slavery in its overseas territories; August 1, Emancipation Day in the empire, was warmly celebrated by Liberians each year with speeches, banquets, and toasts. And it was the British who in 1847 became the first nation to enter into diplomacy with Africa's first black republic, a full fifteen years ahead of the United States.* But the friendship had its limits. Britain's unrivaled power and wealth had been built on the ruthless pursuit of trade; when its merchants demanded unimpeded access to markets, whether in 1770s Boston or 1840s Liberia, London backed them without hesitation. The 1840s in Liberia were in part defined by a series of confrontations between British traders and officials in Sierra Leone on the one hand and Liberia's merchants and commonwealth government on the other.

"I have the honor to inform you that I have received a complaint from Mr. Dring, master of the British brig Ranger, stating that property to a considerable amount, belonging to him, has been seized at Bassa Cove, by Liberia authorities, under the pretence of an infraction of the laws."[19] So began a lengthy correspondence over 1841 and

---

*Washington's hesitation in recognizing the black republic—a republic created in part by the doings of some of America's most distinguished statesmen—was based on, among other things, the pettiest of principles. If the United States established formal relations with Liberia, it would have to host a diplomat from that country. And a Liberian ambassador could not be asked to eat in the kitchen with the help.

1842 between Captain Joseph Denman, commander of the Royal Navy's Sierra Leone division, and Governor Roberts. The issue was whether British merchants had to pay the commonwealth's port duties, which would make the goods they were peddling less competitive in the cutthroat competition that marked West African trade. Denman and other officials claimed the right of custom: British subjects had engaged in trade with African tribes and established factories, or trading posts in American parlance, on the Windward Coast long before Liberia's settlers had shown up, and claimed to have the treaties to prove it.

Roberts countered that the occasional trading voyage did not constitute custom, nor did it give the British the right to ignore Liberian law. And he challenged Denman to produce the treaties. But in a letter begging the ACS board to get Washington to look into the matter, Roberts sounded both more desperate and self-serving. "[British traders] sell goods at such reduced prices as to entirely disable the colonists to compete with them. This they [the British] can do without loss, because their goods are bought in England, and the poor colonist can only be furnished with goods second handed, and very frequently has to pay higher prices than what the natives have to pay at those British factories."[20]

Past practices and treaties aside, Denman proffered a more fundamental challenge to the duties: Liberia did not have the authority to impose them. Liberia, a philanthropically inspired exercise in black self-governance, had, before 1847, no legal standing in the eyes of Great Britain. International custom and law simply did not recognize the sovereignty of a privately sponsored territorial entity. In making a case for independence to the ACS board several years after the Denman exchange, Roberts himself admitted as much. "[W]hat seems most difficult to be understood in our organization, and which is constantly seized upon as a proof of the dependence of Liberia is, that the chief executive officer of the government is appointed and paid by the Colonization Society; and that all laws enacted by the Liberian Legislature, shall be subject to a revocation of the Society," he wrote to the board in his annual official message of 1846. "That an arrangement so novel and without precedence should, in its operations experience some jarrings, is not surprising; nor is it a matter of much astonishment that foreigners, at first view, should consider it complicated and perplexing."[21]

Lost in the considered language of official correspondence is the outrage of Liberians that a black-run government should be treated with such disrespect. "[I]t has been already said by the British that we have no right to demand Anchorage Duties &c of them," Peyton Skipwith wrote to his former master, John Cocke. "If we are to remain in the state we are now in, it is deplorable."[22] British merchants could be imperious. "British traders have become so inveterate against our speculators, that they allow them but a small share in the trade along the coast," Roberts noted to the board. "They effect this, sometimes, by ordering our traders from the spots they have selected to trade."[23] Backed by the nineteenth century's greatest naval power, the traders had little to fear. Whenever disputes arose, as in the Dring affair, Her Majesty's Government in Sierra Leone was quick to dispatch warships to Liberia's defenseless ports. As Blyden later wrote in his history of his adopted country, British actions called Liberia and all it represented into question. The settlers learned they "had no rights which the laws of nations could respect. These facts aroused the thinking people . . . to the desire for an independent national existence."[24]

The Reverend Beverly R. Wilson was such a "thinking" person. A free black of "unmixed African descent," Wilson had emigrated from Norfolk with his two sons in 1834. Although he lost one of them to native gunfire—on a supposed "peace mission" to a rebellious chief—he never looked back, expressing "almost uninterrupted pleasure" in his decision to take up what he called his African "inheritance."[25] And for good reason. Despite being functionally illiterate, Wilson achieved a stature and a level of prosperity unattainable to a black man in his native Virginia. By July 1847, when he served as one of eleven delegates to the Liberian constitutional convention, he was a leading merchant who owned two Monrovian warehouses valued at thousands of dollars and a lay official of the Methodist church.

At the convention, which was called by Roberts and other merchant leaders, he wasted no time asserting his views. In the words of the white physician J. W. Lugenbeel, whose private journal remains the only extant account of the proceedings, Wilson stood up on the very first day of deliberations and "stated that the people of Liberia do not require the assistance of 'white people' to enable them to make a Constitution for the government of themselves." At question was a draft constitution, drawn up at the request of the ACS board by the Harvard law professor and Massachusetts Colonization Society officer Simon Greenleaf. Three days later, Wilson was on his feet again. "The people of Liberia have heretofore allowed the Colonization Society to act as their trustees and guardians," he insisted, "but that they have now become of age, and are determined to manage their own affairs on their own territory."[26]

To Lugenbeel, Wilson's outrage was "really sickening," a display of "nonsensical egotism."[27] Putting aside Lugenbeel's contempt for the political efforts of the black Liberians, his commentary is revealing. In challenging ACS authority, Wilson and the other fire-eaters at the convention were arguing against a straw man. For if they wanted little to do with the ACS, the society by 1847 wanted even less to do with them. The 1839 commonwealth constitution had failed to resolve the existential problem of what Liberia was, as evidenced by the continuing mercantile disputes with Britain. Meanwhile, at home, the ACS continued to be ground down, like other institutions attempting to find common ground on the slavery question, by the forces of relentless polarization. In the South, supporters of colonization were seen as virtual co-conspirators of the abolitionists—a laughable charge to the latter group, who now ignored the ACS, having already won the battle for the hearts, minds, and wallets of antislavery Northern philanthropists. Recognizing that turning over sovereignty and governance of the colony to its residents would free up funds for emigrant expeditions, the ACS, at its thirtieth annual meeting, in January 1846, notified officials in Liberia that a new constitution would be drafted. Liberian independence, momentous as it was, was no act of revolution.

At the time, independence was not even a notably popular idea among Liberians, as the November 1846 balloting on the ACS resolution made clear. A poll called by Roberts in November 1846, even though it excluded natives, women, and any settler with less than $25 in real property, three groups that would have had more reason than any others to fear true independence and the dominance of the merchant elite, resulted in a discouragingly narrow victory for the pro-independence forces. "I regret exceedingly, to find by official returns that not more than two thirds of the legal voters of the Commonwealth attended the poles to record their opinion respecting this highly important question," Roberts told the legislature. And of those that did vote, only a "small majority" cast a "yes" ballot. Predictably, the governor laid the blame on demagogues like Seys who fueled public "ignorance . . . [that] the Legislature contemplated forming a new government without asking the consent of the people." He called the charge "preposterous" and lamented the whole acrimonious debate, which "prevented that unanimity of action so desirable on the adoption of any great and important measure."[28]

Indeed, many settlers who could vote, as well as the poor, saw the agitation for immediate independence as a *coup des marchands*. Again rallying around Seys, these poor and middling Liberians—the latter consisting of the commonwealth's petty traders, small farmers, and tiny professional class—presented a proposal to the convention that pointed out, of all things, the beneficence of the ACS: "1st *Resolved*, That the Citizens of the [Grand Bassa] County as yet see no cause for a dissolution of the present relation that the Commonwealth of Liberia sustains to its benefactors, the American Colonization Society; and that, under existing circumstances, we consider it a step not only imprudent, but ungrateful in the extreme."[29] It was an untenable position. Outnumbered by the Monrovia party at the convention and defending the unpopular status quo of ACS oversight, the opposition lost to the merchants, just as they had in the 1840 elections.

But in insisting upon and achieving independence, the merchant delegates did not act on greed alone. To be sure, they were likely to—and, in fact, did—benefit financially from full sovereignty. They also preferred in their declaration the "right to acquire, possess, enjoy and defend property" over the "pursuit of happiness."[30] But what else could be expected, considering their experiences in America? For freeborn blacks and former slaves, property ownership was one of the few rights they enjoyed under law. Property also assured the black family a modicum of freedom from an oppressive racial order. To the pro-independence delegates, the pursuit of happiness was a luxury of the enfranchised, while property rights were a necessity for those aspiring to that status.

In combining higher ideals with self-interest, Liberia's founders were not so different from the framers of the American Constitution. A few of the 1847 delegates were well versed in European political theory, and all were deeply committed to the small-r republicanism—economic opportunity, political participation, and equality before the law—from which they had been excluded in America. Christian benevolence permeated the early Liberian republic, just as it did the American.* But whereas the framers of the U.S. Constitution shied away from any explicit mention of divine guidance, their Liberian counterparts invoked Christianity from the start and enshrined its place in the nation. In an official statement that prefaced the constitution, and served as a kind of declaration of independence, the delegates openly declared, "We the People of the Commonwealth of Liberia, in Africa, acknowledging with devout gratitude, the goodness of God, in granting to us the blessings of the Christian religion,

---

*Until 1825, for instance, Monrovia was known as Christopolis.

and political, religious, and civil liberty do . . . constitute ourselves a Free, Sovereign and Independent State."[31] When the delegate Samuel Benedict presented the document to the citizenry for their approval, he declared, "It is our earnest desire that the affairs of this government may be so conducted as to merit the approbation of all Christendom."[32] Like the vast majority of their compatriots, the delegates were devout men; more than half were preachers or lay officials in the dominant Baptist and Methodist churches. Not only had faith helped African Americans endure slavery and discrimination, but it provided the moral framework for the colonization idea. Both white sponsors and black settlers ritualistically invoked Psalms 68:31: "Ethiopia shall soon stretch forth its hand unto God."

In the final analysis, however, race outweighed all other considerations in the thinking behind and the writing of the Liberian constitution, which was officially called the "Declaration of Rights." Slavery, needless to say, was explicitly banned by the Declaration, but the framers pressed the matter further. "The great object of forming these Colonies, being to provide a home for the dispersed and oppressed children of Africa, and to regenerate and enlighten this benighted continent," Article V, Section 13 read, "None but persons of color shall be admitted to citizenship in this Republic."[33] The framers justified the clause as a defensive measure necessary to prevent white outsiders from buying up land and businesses in the new republic; a separate clause stated that only citizens could own land.

In essence, the delegates re-created in their constitution the truth hiding behind the principles of the American constitution: the "people" in the Liberian constitution's "we the people" explicitly meant black men and women only. As the ringing cadences of the delegate Hilary Teage's preface to the Liberian constitution, which the eleven delegates of the convention offered to the Liberian citizenry and the world on July 26, 1847, intoned:

We, the people of the Republic of Liberia were originally inhabitants of the United States of North America. In some parts of that country, we were debarred by law all the rights and privileges of men—in other parts, public sentiment, more powerful than law, frowned us down.

We were every where shut out from all civil office.

We were excluded from all participation in government.

We were taxed without our consent.

We were made a separate and distinct class, and against us

Every avenue to improvement was effectually closed . . .

We uttered our complaints, but they were unattended to . . .

All hope of a favorable change in our country was thus wholly extinguished in our bosoms, and we looked with anxiety abroad for some asylum from the deep degradation.[34]

Exactly two months later, the constitution was put to a popular vote. Feelings still ran high; many in the Seys faction refused to participate. Of the 214 votes cast for the constitution, out of a total of only 270, more than half came from Monrovia, where the lopsided count was 111 to 0. Even had there been no boycott, it probably would have passed, though by a narrower margin of perhaps 50. In any event, these numbers are remarkably low. In 1843, the last year before independence that a census was taken, the settler population stood at 2,390. Four years later, it had probably grown by a few hundred, meaning that just 10 percent of the population voted. Only twice that number was even eligible to vote, of course, after the exclusion of women, minors, and the landless. Far more conspicuous in their absence were the natives, tens of thousands of whom lived in the territory claimed by the new republic. But to have included them in the the ranks of citizens would have swamped the settlers and eroded the very reasons for the republic in the first place—as a refuge for free blacks and freed slaves from America.

The constitution did not ignore the native population altogether,

however. Article V, Section 14 forbade individual settlers from purchasing native lands, presumably to ward off unscrupulous speculators. Section 15 aimed at weaning the natives from the slave trade:
"the improvement of the native tribes and their advancement in the
arts of agriculture and husbandry being a cherished object of this
government, it shall be the duty of the President to appoint in each
county some discreet person whose duty it shall be to make regular
and periodical tours through the country for the purposes of calling the
attention of the natives to these wholesome branches of industry."*[35]
Despite these provisions, however, the natives, who outnumbered
the settlers by 25 or 50 to 1, depending on how far Liberian jurisdiction actually extended, were strangers in their own land, subject to
Liberian law but excluded from citizenship, as were the recaptive
slaves who remained under the guardianship of the U.S. government
agent in Monrovia. The country was divided into coastal counties,
where Americo residents were citizens, and inland territories with
virtually no voice in the government. Paternalism won out over racial
solidarity. For those natives or recaptives who shed tribal language,
dress, and custom, there was a path to citizenship. But those who resisted Liberian authority would be declared enemies, and made war
upon.

Some black men, in other words, were less equal than others.
The delegates could seem blind to this reality. During a particularly
contentious convention debate over whether the ACS should retain
any rights to territory in the new republic, Lugenbeel quoted Reverend Wilson as saying that "the territory of Liberia belongs to the citizens of Liberia, as *an inheritance from their forefathers*'; that they are
'the proper descendants of the original proprietors of the soil; and,
therefore, that they are 'the proper inheritors of the whole country.'"[36] Thus, amid celebrations accompanying the unfurling of the
Liberian flag and the first look at the national seal that declared "the

---

*These appointments were not adequately made until the early twentieth century.

love of liberty brought us here," the original inhabitants of the land were all but forgotten. As the convention's independence declaration had it, "We, the people of the Republic of Liberia were originally inhabitants of the United States of North America." The omission would haunt the republic for the rest of its days.

FIVE

A Matter of Color

Edward Wilmot Blyden never really trusted mulattoes, and he wasn't shy about saying so. To the West Indian–born intellectual, who immigrated to Liberia shortly after its independence, the "half-whites" were traitors to their own African blood. "[T]here is more Negro hate in those men than they are aware of," he told the Maine State Colonization Society in 1862, "more want of confidence and trust in their mother's blood than they are willing to admit . . . They cling to the side of their [white] father."[1] A dozen years later he was pleading with the American Colonization Society to do everything in its power to stop them from going to Liberia. "You are planting here a nest of vipers who hate the country and the race," he argued in a letter to the society's secretary William Coppinger. "Do save us from this inundation."[2]

Blyden, who proudly described himself as being of "ebony hue," claimed that mulattoes held dangerous power, on both sides of the Atlantic, over a race that they secretly despised. They "have set themselves up as representatives and leaders of the coloured people of this country [America]," he noted, "[but] who have no faith in Negro ability to stand alone." They were men who "love to sit in the highest places at public gatherings and conventions held by blacks," but refused to open their homes and shops to those darker than themselves.[3]

They had used this power to stymie the very thing Blyden had devoted his life to: integrating a thriving Liberia into a prosperous and civilizing Africa. In the United States, they "scatter[ed] pestilential teachings" about the motherland, "counsel[ing] poor blacks to remain [in America] . . . fearful that . . . emigration will unsettle their hold upon their followers, and eventually leave none in the land low enough to do them honour."[4] And in Liberia, mulattoes did everything in their power to thwart what Blyden felt was the country's destiny as a convergence of Africa and the West, a place where the best of each world would foster black self-rule. "They oppose all interior openings [that is, outreach to the interior of Africa] and do not disguise the most impetuous contempt for the natives except in their public speeches for foreign consumption," he informed Coppinger.[5] In Liberia as in America, Blyden believed, a simple racialist reality held true: a small, light-skinned elite worked against the will of the black masses.

As with most things Liberia, though, the nation's mulattoes were more complicated than they at first appeared. Blyden would know; he married a daughter of Monrovia's mulatto elite, even though, like the white racial theorists of his day, he held that the mixing of white and black blood produced a race of weak half-breeds. The Liberian color line was not as hard and fast as Blyden made it out to be. It was true that mulattoes dominated the higher reaches of political and economic life in early Liberia, and that many of the darker-skinned settlers resented their influence. But men such as Stephen Benson and Edmund Roye, whose African lineage was evident in their features and skin tone, served as presidents in the first quarter century after Liberia's independence and were some of the richest men in the country. Indeed, class and birth status—free-born versus slave-born—were often just as influential as racial lineage. Nevertheless, the matter of color resonated in every corner of Liberian life.

Like many members of the Liberian elite he criticized, Blyden was raised with all the privilege a black man in a nineteenth-century slave society—in his case, the Danish West Indies island of St. Thomas—

could hope for. Both his father, Romeo, a tailor, and his mother, Judith, a schoolteacher, were free and, even rarer, literate and relatively prosperous. On the streets of Synagogue Hill, home to the island's sizeable Sephardic Jewish population, the young Blyden played alongside future Confederate secretary of state Judah Benjamin.

Educated in school and tutored at home by his mother, Blyden demonstrated an aptitude for learning, particularly foreign languages. After his family briefly lived in Venezuela in the early 1840s, Blyden returned to St. Thomas fluent in Spanish, and in the grip of an incipient racial consciousness. As he later wrote, he could not help but notice that while the newly liberated republic of Venezuela had banned slavery, blacks performed the most menial tasks and were treated as second-class citizens. That lesson was further reinforced during his first brief stay in the United States in 1850. Encouraged by John Knox, an American clergyman in St. Thomas, Blyden traveled to New Jersey to attend the Theological College at Rutgers. But the scholarly, polyglot eighteen-year-old's application was turned down by school officials, who did little to disguise that race was the only factor in their decision. After similar experiences with several other schools, Blyden concluded that America was no place for people of color.

He considered both a return to St. Thomas and continuing north, to Canada. But the former offered few opportunities for intellectually ambitious individuals, and Canada, to the young black nationalist, was just another place where white men ruled over black men, if a bit more politely. There was, however, another option, according to Knox's American friends, many of them connected to the colonization project: Liberia. They claimed that the world's only black republic—other than ill-starred Haiti—was the one place where a talented young black man could realize his potential.

For Blyden, the decision was not a difficult one. Like most educated blacks of his day, even abolitionists who considered the white-led colonization movement a conspiracy to drive free blacks from America, Blyden was convinced that benighted Africa was calling out for its long-lost sons to return and lead it out of darkness. His idealism was manifest in a December 1850 article in the *New York Colonization Journal*, one of the first published pieces in his prodigious career as a polemicist. Liberia, he predicted, would one day "include within its limits the dark regions of Ashantee and Dahomey and bring those barbarous tribes under civilized and enlightened influences."[6] Three weeks later, he was sailing out of Baltimore Harbor.

At the time, the shift within Liberian immigration from free blacks and mulattoes to poor and less worldly manumitted slaves—from the likes of Coker and Carey to people like Peyton Skipwith and his family—had already occurred. The sudden surge of free black emigration in 1850 and 1851, a response to passage of the Fugitive Slave Act, which put every free black on either side of the Mason-Dixon Line at risk of abduction and enslavement, was an aberration. By 1861, when the Civil War effectively put an end to emigration from the United States, manumitted slaves and their descendants outnumbered free blacks and their descendants by roughly three to two.

But their numerical strength did not translate into political or economic power. To the ACS, the settlers' two-tier society had from the beginning been rooted in the slave experience. Manumitted slaves, "having never been permitted to act or think for themselves," noted Joseph Mechlin in 1831, "are in point of industry and intelligence far below the free people of colour, and really know not how to provide for their future wants."[7] As usual, the white agent missed the point. True, manumitted slaves were less educated and perhaps unused to fending for themselves, but they were also poorer, in every sense of the word. They came with little money and few connections, to white and free black businessmen back in the States (who might forward them capital or serve as partners in trading enterprises) or to the close-knit mercantile community in Monrovia. By the time the bulk of former slaves arrived in the 1840s and 1850s, the earlier emigrants had already established themselves as an effective ruling class.

Merchant wealth bred resentment among ordinary settlers, who felt the elite used their advantaged position to secure power for themselves and deny opportunities to others. While the elites' power and wealth was most noticeable in Monrovia, it also pervaded the smaller settlements of the interior and along the coast, as Augustus Washington noted in an 1854 letter addressed to Frederick Douglass. A teacher and daguerrotypist, Washington was neither an impoverished farmer nor one of the merchant elite but, like Blyden, a member of Liberia's tiny middle class. As Washington explained, "in nearly every town and county, there is a one-man power, for that county; a man may hold all the offices of government and besides be lawyer, merchant, judge, and agent for the [American Colonization] Society, and, if he chooses, it is not difficult to turn the money and offices of these people into his own coffers."[8]

Most settlers would have nodded knowingly at Washington's observation. But they might have added that the big men, the ones who owned the ships and enacted the legislation and lived in the grand houses, were more likely than not mulattoes. This tension had its roots in America, where mulattoes were better situated than blacks as a result of their status as the offspring of white fathers (and occasionally mothers) and because whites were more likely to do business with them. Mulattoes typically had more money, better skills, and a higher level of education. In the South, they were far more likely than darker-skinned blacks to be free: according to the 1850 census, mulattoes constituted 65 percent of Virginia's free black population but just 22 percent of its slave force. Though elite blacks and mulattoes in most free African American communities in the United States were bound together by class and white animus, they remained communities apart. They might live together in the black part of town, but in different wards. And while economically successful free black males frequently married into mulatto families, the reverse was a rare occurrence. In late antebellum Cincinnati, for example, more than 90 percent of mulatto men married their own kind.

Suspicion, hostility, and contempt were inevitable. Mulatto haughtiness toward blacks was common enough that even whites noticed it. After visiting a Methodist church in Charleston, a colonization agent noted that the mulatto congregants "utterly refused to sit promiscuously with the blacks; and that, in all relations in life, they maintain the same dignified reserve; that the two classes are as totally distinct as it is possible for them to be."[9] In fact, some mulattoes bridled at the idea of immigrating to Liberia, if only because they could not imagine blacks being on equal footing with them. One group of mulattoes went so far as to tell the ACS secretary Ralph Gurley that they would only go "*provided* they could have a colony to *themselves*."[10] William Kellogg, a mulatto slave from North Carolina, was even more explicit, telling his master he would prefer slavery in America if freedom in Liberia meant falling "into the hands of my inferiors."[11]

Many blacks in turn resented and distrusted mulattoes. After the failed Denmark Vesey slave uprising of 1822, the blacks of Charleston blamed mulattoes for informing the white authorities of the plan. In a speech to that city's elite light-skinned Friendly Moralist Society, Michael Eggart acknowledged the hostility, stating that as mulattoes they faced not only the "prejudice of the white man" but "the deeper hate of our more sable brethren."[12] De Toqueville picked up on the tension and put it another context, noting that "when quarrels originating in differences of color take place, they [mulattoes] generally side with whites, just as the lackeys of the great in Europe assume the contemptuous airs of nobility towards the lower orders."[13]

Still, for most mulattoes and blacks in America, white racism was the larger problem. Thus in Liberia, where there were few whites and, after 1847, none in power, the prejudices mulattoes and blacks brought with them became magnified.

The nineteen-year-old Blyden arrived in Monrovia in January 1851 and immediately his idealism ran up against the realities of Liberian life. He had apprenticed with his father as a tailor but found that his skills were not in demand; the poor could not afford his services while the upper classes had their clothes imported from Paris and New York. So he became a clerk for the merchant (and future president) Stephen Benson, and resumed his studies, between predictable bouts with "acclimating sickness."[14]

Although housed in a dank onetime grocery store, the newly founded Presbyterian-run Alexander High School Blyden attended was Monrovia's most prestigious educational institution and, in the absence of any college, offered the most advanced education available. Its dozen or so settler pupils, under the tutelage of the Princeton Theological Seminary graduate D. A. Wilson, studied the classical curriculum of the best American secondary schools back home: Greek, Latin, theology, mathematics, geography. With his linguistic gifts, Blyden excelled and within a couple of years was earning money as a tutor and as acting schoolmaster during Wilson's many absences due to fever.

Blyden also devoted himself to learning Hebrew, a language he had first heard growing up on Synagogue Hill. He intended to correct the bias of most interpretations of biblical passages relating to Africa and Africans, and in 1857 wrote his first scholarly essay, which refuted the accepted notion that the curse on Noah's son Ham was justification for the enslavement of the Negro race.

He learned a more profound lesson outside of school, one that put him on a collision course with the country's mulatto elite. For all of his budding intellectual convictions about African destiny and his growing suspicion that a "foreign race" had taught the black man a "thoroughly injurious and false" version of his heritage, he had no engagement with the real-life natives in Monrovia or the hinterland.[15] He still subscribed to the notion of the settlers' divinely sanctioned mission to bring civilization to the "dark continent." In a letter to Knox, he expressed approval of an 1852 militia expedition against the Kru, noting that the "enemy" had been "subdued," before reflexively adding, "Surely, God is on our side."[16]

Like most Liberian men under forty, Blyden, though he was "physically unprepossessing," was expected to shoulder his share of the republic's defense.[17] In 1853, a year after praising the victory over the Kru, he was recruited into the militia for a punitive expedition against the rebellious Vai, a tribe to the north that would resist paying taxes to Monrovia into the early years of the twentieth century. Although vexing, the Vai commanded the settlers' respect; they were one of the few African peoples to develop their own system of writing independent of Arabic or European languages.* President Benson even claimed that the Vai were "intellectually in advance of many of the immigrants to this country from the United States."[18] Blyden was impressed as well. On the military expedition, Blyden found the Vai "capital . . . remarkably fortified," a testament to "the inventive genius of the natives" and a refutation of "the unfairness of those who represented the native Africans as naturally indolent, and living in a state of ease and supineness."[19]

Blyden never looked back from this first encounter with natives. He began to venture into the hinterland to learn more about the peoples there. He was struck by their learning, commenting on the "extensive manuscripts in poetry and prose" he encountered.[20] As Blyden established himself in settler society—he became editor of the *Liberia Herald* in 1855, an ordained Presbyterian minister and principal of Alexander High School in 1858, and professor of classics at the newly opened Liberia College in 1862—his respect for native African thought and custom only grew. He praised everything that Europeans and Liberians disparaged, even polygamy, which was especially repellant to the Protestant settlers.

Indeed, Blyden came to prefer native culture to settler culture. The natives, Blyden wrote, after a journey to Boporu in 1871, were "more independent than our independent republic . . . Interior people have the advantage over us in never having been under foreign masters, in never having imbibed a sense of inferiority or a

---

*Momolu Duala Bukare, the Vai scholar who devised the system, was said to have been inspired by Sequoyah, the Native American linguist who developed the famed Cherokee syllabary, whom he may have learned about while attending Lott Carey's short-lived school for natives in Cape Mount in the 1820s.

feeling of self-depreciation. They had never had to look up to white men for anything . . . They are entirely free from the mental and moral trammels which the touch of the Caucasian has imposed upon us."[21] To Blyden, Liberians had much to learn from the "half-naked savages" they shunned. As opposed to the acquisitive Western culture of the settlers—which in Blyden's mind was a sure path to "poverty, criminality and insanity"—"the African system of communal property and co-operative effort" assured that "every member of a community has a home and a sufficiency of food and clothing and other resources of life and for life."[22]

Blyden, ever the idealist, believed that Liberia should not be a crude facsimile of a Western nation, but should draw on the native example to create an entirely new kind of society. "How shall we make ourselves sublime?" he asked readers of the *Herald*. "Not by imitating and thus not only cut a most ungainly figure, but accomplish nothing either for ourselves or the world." Liberians, he charged, had imbibed the white man's contempt for Africa. "The notion still common among us is that the most important [part] of our education or knowledge consists in knowing what foreigners have said about things . . . about Africa. Hence some of us are found repeating things against ourselves which are thoroughly false and injurious to us because we read them in books."[23] But Liberia had its own "manifest destiny" beyond the coastal settlements, in Africa's forests and savanna. Expansion into the hinterland promised not just prosperity but life itself for the settlers. "Here we are after fifty years," he complained to the ACS, "lingering, nay perishing on the coast . . . Our backs are still to be turned on the inviting and healthful interior . . ."[24]

His point of view was not, in this respect, unique. European explorers had long emphasized in their writings the contrast between the feverish coast and the salubrious hinterland. But Blyden's goal was different, and profound: the forging of a black empire of both settlers and natives. "We must show that we are able to go alone, to carve our own way," he would write upon accepting the presidency of Liberia College in 1881. "We must not suppose that the Anglo-Saxon methods are final . . . We must study our brethren in the interior who knows more than we do the laws of growth for the race."[25] The path forward was plain to see. Liberians should "amalgamate" with the "athletic and vigorous" Africans of the interior, particularly the Mandingo, both literally, through marriage, but also in the political sense.[26] "I am confident," he wrote, "that when this Republic comes to herself—I mean her African self . . . and understands how to co-operate with and utilize her aboriginal population, she will have many things to teach the world for the welfare and advancement of humanity."[27]

While informed by his Liberian experience, Blyden's ideas about a global African identity—uniting blacks in the diaspora and on the mother continent—ultimately transcended it. No thinker before him had more forcefully and eloquently framed the idea of an African society that, adapted to the modern world, would provide blacks around the world a path out of political, economic, and, perhaps most important, psychological servitude to the white race. When the Republic fell in 1980, Blyden still represented Liberia's greatest intellectual contribution to global civilization, a pioneer who had made possible the careers and thought of black nationalist thinkers from Marcus Garvey to Kwame Nkrumah.

But, in the mid to late nineteenth century, his influence was yet to be felt—especially in Liberia. He despaired of his adopted nation. "It is difficult for me to repress the tears in my eyes when I consider what a noble opportunity Liberia has allowed almost to slip by. Native chiefs of power and widespread influence were ready to place their talents at the service of the Republic," he wrote in 1871. "But they were persistently ignored and became enemies."[28] What, then, was the purpose of Liberia? The Republic demonstrated no "special or peculiar adaptation to the situation it occupies. It has not given evidence of such distinct individuality as makes a man or a nation interesting and indispensable. Any European colony could have done as much and more on the line we have been pursuing."[29]

Blyden blamed Liberia's leadership, who, lacking imagination and statecraft, simply "did not understand their opportunity in the work which devolved upon them." He was referring to the mulatto elite, who kept Liberians facing the West. "Any forward movement is looked upon with alarm," he told the ACS secretary Coppinger. "They love to settle on the sea coast in a selfish clanship caring only to rule with no instinctive care for a future which they know they will never enjoy." The issue, to him, was one of race, not class. "[The mulattoes] discourage all earnest patriotism and enterprise which look to the interior," he said, because of their "fear of being absorbed by a people [i.e., Africans] . . . [they] strangely persist in regarding as a foreign element." It was for that reason, he told Coppinger, as he had told the Maine colonizationists a decade before, that Liberia's "peace and prosperity depend altogether upon keeping [mulattoes] in America. They will never succeed here or suffer us [black settlers] to succeed. And they can never be welded into the life of this African nation."[30]

The bitter 1869 presidential contest gave Blyden hope that the mulatto "clique" might be losing its grip on power and that the dark-skinned former slaves would finally take their rightful place at the helm of state. "The election of Mr. [Edmund James] Roye," he wrote of his close friend and political ally, in a dispatch to the ACS's *African Repository*, "is the triumph of a party which have been striving for several years to obtain such a position in the country as would enable them to carry out certain principles which they regard as indispensable to the proper growth of that African [i.e., nonmulatto] nationality."[31]

Like the "revolution of 1800," the term Thomas Jefferson's supporters gave his electoral victory, the 1869 election in Liberia brought to power a man who spoke of overthrowing a political aristocracy, restoring a republic, and returning a government to its people. And just like the wealthy Jefferson, a son of the same ruling class he railed against, Roye seemed at first glance an unusual candidate to lead such a revolution. He was not just an experienced politician, but was said to be the richest man in the country, with a small fleet of ships and lucrative trading contacts on three continents. And, aside from the deep sable of his skin, his background was remarkably similar to the leader of the mulatto ruling elite, the venerable first president of the republic, Joseph Jenkins Roberts.

Roye was born in 1815, in the small Ohio town of Newark. His father, according to some accounts, was a runaway slave from Kentucky; little is known of his mother, other than that she came from Virginia. Seeing the same opportunity as many of his white neighbors, John Roye—a farmer, boatman, and teamster who spent much of his time in Indiana and Illinois, hundreds of miles from his family—speculated in the Midwestern real estate market of the 1820s, leaving his family well taken care of upon his death in 1829. His bookish heir Edward used some of the estate to obtain an exceptional education for a black youth of his day, including a three-year stint at Ohio University in Athens. A schoolteacher for a time, Roye then went into business for himself, dealing in sheep and eventually, like his father, dabbling in real estate, picking up discounted properties during the economic panic of the late 1830s and building up a small fortune of his own. He married and fathered two children, only to see his wife die shortly after the birth of the second.

Reminiscing later in life, he tried to evoke his thoughts at the time of his decision, in the 1840s, to emigrate: "I have steadily had [my] mind fixed upon a foreign land, since my early youth; a land of African government; for there I believed our elevation would take place."*[32] Such reasoning, whether or not it was true to his younger self's motivations, served him politically in Liberia; fellow émigrés were eager to support a man who claimed that the decision to come to Liberia was inspired by ideals rather than by deteriorating circumstances for free blacks in Ohio in the wake of the bloody, anti-black Cincinnati race riots of 1829.

Roye arrived in Monrovia in June 1846 with a developed talent

---

*By "African government," Roye meant, in the usage of the day, any government run by persons of African descent. His attendance at French-language classes at Oberlin College in 1845 suggests that he contemplated Haiti, the choice of some free black émigrés from the United States, as a new home as well.

for business and a shipload of goods to sell. Within a few years, he established himself as one of the country's leading merchants, launching the first international shipping line to fly the Liberian flag. Political power in Liberia typically coinciding with economic power, he served as speaker of the house in 1849 and, for four years, in the mid-1860s, as the country's chief justice. During this period, he built a political coalition, in both Monrovia and the upriver settlements, among Liberia's growing population of striving former slaves and African recaptives.

As he rose to prominence in Liberian life, Roye developed a close personal friendship with Blyden. Both were well-read, which surely contributed to the bond. But they also shared a pride in their blackness—Roye referred to himself as "a pure descendant of the Ibo tribe"—and a resentment of the mercantile elite.[33] Roye agreed with Blyden that the mulatto minority was holding Liberia back from its African destiny. In the 1860s the two established the National True Whig Party, to challenge the ruling Republicans. Roye, who was the more personable of the two and possessed the resources to run the kind of American-style ballyhoo campaigns the electorate expected, became the party's leader. The National True Whig Party did not meet immediate electoral success, but Roye and Blyden nevertheless expanded their base of support to include up-country farmers, the middling classes of Monrovia, and freed slave immigrants like the Skipwiths. In the presidential election of 1869, it was these constituencies that ousted the lackluster James Payne and replaced him with Roye.

From the start, Roye and Blyden attempted to turn their idealism and ambitions into policy. In his inaugural address, Roye spoke of a central bank, railroads to the interior, and a public school system. Though not a particularly religious man himself, he invoked the hand of Providence, a required refrain in public speech. But this did not lessen the impact of his overt references to black pride as the guiding principle of his administration. "It is our duty," he told the assembled citizens and dignitaries in front of Government House, "to prove that the mental and other disabilities under which the Negro labors as a result of his service antecedents are not inherent . . . but that they are solely the result of circumstances, to be altogether re-moved when those circumstances are altered."[34]

Roye proclaimed that he would redirect the country's energies toward the interior, which was also standard political cant for Monrovia politicians—Liberia's own "city upon a hill" theme—but gave it a spe-cial edge: "I believe that the object of our residence on this coast is to bear some humble part in bringing out the fulfillment of that cheer-ing prophecy, that Ethiopia shall stretch forth her hands unto God." To the light-skinned members of his audience, he then issued a veiled warning. "Who among us," he said, "will prove recreant to a trust of such magnitude, and involving such important consequences?"[35] Blyden, who no doubt had helped to write the speech, was delighted, especially by Roye's plan for schools in native villages. Shortly after the inauguration, he headed up-country, a one-man legation to the chiefs of Boporu, a key administrative and trade center in the near hin-terland, where he spread the good word that a new day had dawned in Monrovia and a new era in settler-native relations had begun.

But change in Monrovia was not immediately forthcoming. The election had produced a divided government—Republicans still con-trolled the Senate—and the makings of a constitutional crisis. On the same ballot that put Roye in the Executive Mansion was an amend-ment that would extend the presidential term from two years to four and double the terms of senators and representatives. These were popular ideas. Most Liberians believed that the two-year election cycle produced a nonstop campaign that hampered good governance, and, moreover, were sensitive to white criticism that the country was something of a political circus.

The measure passed in a landslide since both Republican and Whig voters expected their candidates to win. When Roye came out on top, however, the Republican Senate balked, putting the measure on the ballot again in a special plebiscite. But the votes on the second referendum were never counted, at least publicly. Instead, the Senate seized the ballots and then issued a "resolution" declaring the amendment had not received the two-thirds necessary for passage. Roye, with a typical Liberian emphasis on legal niceties, noted the word *resolution* in the Senate's declaration and cited his own constitutional right to veto such legislative decisions. He then declared the second referendum null and void and made sure the first was put into effect.

But the Republicans, the party of the mulatto mercantile elite, were determined to press forward. They persuaded Roberts to return to political life and run for the presidency in May 1871, despite the fact that Roye had declared such an election, just two years after his own, a violation of the amended constitution. Running unopposed, Liberia's founding father "won," then left for Europe to wait out the long period the constitution called for between election and inauguration on the first Monday of the following year. Even with Roberts gone, however, a political showdown, and perhaps even an outbreak of violence, seemed inevitable. "Matters stand in a very serious condition here," reported the Monrovia correspondent of Britain's *African Times*. "The country is in a great uproar . . . Every man seems to have the law in his hands."[36]

In Monrovia's close-knit elite society, few secrets stayed that way for long. It had been public knowledge for some time that Blyden's fifteen-year-old marriage to Sarah Yates was an unhappy one. The race-proud Blyden had, for reasons unknown (but which can be guessed at), wedded the niece of one of the wealthiest mulatto businessmen in Monrovia who was also the country's vice president. The match had not been a congenial one; the barely literate Sarah showed little interest in her husband's intellectual pursuits and could not have been pleased at Blyden's genteel poverty or utter lack of commercial ambition, a conspicuous shortcoming in Liberia's high society.

Blyden chose to put a political spin on things, claiming that the discord was due to his wife being more loyal to her clan than to her husband. Indeed, in a letter to a friend in the United States, he depicted Sarah as an enemy in his home. "I live among an unsympathetic people—and, I regret to say, an unsympathizing family," he wrote. "My wife seems entirely unimproveable. She is of the mind and temperament of the people around her . . . I am persecuted *outside* but more inside. Uncongenial, incompatible, unsympathetic, my wife makes the burden of my life sore and heavy."*[37]

Blyden's opinion of the first lady, Mrs. Edward Roye, was more favorable. He once told Roye he respected him for choosing a wife from the ranks of black settlers, something his wealthier dark-skinned predecessors had not done. And, indeed, Blyden enjoyed a close relationship with the first lady, which, given his own marital problems, left him open to charges from Republicans that he had been carrying on an affair with her. In the heated political atmosphere of the disputed election, the charges led to violence, as a mob claiming to stand up for the president's honor, and made up of what Blyden called "forty poverty-stricken and ignorant blacks," put a rope around Blyden's neck and dragged him through the streets of Monrovia. Blyden said the mob was "mulatto-incited."[38] But some observers saw Roye's hand in it, and not because he believed the rumors of an affair, but because he saw Blyden as a means to deflect mulatto anger away from himself.

Roye may have felt he had no choice. Long a polarizing figure in Liberian politics, Blyden got caught up in a controversy when a confidential letter to the New York Colonization Society, the professor's benefactor, was printed in the Smithsonian Institution's annual report for 1870 and reprinted in Monrovia newspapers. While Blyden's disdain for the merchant elite was hardly a secret, the contents of the letter were especially inflammatory; in it, Blyden urged American philanthropists to cut off funding to mulatto students. Citing statisti-

---

*Blyden would later move in with a dark-skinned settler named Anna Erskine, thereby flouting the social customs of the Monrovia elite, which dictated that mistresses be taken from the African population and kept at upriver plantations.

cal evidence, Blyden argued that the death rate among mulattoes was so high that it made little sense to pay for their education. That and claims that "decadent mulattoes in important positions" were responsible "for Liberia's want of enterprise and progress" produced such outrage that Roye opted to distance himself from his longtime friend and ally.[39]

In the end, Blyden was saved from a lynching by the last-minute intervention of another powerful friend, the former president Daniel Warner, who urged him, for his own safety, to leave the country. Blyden needed little persuading. He fled to Sierra Leone, where, for two years, he edited a Freetown paper and served as agent to the interior for the local colonial government. The forced absence, while no doubt upsetting to a man who considered himself a Liberian patriot, saved his life.

Roye's expansive plans were also expensive ones, especially for a government as impoverished as Liberia's. Virtually all of the country's revenue came from import and export duties and, as the legislature was dominated by merchants who paid these customs, collection was haphazard and payment usually honored in the breach. So Roye tried a different tack. All civilized governments, he lectured the legislature, ran a public debt, which they "converted into a sort of available capital and circulate as money upon the faith of the government which renders itself worthy of credit."[40] Why shouldn't Africa's only black republic do likewise?

But opposition lawmakers refused to authorize a loan. Undeterred, in the summer of 1871, shortly after Blyden's escape to Sierra Leone, Roye contacted Liberia's representative in London, David Chinery, to make inquiries in the city's financial markets. Essentially an ambassador for hire, Chinery, a British national, operated on the fringes of London's diplomatic and banking circles. He wrote Roye to say that he had found willing bankers. The president then dispatched two high-level allies, House Speaker W. S. Anderson and Interior Secretary

H. W. Johnson, to conclude the negotiations for a half-million-dollar loan.*

Anderson and Johnson were out of their depth in the sophisticated and complex world of international finance; the deal they agreed to was a terrible one by any standard. Citing Liberia's precarious finances—and, no doubt, charging an unstated premium on a loan destined for a black republic—the bankers demanded a discount of 30 percent merely for extending the loan. They also required that three years' interest be paid up front. This meant that Anderson and Johnson would return home with less than half the borrowed amount. Moreover, with interest set at a high 7 percent over fifteen years (and on the full $500,000), the Liberian government would end up paying more than $650,000 for a payment of less than $250,000.

When word of the extortionate terms reached Liberia, the political classes erupted in anger, especially as rumors began to circulate that Roye, who had gone to London to ink the deal, had siphoned off another $50,000 for himself. Even when it turned out the money had been spent on government supplies, the president's critics were not placated; Roberts labeled the purchases "inferior" and "useless" and paid for "in excess of their market value." Regardless, the spent funds made it impossible for the Liberian government to back out of the deal. The whole episode, an indignant Roberts said, consisted of "charges, peculations and frauds unparalleled, I presume, in any public loan transaction of modern times."[41]

Roye's return to Liberia at the beginning of October precipitated a crisis over the very legitimacy of his presidency. Citing the alleged repeal of the constitutional amendment extending the presidential term and emboldened by their victory in the strange election of the previous May, Roberts and his Republican supporters insisted that Roye's term would come to an end in January 1872. When the president issued a proclamation that he intended to serve four full years in

---

*A rough estimate puts the amount at $8–$10 million in twenty-first-century funds. A half million dollars was an enormous sum to a country whose annual government revenues were never more than $100,000 a year in the nineteenth century.

office, his opponents hinted darkly that Roye was planning a Latin American–style coup and on becoming the dictator of Liberia. Roye countered that it was the Republicans who were the coup plotters. As the charges flew, both sides began to arm themselves in Monrovia and the outlying settlements, each side insisting it was acting in defense of the constitution.

Who started the violence is, like so much else, lost to history. The surviving accounts, largely written by anti-Roye forces, claim that the president's supporters moved first, forcibly seizing a Monrovia bank owned by a pro-Republican upriver cooperative. The rioting that followed engulfed the capital and led to an armed siege of the president's house. Eyewitnesses claimed that they saw Roye himself lobbing grenades at the crowd from an upstairs window. But after the mob fired a cannon into the house, resistance collapsed; the rioters ransacked the place, seizing Roye and his eldest son, who served as the treasury secretary.

While the crowd escorted the Royes to jail, the legislature met in joint session. Discussion was heated, even though Roye had few defenders left. Impeachment, they decided, was too slow a process, and promised to divide the country further. Instead, they took the unconstitutional step of deposing the president. In public speeches, anti-Roye politicians cited him for "contract[ing] a foreign loan contrary to the law . . . distribut[ing] arms and munitions of war . . . to crush the liberties of the people" and "contrary to the Constitution, proclaim[ing] himself President for four years, although elected for only two years." [42]

The Republicans, careful, like all Liberians, to keep up appearances and ward off criticism from Washington and the capitals of Europe—to maintain their pride and their commerce—decided they needed constitutional cover for their actions. So they put Roye and most of his cabinet on trial for treason. But when the inevitable guilty verdict and hanging sentence came down on February 10, 1872, the results triggered a still greater embarrassment for the young republic.

•

In the gathering darkness of the near moonless Saturday night of February 10, the Royes broke through a second-floor window of Monrovia's stone courthouse and slid to the ground on a rope that a supporter of Edward Jr.'s had smuggled into his cell. The two then made their way to the outskirts of Monrovia, where they attempted to bribe some Kru boatmen to row them to the English mail steamer anchored in the waters off Cape Mesurado. But word of the escape had already spread and the Kru men quickly recognized the burly, balding ex-president. They gave chase. Roye and his son, one step ahead of them, disappeared into the jungle and then became separated. Through the night and into the morning a posse searched the edge of the cape as each Roye, father and son, listened to the muffled voices of their pursuers above the crashing Atlantic surf and contemplated his next move.

In the early afternoon, the elder Roye, perhaps betting that his pursuers were waiting in the shade to avoid the dry-season sun, took his chance. A witness in Krutown said he saw "a naked man . . . emerge from the bushes" sometime between two and three, "with something like a bag about his waist."[43] Hoping that his dark skin and bulky build would let him pass for a Kru man out for a swim, Roye had stripped down to a breechcloth and dived into the surf, heading for the steamer. He didn't make it. A gathering crowd on the beach watched him slowly go under. Some said they heard shots ring out. Most, however, were convinced he was brought down by gold coins in the bag strapped around his waist.

The younger Roye was apprehended a couple of hours later, cowering in the bush. He was eventually acquitted of treason but fled for England before a second trial, for misconduct in office, could begin. As for his father, a team of Kru men sent to recover his body found no bag of gold, setting off a new controversy. Roye's supporters claimed that the president was a martyr, innocently gunned down as he fled his tormentors. But opponents replied that the Kru men must have made off with the loot. And, indeed, one of them, who swore that he had been cheated of his share, admitted as much to Liberian authorities weeks later.

Whatever the case, the drowning cast a pall over Monrovia's citizenry. "The long excited passions of the populace seemed to have lost all their recent vehemence on that holy Sabbath afternoon," a correspondent for the *African Repository* reported, "as following in silence the lifeless body of him, once their ruler, so lamentably misled, so deplorably ambitious, borne to the prison which, scarcely four and twenty hours before, he had left, animated doubtless by most sanguine hopes. So perished the deposed President E. J. Roye, fifth President of Liberia."[44]

Roye's death reverberated across Liberia. In the upriver settlements, black Liberians met to discuss secession in view of what they believed was an illegal usurpation of power by the mulatto elite. And while these discussions led nowhere, the former president's True Whig supporters never accepted the legitimacy of the Roberts administration. The Liberia College philosophy professor and Blyden ally Alexander Crummel, whose son, a Roye supporter, was briefly imprisoned during the coup, denounced the whole affair as "an uprising of a whole class of persons, who are opposed to culture, improvement, and native elevation. These men have now at last made a deed set against civilization, enlightenment, and mission."[45]

Roberts, who took office uneventfully in January 1872, proposed reconciliation with the True Whigs, recognizing that, while defeated, they nevertheless represented a growing force in Liberian politics. In his inaugural address, he spoke of meeting them halfway on the native question that had divided the black nationalists from the mulattoes, though his vision was traditionally condescending. "It is extremely desirable that the whole aboriginal population of the Republic should be drawn as rapidly as possible within the circle of civilization," he declared, "and be fitted by suitable educational training for all duties of civil and social life; and thus too we shall be exerting a hallowed influence upon the tribes of our far interior."[46] But when the new president tried to recruit the Whigs' intellectual leader as his secretary of state, Blyden, now back in Monrovia, turned him down, describing the Republican-led government as "inefficient and imbecile."[47] Blyden preferred to continue his educational work among the natives.

The stark divisions between black working class and mulatto elite were beginning to dissipate even as the passions quieted. With increasing intermarriage between the two groups, it became more and more difficult to make distinctions based on skin color. As a discrete political and economic group, the mulattoes were becoming no more, even if their light skin would remain a badge of elite distinction and their notion of a settler civilization beset by savage natives would inform Liberian self-conception for generations to come.

After their dramatic losses in the 1878 elections and their decision to endorse the True Whig candidate for president four years later, the Republicans were effectively done as a viable party, their elitist politics no longer viable against the rising populist True Whig machine. Roye may have met an untimely end but the political party he founded survived him in spectacular fashion: the True Whigs maintained a one-party grip on power into the late twentieth century, the longest reign for a political party in modern world history. It would require a bloody native-led coup to finally force them out; the party's final leader, like its first, would die violently while still in office.

Long before that circle closed, Liberians of all political stripes had to deal with the consequences of the disastrous Roye loan, a financial hole out of which their government would not dig itself until early in the twentieth century. After decades of conflict with the natives, harassment by European traders, and political strife, this fiscal burden was only the latest existential threat to the young republic. Graver ones would soon follow.

SIX

The African Banquet

If a country founded by a small group of former slaves and oppressed free blacks from America, nominally ruling over a vast and often hostile native African population and disdained by much of the outside world as an affront to the natural racial order of things, can be said to have a golden age, it was Liberia in the 1850s and 1860s.

John Seys, former gadfly missionary and leader of the anti-Monrovia political opposition in the 1840s, who was, during this period, the American vice consul in Liberia, captured the moment in an August 1859 dispatch to U.S. Secretary of State Lewis Cass: "Among the many instances of their prosperity, their commerce with the United States and Europe is becoming so extensive that they are purchasing vessels of sufficient size to cross the Atlantic and sending them laden with the rich products of their country, to foreign markets, under their own flag and manned by their own citizens."[1]

The business of the four McGill brothers, free black emigrants from Baltimore, epitomized Liberia's new prosperity. Launching their firm in 1847, the birth year of the republic, the brothers saw their business grow dramatically; they built stores in Monrovia and the southeastern settlement of Harper, established trading posts up and down the coast, and purchased more than a dozen ships to export camwood (a dye source) and palm oil. Indeed, it had been a Grand Bassa planter named Samuel Herring who, in 1848, invented a palm-kernel pressing machine and transported the first palm oil to Europe. By the end of the century, the mango-colored liquid would become West Africa's leading export commodity, used in Europe to lubricate machines and, as soap, to wash the grit off the workers tending them. Small but prosperous coffee, cotton, and sugar industries also arose in Liberia in these years, with local merchants shipping these products to eager buyers overseas.

Liberia was also attracting waves of newcomers. Abolitionists in America had long questioned its reputation as the last safe haven for free blacks and manumitted slaves, but in the 1850s, Liberia lived up to its purpose, to an extent. With the Southern states exerting their influence in Washington, thousands of African Americans emigrated. Whereas fewer than 2,000 emigrants arrived in Liberia between the mid-1830s and late 1840s, nearly 6,000 came in the dozen years leading up to the American Civil War. And when the war and the brief success of Reconstruction all but ended emigration, Liberia began to benefit from the arrival of small numbers of highly educated and skilled West Indians.

The biggest single year for new arrivals involved a very different kind of settler. Recaptives, seized from smugglers by U.S. naval patrols, had been sent to Liberia since the mid-1820s. Indeed, the ACS had initially won congressional backing for its African experiment on the condition that the colony serve as a sanctuary for these people. As sectional tensions in the United States reached a breaking point in 1860, prices for illegally imported slaves rose dramatically, triggering both a smuggling boom and an increase in seized slave cargoes. Between June 1860 and June 1861, nearly 4,500 recaptives were brought to Liberia. While the influx taxed the resources of both a much-diminished ACS and the Liberian government, the recaptives were welcomed, as they proved to be adept farmers, loyal militiamen, and eager assimilators into settler culture.

Not surprisingly, this era of prosperity and growth was also one of peace. Other than a brief war in the mid-1850s between the Grebo and the colonists of Maryland, then still an independent settler-run state, the Liberian hinterland was more or less calm through the 1850s and 1860s, though this had as much to do with intertribal politics as it did Liberian diplomacy or military prowess. Europeans, too, left the Liberians largely to themselves. The transatlantic slave trade along the Grain Coast had all but died out by the late 1860s, a victim of the American Civil War, Western naval patrols, and Liberian expeditions against local barracoons. London and Freetown authorities seemed willing to abide the uncharted border between Liberia and the colony at Sierra Leone, even if British traders tested Monrovia's authority from time to time. As for the French, who would become Liberia's prime imperialist adversary during the late nineteenth and early twentieth centuries, their ambitions for a West African empire had yet to crystallize.

But this halcyon period would not last. Liberia's commodity-based export economy shriveled in the face of competition and the relentless march of nineteenth-century technology and science. By the 1870s, German chemists had learned to synthesize aniline dyes, ending the market for Liberian camwood, which had already been in decline as a result of, in the words of the American consul general in Monrovia, "the destruction of the forests, and the grubbing up of the roots, the more valued part of the cam tree for commercial ends."[2] Around the same time, European agronomists had perfected a method for extracting sugar from local beets, causing the price of imported cane to plummet and putting small and less efficient sugar producers, like those in Liberia, out of business. Vast new plantations in Brazil, meanwhile, had driven down the wholesale price of coffee to a point where Liberian growers could barely make a profit. Even the lucrative palm oil business never reached its potential; growers in British Nigeria grabbed the lion's share of the market, which began to shrink anyway as mineral oil became the machine lubricant of choice by the end of the century.

As their economy shrank, Liberians lost control of it. What had once been the pride of the nation—its robust merchant marine—was fast disappearing. Liberian-owned and -operated ships and coastal schooners could not compete against European steamers; a national fleet that numbered fifty-four vessels in 1875 was reduced to "one solitary schooner" by 1900.[3] And while European steamships allowed Liberian products to reach overseas markets that much cheaper and faster, their frequent calls also made it easier for foreign traders to establish themselves in Liberian ports, where they struck exclusive deals with their compatriots' shipping companies, locking out weaker Liberian competitors. "What has become of all those crafts that were once owned by Liberian traders?" the *Liberian Recorder* asked in 1902. "Where are all their stores and business houses with clerks, porters, and attendants? I guess you will say that they like their vessels and stores are all gone."[4]

In the gray gloom of late-autumn Berlin, Prince Otto von Bismarck's yellow-brick residence on Wilhelmstrasse could not have appeared more resplendent. Lit by chandeliers ensconced in vaulted ceilings, the formally attired officials sat down at a horseshoe-shaped table, chatting in French and glancing through the windows at the dormant gardens outside. Counts and colonels, ministers and diplomats, even a vizier from the Sublime Porte of the Ottomans, they represented all the major powers of Europe. They had come in November 1884 at the behest of the German chancellor, who now sat at the top of the horseshoe, garbed in scarlet court dress, to decide the fate of a continent.

For four centuries, sub-Saharan Africa had seemed big enough for every ambitious European nation to stake its claim. Europeans had built forts and trading posts along its sinuous 20,000-mile coastline and launched expeditions to explore the interior. Here and there, as at the Cape of Good Hope, they had even put down roots. And, of course, they had forcibly carried off millions of Africa's sons and daughters, till their consciences finally caught up with them in the early and middle years of the nineteenth century, helped along by the fact that slavery was becoming economically untenable. But for the most part, white men had kept their distance. Held at bay by an array of diseases, the Spanish, the British, the French, and the Dutch had turned elsewhere for territory and glory. Now there was new interest in Africa. Evolving public health measures—and weaponry—made the idea of occupying and administering the vast reaches of the world's second-largest continent seem possible. Tantalizing riches were a part of the imperialists' strategic calculation but perhaps the truest motivation was simply the glory of it all, especially for new nations like Belgium, Italy, and Germany which had never had a chance at empire in the Americas and Asia.

But Europeans agreed that there had to be rules for the carving up of Africa. Over fifteen weeks, between 21-course dinners, all-night balls, and leisurely carriage rides down the Unter den Linden, the attendees hashed out rules of navigation and trade and occupancy. Existing possessions were acknowledged as legitimate, including those of the only black republic on the continent, though no Liberians, or any Africans for that matter, were invited to the conference. A little-noticed provision, known as the "principle of effectivity," would have the most far-reaching implications for Africa. To prevent a government from simply planting its flag and claiming ownership, the attendees at the conference agreed that a nation had to set up a colonial administration, establish an economic presence, make some effort at treaties with native chiefs, and deploy a police force adequate to pacify the natives before it could claim the land as its own. The purpose of the conference was to make the conquest of the "dark" continent an orderly affair, but as it turned out, the "scramble" for Africa that ensued over the next few decades was anything but.

For almost half a century, Liberians practiced an older form of colonialism. Sign a treaty with a local chief and the territory, in European eyes, was yours. Venture into the interior, plant the flag, and other nations would honor the claim. Liberians had done this, to the best of their limited means, laying claim to 180,000 square miles of West African shore, jungle, savanna, and highland, from just south of Sierra Leone's Sherbro Island, where the first, ill-fated settlers from

America had landed, to the San Pedro River, deep inside what is now Ivory Coast, to the long uncharted headwaters of the Niger in modern-day Guinea. But in Berlin in 1884 Liberia's claims were rendered, without the knowledge or consent of the black republic, meaningless. Treaties and exploration were no longer enough to secure sovereignty; now, occupation and pacification were necessary.

Though Great Britain was the first to recognize the Republic of Liberia in 1847, one result was territorial disputes between the two nations along the uncharted fringe of settlement, most notably over the Gallinas, a rich trading territory lying in what is now southeastern Sierra Leone. Liberians claimed sovereignty based on treaties they had signed with local chiefs. Britain disputed the validity of the treaties and then, when the evidence in Liberia's favor appeared to be overwhelming, ignored them altogether. The two sides met many times in the 1870s and 1880s, in London, Freetown, and even aboard an American warship, but could not come to an understanding, so the British simply took the lion's share for themselves. The Roye loan, indebting Liberia to London bankers to the tune of hundreds of thousands of dollars, hardly helped Monrovia's negotiating position. Still, humiliating as it was for the Liberians, the episode marked the last time London would force them to adjust their colony's borders. The French, however, would be another matter.

Relations between Monrovia and Paris got off to an auspicious start. A year after leading his country to independence, President Roberts had visited the capitals of Europe. At the Louvre, Napoleon III kissed him on both cheeks and duly extended French recognition to the world's second black republic; it had taken thirty years for the French to officially acknowledge the first, their former colony of Haiti. A decade later, when Kru laborers on the ship *Regina Coeli*, convinced they were being sold into West Indian slavery, mutinied and slayed every Frenchman aboard save the doctor, Paris absolved Monrovia of responsibility.

In the 1850s and '60s, French desire for an African empire was expressed, for the most part, in Algeria in the north and Senegal in the far west. But that would soon change. France, like other European nations, had already negotiated trade and protection treaties with tribal leaders along the coast and had built forts and factories to enforce them, notably on Côte d'Ivoire, to the east of Liberia. Then, after mid-century, exploration became a European obsession; many expeditions set out in the 1860s and 1870s to find the headwaters of Africa's great rivers, including the Liberian-claimed Niger. Yet after the Berlin conference, France began to covet something greater: an unbroken empire stretching across Sahara, savanna, and rain forest, from the azure waters of the Mediterranean to the steamy Gulf of Guinea. Potential economic opportunities helped spur the ambitious plans but mostly it was for *la gloire de la France*, and to prevent rivals such as Germany and Britain from grabbing it all first. There were obstacles to realizing this vision. It was unlikely the British could be dislodged from Sierra Leone or their possessions on the Gold Coast. And resistance from the more martial tribes and native confederations, particularly in the interior, would require substantial applications of force.

But Liberia, the military strategists and diplomats of the Quai d'Orsay decided, could be more easily had. The first French interest in Liberia had occurred in the waning days of ACS rule in the 1840s, when French naval officers—crates of rum, guns, and iron bars, the legal tender of West African trade, piled on the beach beside them—signed annexation treaties with local chiefs along the coast. Liberia protested, then appealed to London and Washington, which issued stern diplomatic warnings, forcing Paris to back down.

When Monrovia, in the mid-1880s, proved unable to quell continuing unrest among the Grebos, the main tribal confederation along the border with Côte d'Ivoire, French officials dusted off the old treaties, laying claim not only to Maryland and the rest of eastern Liberia but to bays and coves all the way up the coast to Sierra Leone. French naval officers also began signing new treaties with Grebo chiefs, prompting Liberian officials to produce an 1882 map of the region, issued by the French War Office, showing all of Greboland under Liberian control. Unswayed, Paris pressed the issue, citing Liberia's failure to pacify the natives or plant settlers on its eastern marches. In response, Liberia claimed that it was the French themselves who were stirring up the trouble. Whatever the case, the unrest was all the justification the French needed, under the rules set forth at the Berlin conference, to nullify Liberian claims.

Hilary Johnson, the newly elected Liberian president, was the first Liberian-born Americo to hold the office and the son of the patriot-hero Elijah, whose challenge to an offer of British protection— "We want no flagstaff put up here that it will cost us more to get down than it will to flog the natives!"—inspired generations of settler youth. The younger Johnson did not make such a rhetorical stand. Instead, he played what would soon become Liberia's diplomatic ploy of last resort. He turned to America for protection. Washington went through the motions, dutifully but halfheartedly issuing a protest. But Paris was more perturbed than persuaded, with the Foreign Office warning the Liberians that if they continued "to cloud every issue" by appealing to their American mentors, France would be forced to sever diplomatic relations with Monrovia.[5]

Johnson then decided on a new and desperate measure to get Washington involved. In 1887, he gave permission for American evangelists to set up a mission in the heart of Greboland, knowing full well they would soon need to be rescued. While Washington, the Liberian president figured, might ignore its protection pledge to Liberia—signed two years before to get Monrovia to acquiesce to Britain's seizing of the Gallinas—it was unlikely to leave its own nationals in danger. But the Grover Cleveland administration soon saw through the ruse. "Even if . . . the government of Liberia were the judge of the emergency requiring the intervention of the government of the United States to protect its own citizens under article 8 of the [recognition] treaty of 1862," Secretary of State Thomas Bayard notified the American consul in Monrovia, Ezekiel Smith, "it could hardly be deemed within the legitimate bounds of Liberian discretion to provoke the issue by sending our citizens or encouraging them to go into regions inhabited by aborigines [over] whom no effective control is or has been exercised."[6] Though he dispatched a warship to bring the missionaries home, Bayard left Liberia to fend for itself diplomatically, for the time being at least.

Meanwhile, French expeditions signed treaties with local Grebo chiefs, encouraging them to look to Paris, rather than Monrovia, for protection. Given the long history of disputes between the Liberian settlers and the Grebo—over trade, land, political representation, and simple human dignity (the settlers had acquired the unfortunate habit of referring to Grebos of any age as "boy")—the French found the Grebos receptive. Desperate, the Liberians sent their attorney general to Washington, where the new secretary of state, James Blaine, found a few minutes in his schedule for pleasantries, but not substantive talks. Nevertheless, the message somehow got through, as America's Paris ambassador was instructed to inform the French government that Liberia and the United States were "bound . . . by special ties . . . [and] this government [i.e., America's] and people could not behold unmoved much less acquiesce in any proceedings on the part of the neighbors of Liberia which might assume to dispose of any territory justly claimed and long admitted to belong to the Republic."[7]

As with past American appeals, Blaine's had only a small effect on the French, who continued to pressure Monrovia. Anxious Marylanders issued an appeal to the world's conscience, in Monrovia papers: "Is there not to be a foot of land in Africa, that the African, whether civilized or savage, can call his own? We only ask, in all fairness, to be allowed just what any other people would require—free scope for operation. Do not wrest our territory from us . . . Give us a fair chance, and then if we utterly fail, we shall yield the point."[8] Eventually, the Liberians were forced to accept the inevitable and sign the treaty, which included a troubling clause, inserted by Paris at the last minute, allowing the French to unilaterally abrogate the treaty should "[Liberian] independence . . . be impaired or in case the Liberian Republic should abandon any part of the territory which has been accorded to her by the present agreement."[9]

If the clause worried officials in Monrovia, it also concerned London, which wanted to maintain Liberia as a buffer between its holdings and those of France. The French, after reserving the right to occupy even more Liberian territory, proceeded to do just that in 1892, a few years after signing the Greboland treaty. They used the Berlin Conference rules as pretext, claiming once again that Liberia was unable to pacify or settle its hinterland. In pursuit of Samory Touré, an Islamic rebel, the French occupied the Guinea Highlands and the headwaters of the Niger, laying claim to roughly a third of Liberia. They began to talk of establishing a protectorate over the whole country, reviving an offer they had made, and the settlers had spurned, two decades before.

As if French ambitions were not worrisome enough, yet another threat soon emerged when, on a hot and cloudless January day in 1898, the German man-of-war *Vixe* steamed into the blue waters off Cape Mesurado. The governor-general of the new Teutonic colony at Kamerun, Baron von Soden, was demanding satisfaction—$13,000—for the "outrage" committed by "uncivilized Liberians" on one of his national's coffee plantations. Knowing full well that Monrovia could not pay the indemnity, von Soden proposed an alternative. Berlin would drop its demand in exchange for Liberia agreeing to a German protectorate, a not unreasonable offer, the baron felt, given that his countrymen had already wrested most of Liberia's foreign trade away from the British.

Beset by imperialists in Paris and Berlin and creditors in London, Liberians grew so desperate that some members of the government began to consider the unthinkable: a return to American guardianship. The future president Charles King, at the time a senator fresh out of law school, noted that Liberia's treaties with foreign powers were "not worth the paper upon which they were written" and that it was time the country "accept any terms laid out or even dictated by the Government of the United States of America." In Washington, the assessment was equally dire. "The extinction of Liberian independence is only a question of time," a State Department official informed the secretary in an internal memo. "The only practical question is whether Liberia shall be absorbed by a European power or become a virtual colony of the United States through a treaty of protection."[10] But, as before, the pleas and warnings fell on deaf ears, as the McKinley administration, preparing for war with Spain, did little more than its predecessors had.

So Liberian diplomats turned to the British, now seen as the least threatening of their neighbors. London, increasingly suspicious of Berlin's territorial ambitions in the vicinity of Sierra Leone, dispatched a warship to Liberian waters as a warning to von Soden, which temporarily neutralized the German threat.

Meanwhile the French challenged Liberia's most substantive claim on its hinterland, and one of the republic's proudest achievements: the explorations of Benjamin Anderson. In 1868, the Baltimore-born Anderson—a former militia captain and trained accountant who had risen to become Liberia's secretary of the treasury at twenty-nine— set off for the interior with a group of Kru porters. His ultimate goal was the city of Musardu, near the headwaters of the Niger, in present-day Guinea, a place no white man, or Liberian, had ever seen.

Just as legendary Timbuktu, a thousand miles down the Niger River, held a centuries-long fascination for British and French explorers, so Musardu had cast its spell over Monrovia's merchant elite for more than a generation, and for much the same reason. West Africa, educated Westerners of the day decided, was essentially two distinct regions with two very different kinds of people inhabiting them. Along the damp and miasmic coast, pagan savages, immersed in superstition and divided into a myriad of eternally squabbling tribes, existed in a Hobbesian world of all against all.

But deep into the interior, indigenous African society was supposedly far different. Hundreds of miles to the east and north of the

jungled coast, in the salubrious highlands and savannas of the hinterland, was another Africa—a land of wealth, learning, and law, ruled
over by the Mandingo, a literate, Islamicized people whose mercantile acumen was legendary. Musardu, or Moses' Town in the Mandingo language, was the southwestern outpost and, hence, the closest
access Liberians had to this empire of, in the words of one Liberian
missionary, "the most famous, most cultured, and most enterprising
tribe in Western Africa."[11] But Musardu offered more than just trading opportunities, as far as Monrovia was concerned. Its leaders were
believed to wield great influence over the interior. An alliance with
Musardu offered Liberian officialdom a means for pacifying the war-
ring and hostile tribes surrounding the settlers' constricted coastal
enclaves. Allied with the Mandingo, the Liberian merchants' self-
declared mission of civilizing Africa and realizing its commercial potential could proceed apace.

After ten months of setbacks and trials, including the desertion
of his porters and a Mandingo guide who led him astray, Anderson,
whose trip had been sponsored by an American philanthropist, arrived
in Musardu. While Anderson was duly impressed by the haleness and
trading instincts of its people, the city proved a disappointment. By the
late 1860s, its heyday had clearly passed, evidenced by the crumbling
architecture and conspicuous lack of wealth. Rather than a seat of
power, it was a town besieged by rivals on all sides, which may have
been why the inhabitants were so eager to establish diplomatic ties
with Monrovia. In this, the Musardu city fathers were as disappointed
as Anderson, who, like his good friend Blyden, soon discovered that
the merchant-led government in Monrovia, despite its claims to the
contrary, had little real interest in establishing closer relations with the
peoples of the interior, even the learned and enterprising Mandingo.

The controversy over Anderson's achievement and Liberia's
claims on the interior began more than three decades after his return
to Monrovia and the publication of his travel journals, with a March
15, 1903, article in *Annales de Géographie*, the French journal of exploration, that was soon picked up by the Parisian press. The author was

Henri d'Ollone, an army captain dispatched to West Africa in the early 1890s to survey newly acquired French territory. He made the extraordinary claim that Anderson was a fraud. As D'Ollone wrote, sarcastically, "[t]he geographers, however, in following their pleasant tradition of being 'abhorred by emptiness' delight in filling this territory with rivers, towns, and mountains . . . And, as assurance that they have not invented all that, they cite with serenity their author: it is the traveler Anderson, whose itinerary, departing from Monrovia up to Moussadougou, in the Sudan, spreads out on all the maps . . . It is time, however that one says it. This itinerary is purely a fantasy."[12]

D'Ollone said he had interviewed numerous inhabitants of the region, none of whom had heard of Anderson. Yet the Frenchman argued that such evidence was not necessary; anyone familiar with the conventions of explorers could see the truth—or rather, the falsehood—in Anderson's own maps, which consisted, according to him, of "long, straight lines with acute angles between. Now, in which country has a traveler ever walked in a straight line?"[13] D'Ollone allowed that it was understandable that geographers had been fooled, for many mistakenly believed that Anderson was English or American. But in fact, he wrote, Anderson "is simply a black Liberian . . . [with] very ordinary education, little in relation [to] the use of instruments that he would have had to carry to make the astronomical calculations."[14] So where did Anderson get his information about the interior? d'Ollone asked. "[C]aptives . . . passed from master to master as far as the coast. Through them, one can know the names of the few villages that have been put on the map more or less judiciously," the Frenchman wrote, provocatively raising yet another issue Europeans routinely used to claim territory, that of the black republic's alleged involvement in a slave trade.[15]

When a British journalist in Paris read the article and had it reprinted in the *West African Mail,* a newspaper out of Sierra Leone, the charges eventually came to Anderson's attention. Unaware that the source of the attack was d'Ollone, the aging explorer aimed his fire at the *Mail*'s reporter. "This gentleman," he wrote, dismissively, "is very late in giving this startling piece of information in a transaction of 1868 and 1874 [Anderson had made a second journey to Musardu in the latter year]."[16] Anderson disputed the charges, first citing his well-known native sobriquet, "Musahdu," and then offering as evidence charts and tables from his travels, some of them never before published, and a letter from the late King Vomfeedolla of Musardu himself.

The exchange continued for another year or so. Blyden and the famed traveler and the diplomat Maurice Delafosse, a former French consul in Liberia, came to Anderson's defense. The matter had important geopolitical ramifications. If Anderson had never ventured to Musardu, then the Liberians—"none of [whom] . . . have ever dared adventure more than 10 km from the sea or navigable river, for fear of being eaten by the natives," d'Ollone averred—had no claim on their hinterland.[17] As Anderson wrote in his initial response, "[t]he gentleman seems to be sounding the signal trumpet for a fresh grab of Liberian territory rather than disproving [my] journey to Musahdu."[18] Not only had Liberians failed to occupy or pacify the interior, the French government was now claiming, they had not even set foot there.

In the face of such attacks on their sovereignty and legitimacy, the Liberian government's options were limited. Settling the hinterland was out of the question, as few Liberians were willing to move inland and the stream of new settlers from America had all but dried up; in 1900, the ACS sent a grand total of one emigrant to Liberia. Nor did the government have the power to pacify the natives. An expedition led by President William Coleman against the Gola in 1900 had been ignominiously routed. Coleman barely escaped with his life, but not with his office; he was forced to resign in the face of near universal condemnation from his cabinet and the legislature.

And so the Liberians reluctantly adopted a practice perfected by their imperial antagonists: indirect rule. Each European nation staking a claim in Africa granted favored natives certain privileges to maintain order as it exploited the resources and manpower of its territory. Liberians had avoided this model for years because the hinterland had been of little concern to the merchant-dominated settler elite, and for reasons of principle. Liberia was not a distant, imperial power, but a republic that in theory represented all of the people within its borders, settler and native alike. Indirect rule implied two or more levels of citizenship, something few Liberians were willing to abide in practice, or at least admit to.

The government had previously tried, and failed, to properly govern the hinterland. An interior administration, manned by settlers, floundered in the late 1860s because few were willing to leave Monrovia and its environs. Under an 1874 law—passed under pressure from the British, who wanted to end native fighting on the border with Sierra Leone—the government had invited two chiefs to represent each tribe as nonvoting delegates in the national legislature, though they were to be consulted only on affairs concerning the natives. But even this limited offer had given rise to fears in Monrovia of a native takeover, and just a year later, the legislature abandoned the plan, promising instead an annual hundred-dollar stipend, "to make [the chiefs] feel more identified and interested in the Government."[19]

Thirty years later, in 1904, the Liberian government was rolling out the red carpet for the kings and chieftains of the hinterland: Gola, Vai, Dey, Pessa, and Mandingo. The occasion was a grand conference that would at long last reconcile "civilized" with "tribal" as members of the same nation. There were speeches, inevitably leavened with the unctuousness of African diplomacy, and a banquet prepared by the First Lady at the Executive Mansion. When it was discovered that a grandson of King Boatswain—the paramount chief who had befriended the American pioneers during the first precarious days of settlement—was in attendance, President Arthur Barclay offered him a prominent role in the new order and pledged his government's support "in rebuilding the country [Boporu] of his father and grandfather."[20]

The plan set forth by the government involved a hinterland administration composed of chiefs and government commissioners and would, in the long run, lead to abuses. As Liberian military prowess and administrative control grew more effective in the 1920s and 1930s, the government's representatives in the hinterland became laws unto themselves, using the troops under their command to humiliate chiefs, seize native property and women, and brutally enforce labor corvées and the hut tax.

At the time, the new arrangement failed to keep European nations at bay. Within a few years, France would impose the most disastrous treaty yet on Monrovia, forcing it to turn over more of the Guinea Highlands and the headwaters of the Niger, roughly a quarter of the country's remaining territory, in 1911. British encroachment proved even more insidious. Bothered by native unrest along the Sierra Leone–Liberia border, London demanded that the Liberian government establish a regular army to patrol the hinterland, and that it be put under British command. Still deeply in debt to London bankers, the Liberian government had little choice but to accede, surrendering yet another piece of its national sovereignty to preserve what little remained of its independence.

The Liberian Frontier Force, as this new army was called, was organized by a British con man styling himself an adventurer. His name was Captain Mackey Cadell, though it is not clear whether the Boer War veteran was even a captain at all. Cadell approached President Barclay on his own volition, while the latter was in London in early 1908 about yet another loan. The president was wary at first but Cadell's powerful friends in the British Foreign Office helped sway Barclay, though it's unlikely that Cadell was acting as a representative of His Majesty's government.

Proceeding to Monrovia, Cadell, who was known for his "indomitable energy," quickly went to work, ordering arms and recruiting some 250 natives, on credit, since the Liberian treasury was virtually depleted.[21] Citizens soon grew suspicious after royal emblems began to show up on the uniforms of Mackey's troops and strange accents were heard among the barracks the men had built in the heart of Monrovia. Nor were Liberians alone in their concern. France's vice-consul claimed the force was, in fact, "a British army of occupation," an assessment perhaps supported by the arrival of a British gunboat off Cape Mesurado.[22]

By December, an increasingly worried president and legislature—Cadell had also unilaterally assumed command of the Monrovia city police and local tax office—had had enough. But their demand that Mackey quit and the force be reorganized was initially ignored by the British officer, and when he finally did resign, it came with a thinly veiled ultimatum. Should the legislature fail to pay his men, he would not answer for the consequences. The threat was soon made real; some seventy of Cadell's former soldiers left their barracks, threatening to seize the arms and ammunition their commander had turned over for safekeeping to a local British mercantile house. Liberia was teetering on the verge of a military coup.

It was the much-maligned militia, ironically enough, that saved the republic. Some four hundred citizen soldiers, in Monrovia for their quarterly drill, occupied Cadell's barracks, quickly defusing the situation. The British officer, his men, and the gunboat all decamped. A government investigation later revealed that many of Mackey's soldiers were, in fact, natives of Sierra Leone and hence British subjects, implying that their loyalties were to Cadell and London rather than Monrovia. Unlike France, Britain had no interest in seizing Liberia, either as a protectorate or a colony. Cadell's army, then, would have given the British Foreign Office and colonial authorities in Freetown exactly what they wanted: the ability to go after uncooperative natives from both sides of the border but without the cost and trouble of having to administer Liberia and deal with what would inevitably become a very disgruntled Americo population.

As for Cadell, he would return to Liberia in a few years, though not as a military officer. Claiming he had "always loved Liberia" and touting his Washington connections this time, he would come as the front man for a quasi-philanthropic but primarily profit-making venture known as the Cavalla River Company.[23] Ever the opportunist, he had recognized that Liberia had turned away from Europe and toward America. His abortive coup would prove to be the last attempt by a European government to assert its dominance over Africa's first republic.

In September 1907, Booker T. Washington wrote to President Theodore Roosevelt about Liberia. "You know, I think . . . how it was established by Americans . . . and how its interests have been safeguarded in many ways by Americans ever since its foundation," Washington prefaced, before making his appeal. "I have information from reliable sources that both France and England are seeking to take large parts of the Liberian territory. I am sure that you will prevent this, if it can be done."[24]

Washington, the founder of the famed Tuskegee Normal and Industrial Institute in Alabama, was Roosevelt's friend, in part because they agreed that blacks should focus on working hard instead of politics. Just a month after taking office in 1901, Roosevelt had set off a political firestorm by dining with Washington at the White House. And while the black educator was an opponent of Roosevelt's imperialism, especially U.S. actions in the Philippines, he nevertheless shared the president's view that America and its values had a role to play in lifting up the darker peoples of the world.

Washington's feelings about Liberia were similarly mixed. He was a longtime opponent of emigration, on practical grounds; in his mind the rural South offered the most suitable environment for hardworking, self-effacing blacks to improve their lot. Still, he believed that an independent Liberia represented hope for Africa and should for this reason be protected by America. When a Liberian delegation came to visit the U.S. capital in 1908 with yet another appeal for American protection from European aggressors, Washington worked to get them a hearing with the president, while making sure they did not have to confront the crude racialism of the era. "This is the first

Reverend Daniel Coker sailed on the *Elizabeth* in 1820 but never made it to Liberia, choosing to remain in Sierra Leone to missionize when most of the other settlers decamped in 1822 to Cape Mesurado. (New York Public Library)

Lott Carey arrived in West Africa on the second boat sent by the ACS. Like Coker, he had missionary ambitions, but quickly found himself defending the settlement of Monrovia against the very natives he had hoped to convert. (Lott Carey Foreign Mission Convention)

Emigrants from all over the United States sometimes waited months in New York and other port cities for the American Colonization Society to arrange their transport to Liberia. The people in this post–Civil War illustration are from Arkansas. (New York Public Library)

Liberia's first president, the mulatto Joseph Jenkins Roberts, was described by one settler as "a very fine gentleman, but . . . more white than black." (New York Public Library)

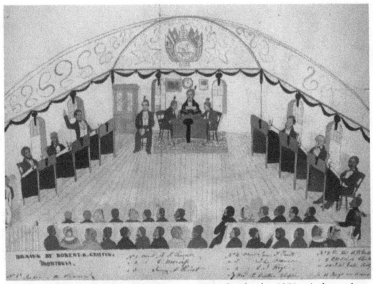

An illustration depicting a Liberian senate session in the 1850s. At least three future presidents were in attendance, including Edmund James Roye, with arm raised at left. (Library of Congress)

Roye was a successful real estate speculator in Ohio before emigrating and becoming one of the richest men in Liberia. As president he nearly bankrupted the nation by agreeing to a usurious loan from London financiers. He was driven from office and died in mysterious circumstances, with some claiming that he was murdered by political opponents. (Library of Congress)

Edward Blyden, photographed shortly after his arrival in Liberia in 1849, was a pioneer of black nationalism and a political ally of Roye's. He fled the country for a time after Roye's death. (Library of Congress)

NATIVE BOYS from the jungles of AFRICA,

NATIVE AFRICAN BOYS

Many settler families adopted native youth, ostensibly to educate and Christianize them. Showing spears literally turned into ploughshares, these posed photographs reveal the Americo view of natives as warlike savages in need of civilizing. (Library of Congress)

Monrovia, seen here in the late nineteenth century, was built in the image of American towns, with some of its features reflecting nostalgia rather than practicality. In theory, for instance, the city's wide avenues would allow wagons to turn around, but in practice traffic was sparse because most draft animals brought to Liberia quickly died of tropical infections. (Library of Congress)

In the 1920s, Marcus Garvey and his Universal Negro Improvement Association sold shares in the Black Star Line to African Americans in a futile effort to send thousands of emigrants to Liberia. (Mystic Seaport: The Museum of America and the Sea)

Charles D. B. King was president of Liberia from 1920 to 1930. He spoke of his nation as a haven for the world's blacks but, a shrewd politician, he always put Americo interests first. (Library of Congress)

Americo–Liberian Frontier Force officers were criticized by the League of Nations for their role in the Fernando Pó slave trading scheme and for their general poor treatment of native Africans. (New York Public Library)

Seen here with cigar in mouth and holding the arm of his wife, Antoinette, at a diplomatic reception, William V. S. Tubman was president of Liberia from 1944 until his death in 1971. Tubman's cultivation of foreign capital spurred the biggest economic boom in the nation's history. (Indiana University Liberian Collections)

The elite membership of Monrovia Masonic Lodge Number One was rumored to make government policy during secret conclaves. This photograph was taken in the 1970s; in the civil wars of the 1990s and 2000s, the Lodge became home to refugees. (Don White)

Master Sergeant Samuel Doe holds his first press conference after he or soldiers under his command assassinated the country's last Americo-Liberian president, William Tolbert, in April 1980. (Bettmann/CORBIS)

In this Pulitzer Prize–winning photograph, a soldier prepares to shoot Foreign Minister Cecil Dennis on a Monrovia beach on April 22, 1980. Dennis was one of thirteen cabinet members from the Americo regime executed that day. (Copyright © Larry C Price. All Rights Reserved)

Charles McArthur Ghankay Taylor, born to an Americo judge and a native woman, became the first sitting head of state to be indicted for crimes against humanity by the International Criminal Court in The Hague. In the spring of 2012, he was sentenced to fifty years in prison. This photograph, from 2008, shows Taylor at his trial, which was a protracted affair. (Michael Kooren/Reuters/CORBIS)

Ellen Johnson Sirleaf, the "iron lady" of Africa, gives her Nobel Peace Prize acceptance speech in Oslo in 2011. Under her leadership, Liberia has begun to rebuild after fourteen years of civil war. (John McConnico/AP/CORBIS)

time any such commission composed of Negroes, has visited this country and I am anxious that they be treated with just as much courtesy as the customs of the United States will allow," he wrote to Roosevelt, "even if an exception has to be made, I think it will be a fine thing."[25] In the end, the delegation did make it into the White House, but received little more than the usual vague promises of diplomatic support.

Washington did, however, convince Roosevelt and later his successor Taft to take a more hands-on approach with Liberia. A three-man commission, headed by the white economist Roland Falkner, but also including the black educator George Sale and Washington's chief aide at Tuskegee, Emmet Jay Scott, was sent to the nation to attempt, in essence, to fix every part of it that was broken. They arrived in April 1909, just after Cadell's near-coup. Their investigation of Liberia's books revealed that the Americo elite lacked financial acumen. Not only was the treasury empty, but Liberia was in debt to foreign creditors to the tune of nearly a million dollars, more than five times what would have been its GDP, if anybody had tried to measure it.

The financial hole had been forty years in the making. Liberia had been left behind by the rapid technological and economic developments of the era, which had rendered obsolete its export economy and its sail-based merchant marine. But Liberians had not helped themselves either, and not just in their loan choices. Bribery and embezzlement were rife throughout the country. Customs agents in the nation's ports accepted bribes from foreign traders to look the other way while bureaucrats treated their departmental budgets as personal bank accounts. Corruption was so common as to seem banal. As the American anthropologist Frederick Starr wrote at the time, "Liberian officials quite well know the thing which we call junkets. When some crisis arises, and the 'Lark' [Liberia's lone gunboat] must be sent to a seat of danger, high officials, whose relations to the Government are not such that their presence is necessary . . . take advantage of the opportunity for a fine outing. The nation may be in financial difficulty, but good food, good smoking, and good drinks seem easily provided; such an outing not infrequently gives the official opportunity to transact private business [as well]."[26]

In the hinterland, underpaid officials levied arbitrary taxes and fines on the natives and then pocketed the proceeds. Such actions could lead to unrest. James Howard, a barely educated officer in the LFF, was made commissioner over much of the northwest in 1916 and founded a smuggling operation, transferring various goods, including kola nuts, rice, and ivory, across the Liberia–Sierra Leone frontier to avoid customs duties on either side. Forcibly conscripting native carriers and employing the militia as his own private army, he ran his native competitors out of business and then charged exorbitant prices. After two years, the local Gola rebelled, forcing the government to dispatch an expensive military expedition. As for Howard, he was assessed a token fine for his excesses and then reinstated at his former rank in the LFF, a typical response to official malfeasance.

The corruption of the coast and the extortion of the hinterland radiated from Monrovia. The government payroll was bloated. "Every official . . . has a list of dependents," wrote the sympathetic Starr, "[and] once in office, he must provide for others; the number of brothers, sons, nephews, and cousins of officials who find some clerkship or small appointment is relatively large . . ."[27] Nepotism was a problem with no obvious solution, since there were no skilled people to replace its beneficiaries; the Liberian educational system turned out eloquent preachers and an "unnecessarily large" cohort of lawyers but few competent administrators or businessmen.[28] The post of treasury secretary usually went to a political insider with little experience in budgeting or even bookkeeping. The legislature appropriated money arbitrarily and with little concern for what the country could afford, or had to pay back to foreign creditors. And to prevent a presidential veto of its irresponsible spending, the legislature usually submitted its budget, as Barclay complained in his 1904 annual message to the legislature, "just at the last hour or even a little after [they] had adjourned *sine die*."[29]

Virtually everyone in the country tried to avoid paying taxes. Natives either ran away from tax collectors or chased them away, seeing no reason to contribute to a government that had provided them with so little beyond a few tumbledown schoolhouses, some shoddy roads, and the business end of the bayonet whenever they demanded a fairer shake. The natives resented the poll tax above all, which was not unreasonable given that most of them were not even permitted at the polls. As for the Americoes, they, too, resisted tax collection at every turn, contributing less than 5 percent of the country's revenues even though they owned the vast majority of its wealth. The bulk of the government's money in the early twentieth century came, as it always had, from customs revenues and the head tax levied on Kru stevedores seeking work aboard foreign ships—but even this last source of revenue was unreliable, since European traders often underpaid the collectors and then threatened to go to their governments if harassed.

Americo society, living beyond its means, made up the difference by borrowing from abroad. The terms were always extortionate, a result of opportunism and racism on the part of creditors and financial ignorance on the part of the borrower. The 1871 loan arranged by President Roye did not result in much economic development and remained in arrears into the twentieth century, its onerous payments compounded by another desperate but ill-considered borrowing from British bankers in 1906. This £100,000 sterling ($500,000) credit, negotiated through a former African explorer named Harry Johnston, turned out to be even more catastrophic. Most of the money went to the Liberian Development Company, which had been set up by Johnston to build much-needed infrastructure for the country. But after two years, Johnston, who refused to open up the company's books to the Liberian government, had nothing to show for his enterprise outside of a fifteen-mile dirt road from Monrovia to Careysburg and exactly two automobiles to drive on it.

The recommendations of the American commissioners to the incoming Taft administration included another loan, of $1.7 million, a new customs receivership, and a reorganization of the LFF under American officers. There were important differences from earlier deals. This time, the loan, though financed by European and American investors, would be guaranteed by Washington, which meant a more reasonable interest rate. The receivership would also be administered by an official from the United States, a country Liberians understood had no territorial ambitions in Africa. And, finally, the officers assigned to head the LFF would be buffalo soldiers, who had once pacified the natives on the American frontier.

Charles F. Young had come a long way in his nearly fifty years. One of only three African Americans to graduate from West Point in the nineteenth century, this son of freed Kentucky slaves had risen to the rank of U.S. Army captain just after the turn of the twentieth century, a rare achievement in an age when no white soldier could be expected to salute a black officer. He had succeeded despite many obstacles by doing his duty—he had commanded a black regiment against Filipino freedom fighters and served as military attaché to the U.S. legation in Haiti—and because he subscribed to the imperialist assumptions of the day. "The regeneration of [Africa] must come in the same manner as it has to all countries . . . i.e. from the outside," he wrote in his 1912 textbook, *Military Morale of Nations and Races,* published the same year he was seconded to the Liberian government to reorganize its army.[30]

Young, officially designated an attaché to the U.S. mission in 1912—no active-duty officer was permitted to serve in a foreign army—saw the challenges he faced clearly enough. His predecessor as attaché, another black officer and former buffalo soldier named Benjamin Davis, had described the LFF as "worthless" after witnessing 120 soldiers threaten the life of the secretary of war unless they received their back pay. Young may have found Liberian officials more problematic, though. While Barclay and his successor, Daniel Howard, had accepted outside leadership of the LFF as a necessary concession, some Liberian political and military leaders resented the intrusion. They bristled at what they saw as the superior attitudes of Young and the four former U.S. Army officers under his command. Moreover, Young's salary was $2,000 a year, more than any official in the government aside from the president, and under the American loan agreement, the money was to come out of the Liberian treasury.

Nor was Young particularly impressed by the Liberians. As an American missionary close to the officers wrote in a letter to the U.S. minister in Monrovia, "[h]aving served with outstanding leaders in the U.S. black regiments, the Americans were appalled by the lack of leadership within the LFF . . . [and] reported that the [new] Secretary of War knew nothing of his duties, [having] confessed that he was a preacher and only assumed the office because it had been forced upon him."[31]

Young largely failed to rein in the excesses of the LFF. Just a month after his arrival, he brought in the district commissioner James Cooper and the militia colonel William Lomax from their posts along the Sierra Leone border. According to British officials on the other side, Cooper and Lomax, both of whom came from prestigious settler clans, had been running a violent extortion racket. When local Gola chiefs aired their grievances, Cooper and Lomax had eight of them murdered. Yet after a one-day trial in front of Liberia's Supreme Court, in which key witnesses were kept from the stand and incriminating evidence ruled inadmissible, both were acquitted of all charges. Lomax, who openly confessed to the killings and justified them on the grounds that the victims were traitors, did not even have his officer's commission revoked.

The tensions between the American officers and Liberian authorities did not abate. Because the country fielded two forces simultaneously—the militia and the LFF—the chain of command was muddled, resulting in squabbling over jurisdiction and authority. The American officers also went unpaid for months at a time, requiring Young and his successors to appeal to the American who had been put in charge of the nation's customs service to intercede. Young and his men were not entirely blameless, however. They themselves were far from united and were guilty of some of the same crimes against natives as their settler counterparts had been. A 1913 expedition against rebellious Kru, led by one of Young's lieutenants, resulted in what a *New York Times* correspondent described as a "heavy slaughter."[32]

By the early 1920s, Liberian government officials were searching for a way to rid themselves of the American officers. A new deal was finally reached in 1927. Washington would dispatch four "qualified and experienced" officers, but they would not be in command roles. Rather, they would serve as advisors only, an arrangement that would last through World War II and beyond, even surviving the 1980 coup that deposed the last Americo-led government.

Liberia had made it through the worst of the European imperialist grab for Africa, though not without cost. The republic had surrendered two-thirds of its territory and a third of its coastline; it was now a rump state barely the size of Ohio. Still, Liberia had survived, thanks to its strategic retreats at the negotiating table, the competition among its European adversaries, and the reluctant intervention of the nation that had birthed it and to which it was forever bound.

SEVEN

Conquering Hero

They came down from Harlem by the thousands on the west side BMT and east side IRT lines, by bus and on foot, dressed in their Sunday finest. Once inside Madison Square Garden, then an immense Moorish pile on the corner of Twenty-sixth Street and Fifth Avenue, they waved banners of black, green, and crimson and sang along as three brass bands trumpeted "Ethiopia, Thou Land of Our Fathers." Some of the attendees had roots in New York, but most were just a few years removed from a sharecropper's shotgun shack in Georgia or the Carolinas, having fled the poverty and violence of the Jim Crow South for the promise of jobs and freedom in the urban North. On the evening of August 2, 1920, they had come to hear about a new journey to freedom, from a new kind of messenger.

Theirs was an unlikely Moses. A squat, pudgy-cheeked former printer and labor organizer from Jamaica, thirty-three-year-old Marcus Garvey was not much to look at, even dressed as he was in academic cap and gown of purple and gold. But, like most of his audience, he was a dark-skinned man, one who spoke with the pugnacious eloquence of the Harlem streets about long-suffered indignities and new ambitions. "We do not desire what has belonged to others, though others have always sought to deprive us of .that which belonged to us," the founder of the Universal Negro Improvement Association (UNIA) proclaimed through the saucer-sized microphone. "If Europe is for the Europeans, then Africa shall be for the black peoples of the world."[1]

Garvey had launched the organization six years earlier in the Caribbean, to challenge British rule and raise consciousness among the black working classes of the islands. But he made little headway, and moved on to New York, where he quickly adopted a message—of black capitalism and racial solidarity—more suited to his new home. The message caught fire. To electrified audiences in New York and across America, Garvey sold shares in the UNIA and with the proceeds purchased an imposing headquarters on 138th Street, which he dubbed Liberty Hall, and founded a steamship company, the Black Star Line, to realize the most ambitious enterprise of all: the mass emigration of black people to Africa and the continent's liberation from European colonialists. "We shall now organize the four hundred million Negroes of the world into a vast organization to plant the banner of freedom," he announced that August evening to the cheering working-class throng, few of whom knew much about Africa beyond the fact that it was, like America, a place where the white man ruled and the black man suffered.[2]

But at least one of the 25,000 people in attendance had a more nuanced understanding of Africa. Few Liberians could boast a more illustrious pedigree than Gabriel Moore Johnson, mayor of Monrovia. His grandfather, Elijah, a patriot-hero, had rallied the first settlers against the ACS and native armies; his father, Hilary, a four-term president, forged the political alliance that ended a half century of black-mulatto feuding; and his brother-in-law, Charles Dunbar Burgess King, was the sitting president of the republic. Johnson intended to make a little history of his own by wooing the largest back-to-Africa movement America had ever known. "I bring you greetings from Liberia," Johnson addressed a delegates-only meeting at Liberty Hall the night after Garvey's Madison Square Garden rally, "and we hope that this organization will take on the right spirit and with concerted action on your part [and] with our assistance—[t]hat Liberia some day may grow and prosper and be what we all desire it to be—a great Republic."[3]

Garvey wholeheartedly concurred. He announced plans to move the UNIA's headquarters to Monrovia and crowned Johnson "potentate," the titular head of the organization. Two months later, Garvey launched a campaign to raise millions of dollars to build a city on a hill in the African jungle, where tens of thousands of Garveyites could prosper and breathe free.

Johnson and other Liberian leaders understood that this utopian vision would never be realized. Still, they hoped that Garvey's plans might lead to a modest infusion of "civilized" immigrants and, more important, their money. The Liberians also hedged their bets. Skeptical of Garvey's grandiose promises and wary of his talk of pan-African liberation, which might also involve the liberation of Liberia's own native masses, they courted successive administrations in Washington, seeking loans on favorable terms, even if this meant allowing another foreign government control of its finances. They reasoned that, at the very least, America had no territorial ambitions on Africa.

They also made sure to tell all parties what they wanted to hear. When Garvey spoke of international black solidarity, they nodded sympathetically, especially in the first years when it seemed like anything was possible for the UNIA and its growing legions of enthusiastic followers. At the same time, they winked knowingly to U.S. and European governments, assuring them they had no intention of letting Liberia be the staging ground for Garvey's pan-African revolution. Long gone was talk of Liberia as the last great hope and refuge of the black diaspora. In its place was a pragmatic nationalism, a desire to protect the nation's sovereignty above all other considerations and to ward off the potential challenges to elite rule. As Lott Carey had discovered many years before, idealism must be sloughed off when survival is at stake.

Not that Liberians were unified in their response to Garvey. Followers of the late Edward Blyden, who had died less than a decade before the UNIA announced its Liberia plans, could not have helped but be encouraged by this powerful figure from America who talked a lot like their intellectual mentor. Meanwhile, less-well-off Americoes, especially in the upriver settlements where, presumably, the Garveyites would settle, became as enamored with Garvey's talk of black self-help and economic liberation as the thousands of American blacks who filled Madison Square Garden on that August evening in 1920.

But their hopes would soon be dashed. Over the next four years, Johnson, the settler elite, and the UNIA would engage in a dance of deception that, in the end, would see Johnson exiled, the UNIA banned from Liberia, and the government in Monrovia throw itself into the arms of another, very different American savior with a double-edged promise.

Elie Garcia did not ignore the warning signs in Monrovia. The Haitian immigrant, who had risen to the top ranks of the UNIA leadership through his efforts as a salesman of Black Star shares, had been dispatched to Liberia by Garvey several months before the Garden event, to meet with officials, explain his organization's plans, and, most important, determine whether these descendants of slavery would welcome their modern African American brethren home.

The initial reception was mixed. Though he was the first Garvey official to visit the country, he was met by two official delegations when he reached Liberia. A day after his arrival, however, the xenophobic *Liberian Commercial*—whose masthead read "LIBERIA is ours to maintain, ours to DEFEND, and ours to ENJOY"—ran an anti-UNIA article claiming that the organization was a scam and urged Liberians to keep their distance from it. When Garcia met with the paper's influential publisher, Abraham Butler, he was grilled in a "very uncivil manner," not unexpectedly, perhaps, given that the man was also Monrovia's chief of police.[4]

From then on, however, he met almost universal acclaim. A meeting of local UNIA chapters, held in the congressional chambers, "was packed," he reported, with the local elite, including the former president Arthur Barclay and Chief Justice F.E.R. Johnson, Gabriel's brother. Over the next month, Garcia took Garvey's message across the country, to similar response. After a visit to the upriver community of Brewerville, he wrote, "I have been traveling in the interest of the U.N.I.A. for a while and it seems to me that nowhere the U.N.I.A. has ever met with more emotionable feelings . . . [O]ne could see on every face the clear indication that those poor souls who had long suffered were sincere in their welcome." In Monrovia, Garcia visited the presidential mansion and was introduced to the newly inaugurated President King, who formally declared that "the Government . . . welcomed the U.N.I.A. to Liberia and that it will be soon when the Headquarters shall be established in Liberia, for which purpose land and other facilities will be granted."[5]

But for all the excitement, Garcia had doubts about Liberia's true feelings concerning the prospective emigration of well-funded, idealistic, and ambitious black nationalists from America. He learned that Americo-Liberian society, particularly its upper reaches, was deeply divided over how to respond to the UNIA's plans for their country. Local supporters hinted of commercial conspiracies, about businessmen not keen on new competition, which may have explained the broadside in the *Liberian Commercial*. "It is said that Mr. Butler's paper is subsidized by firms and that soon after they had learned of my coming, they started the propaganda against us, which was for a while disastrous for the selling of shares of the Black Star Line."[6]

The UNIA envoy soon uncovered something even more insidious at work. "While in Monrovia, I went to a dry goods and bought several yards of khaki to have two pairs of trousers made," Garcia reported to Garvey. "As I was stepping out of the store, my companion (an Americo-Liberian) told [me]: 'Why, I don't suppose you are going to carry this bundle yourself?' 'Why not?' said I; 'it is a very small parcel.' He answered that it was not the custom in Liberia for any gentleman to carry parcels; therefore the usefulness of having slaves."[7]

Visitors to Liberia, particularly white ones, had long accused the Americoes of mistreating the natives, but a similar assessment from Garcia would likely spark a controversy.

Garcia's bold recommendations as to how the organization should proceed, particularly in regards to settler-native relations, reflected the sensitive nature of his findings. In an addendum to his official report that he carefully labeled "for the personal information of the President General, the Hon. Marcus Garvey," Garcia suggested the UNIA simply bypass the Americoes. *"The Liberian politicians understand that they are degenerated and weak morally* and they know that if any number of honest Negroes with brains, energy and experience come to Liberia and are prompted to take part in the ruling of the natives, they [the Americo-Liberians] will be absorbed and ousted in a [very] short time . . . *This intention of the U.N.I.A.* must be kept quiet for a while [emphases in original]."[8]

Whether or not Garvey took Garcia's message into account, several months after the latter's return to New York in August 1920, he dispatched a three-man vanguard to begin acquiring land and establishing businesses in preparation for the emigration of the masses. The trio was led by Cyril Crichlow, a director of the Black Star Line. Tall and heavyset, the University of Nebraska alum and owner of a New York secretarial school was typical of the educated, middle-class Caribbean and North American blacks drawn to the UNIA and its promise of both racial uplift and entrepreneurial opportunity. Joseph Johnson (no relation to the Liberian Johnsons), the black U.S. minister in Monrovia, described the Trinidadian-born Crichlow as a man "thoroughly imbued with the go-ahead American spirit."[9]

Despite a warm reception from ordinary Liberians and government offers of land leases, Crichlow was wary. He had no doubt been briefed by his good friend Garcia. "From our arrival in Monrovia," Crichlow reported to Garvey, "I gradually sensed that the Potentate [Gabriel Johnson] and the Supreme Deputy [George Osborne Mark, a schoolboy chum of Johnson's] were putting their heads together and . . . would do all in their power to embar[r]ass me so that in the end I would be forced out or my wings clipped so the two of them could control the expenditures."[10]

When Johnson's son Hilary was hired to run the UNIA office in Monrovia, the situation deteriorated further. "The son," Crichlow noted, "started at once by coming to work late, and sometimes never showing up until late in the afternoon, and sometimes not showing up at all." Crichlow then instituted a thoroughly American solution: a sign-in timesheet. "This [Hilary] treated with contempt," he noted, "signing it when he pleased and sometimes not signing it at all . . . Then, at the end of April when I looked for the time sheet for that month, it had disappeared." The source of the problem, as Crichlow saw it, was not just that the son felt himself above the job of a mere clerk—"[his] constant grumble was that he was educated in the United States, graduated from some college or other, and had more ability than any of the other men"—but that his loyalties and interests lay elsewhere.[11]

As it turned out, Hilary was spending most of his time seeing to his family's transport business. His father, Crichlow reported, was primarily concerned with the same matter. "He has a number of little pet schemes that he intends to combine with the [UNIA's] program in order to make some money for himself." Among these was "an old, leaky bui[l]ding on Broad St. [downtown Monrovia]" that he planned to sell or lease to the Garveyites, as well as "arrangements whereby settlers would be turned over to certain persons who would board and lodge them, paying His Highness [i.e., Johnson] a consideration."[12] Crichlow declined both deals. He and Johnson continued to bicker over who was in charge of the mission, with Crichlow sending letter upon letter to Garvey, asking him to settle the matter once and for all, but to little effect.

Three months into his stay, an exhausted Crichlow wired his resignation to New York: "on account of serious personal difficulties with Potentate and Supreme Deputy, position untenable."[13] The

UNIA Executive Board refused to accept it. Crichlow fell ill with "chronic enteritis," a painful inflammation of the intestines.[14] Liberia's sanitary and health officer urged him to leave the tropics immediately. But with Johnson in control of UNIA funds, Crichlow was stuck, pleading in vain for his organization to send him money. Eventually, the intercession of the American minister in Monrovia secured his passage on a British steamer. Furious, he dashed off a last letter to Garvey before leaving Monrovia. "An organization that would . . . send a man to his death without compunction . . . would be a very dangerous organization to be in the service of."[15]

While understandably upset at his treatment by UNIA officials, Crichlow still believed in the organization's mission. Like Garcia, he warned Garvey of the pitfalls of working with the Americo-Liberians. He was emphatic: Do not put them in charge of UNIA affairs, as their "clannishness and sensitiveness . . . will but lead to irrecoverable disaster . . . [and] is certain to have things accomplished in the good old-fashioned Liberian way, which is beautifully less than nothing." Reflecting on his own experiences, he concluded, no "self-respecting American or West Indian . . . [would] tolerate being placed under any Liberian for the execution of business." The criticism was reciprocated. "[African Americans] believed they knew too much," is how Crichlow characterized Liberian opinion, and are "more aggressive . . . in their methods." Or as young Hilary Johnson put it during the time-sheet affair, "he [Crichlow] was like the rest of them [African Americans], trying to be too strict."[16]

It was a true clash of cultures. For all their misgivings about their homeland, the Garveyites were Americans, energetic, proud, and naïve in their idealism. When they spoke enthusiastically of great waves of immigrants landing on Liberian shores, new enterprises, and a new day in the country's history, the Americo elite—the survivors of imperialist aggression and financial indenture—heard only invasion, interference, and more threats to their prized sovereignty. Cyril Henry, an African American missionary and longtime resident of Liberia, adopted the voice of a Liberian official to capture local attitudes toward Garveyite plans. " 'You are welcome,' they say, 'but your numbers, your influence and combined power should not be sufficient to supplant our political preferments; i.e., the presidency, the secretary-ship, consulships abroad, customs service, etc.,' " he wrote to a UNIA official. " 'You must adopt our ways, be scattered amongst us, be not over-zealous about the affairs of the aborigines—us first!"[17]

For much of its hundred-year history—except when food and housing was scarce, or when, in the 1860s, J. J. Roberts's ruling party feared an influx of darker-skinned people from the West Indies who might join a Blyden-led opposition—Liberia had done everything it could to lure new settlers from across the Atlantic. A few citizens traveled back to the United States to spread the good word; others wrote letters, articles, and books to persuade African Americans to emigrate. "We are proprietors of the soil we live on; and possess the rights of freeholders," read the "Address of the Colonists to the Free People of Colour in the U.S.," reprinted in an 1827 edition of the ACS organ, the *African Repository*. "Our suffrages, and, what is of more importance, our sentiments and our opinions have their due weight in the government we live under."[18] These were not empty claims. New settlers were given land, offered aid, and, after independence, were awarded citizenship on arrival.

Yet few blacks in America or the West Indies had the means or the inclination to emigrate to a nation still notorious for disease and economic troubles. Isolated and surrounded by hostile powers for two generations, Americo-Liberians grew suspicious of foreigners and paranoid of outside interference. Their impulse to help their oppressed brothers and sisters diminished as their nation sunk into debilitating poverty. The founding generations, renewed by a steady stream of immigrants and by the idea of Liberia as the last best hope for the African diaspora, had given way to a shrewd, hard-nosed—or, in Crichlow's estimation, a more self-serving—ethos. By the 1920s, the Americo elite—like the nation from which their forefathers had emigrated—had become far more selective about whom they let in. "The arrival of settlers . . . is not greatly desired by Liberians.

Americans especially are not particularly wanted," Crichlow noted to Garvey, "unless they have money."[19]

President King embodied this ambivalence. He first encountered the UNIA in the winter and spring of 1919, when, as foreign minister, he led the Liberian delegation to the post–World War I Paris Peace Conference. Eliezer Cadet, a twenty-two-year-old Haitian national representing the UNIA, met with the Liberians in King's hotel suite and immediately tried to push organization pamphlets and newspapers on them, "each containing large headlines and inflammatory wording, emphasizing a day of judgment and retribution for the American people."* As Henry Worley, American financial advisor to Liberia, described the scene, "Cadet called on Secretary King and endeavored to arouse in him some sort of movement but I think did not receive much encouragement . . . King asked him, if the American Negroes were so thoroughly dissatisfied with the social and political conditions in America, why they did not go to Liberia, which is a Negro Republic founded by the United States, and become citizens there where they would have social and political equality."[20]

When he met with Garcia a year and a half later as president and in the Executive Mansion, King was more encouraging, promising land and facilities to the UNIA should it relocate its headquarters to the Liberian capital. But King's public stance was more reserved. He had good reason to hold back. Too close an association with Garvey would jeopardize a much bigger prize: a $5 million U.S. government-backed loan, which King and many other Liberians felt was their due. In the early years of World War I, Liberia had experienced a brief period of prosperity selling much-needed tropical products— most notably, the palm oil that lubricated the war's big guns—to the belligerents. But when the United States entered the war in April

---

*With the postwar American red scare at its height, the Justice Department declared the UNIA a subversive organization with communist ties, and the State Department denied Garveyite officials passports to attend the conference.

1917, it pressured Monrovia to sever ties with Berlin, which, by the early twentieth century, had become the country's leading trade partner. King felt that his nation was owed something for this act of loyalty.

In the spring of 1921, King and several of his advisors traveled to the United States to lobby Washington for the loan but also to take the measure of the UNIA up close. Upon his arrival in New York, he hosted a five-man Garveyite delegation at his suite at the Waldorf-Astoria Hotel, where they discussed UNIA plans for the black republic. Oddly, Garvey was not in attendance. He did, however, write a personal letter to King, attempting to alleviate the latter's concerns about a UNIA takeover of his country. "[T]he purpose of the Universal Negro Improvement Association with respect to the Republic of Liberia," he wrote, "is solely and purely industrial and commercial, with a view of assisting the peoples of Liberia in strengthening and improving their country, generally."[21]

But as Garvey and the UNIA offered promises and assurances, King and his delegation were hearing from African Americans who were disdainful of Garvey's populist theatrics, opposed to his separatist politics, and suspicious of his economic schemes. Just days after the Liberians' arrival in New York, a Bureau of Investigation operative reported to J. Edgar Hoover that "there is a strong feeling among a number of the leading business men (Negro) to find out from President King whether he approves of the Garvey Liberian Loan or whether it is an independent scheme of Garvey's to fleece the public. They seem to feel that Garvey should be openly denounced by King." In early April, King met with Richard Robert Wright, who had been one of the highest ranking black officers in the U.S. military and was then the head of a Negro college in Georgia, who urged "him against the U.N.I.A." King later told a State Department official that Wright "impressed the most of any negro he had met in the United States."[22]

W.E.B. Du Bois had weighed in even before King's arrival. Had Garvey "asked permission of the Liberian government" before making plans to relocate his headquarters there? he asked in an editorial in *The Crisis*, the NAACP paper he edited. "Does he presume to usurp authority in a land which has successfully withstood England, France, and the United States,—but is expected tamely to submit to Marcus Garvey?"[23] America's leading black intellectual had taken exception to Garvey's back-to-Africa program from the start. While he admired and even envied the Jamaican leader's ability to connect with the masses, he felt the black nationalist message was a dangerous distraction. "Give up! Surrender! The struggle [for equal rights in America] is useless; back to Africa and fight the white world," was his mocking assessment of the UNIA's plans.[24] Moreover, Du Bois had come to believe, like the African American businessman the Bureau's agent had reported on, that Garvey's campaign to raise money for his Black Star Line and the Liberian construction loan bonds were, at best, ill-conceived ideas that would only serve to part thousands of working-class blacks from their hard-earned wages.

But as he made his way from New York to Washington, King's focus was on the loan. Like most educated Liberians, he was an astute observer of American politics and was no doubt aware of the isolationist sentiment and fiscal probity that had overtaken the country in the wake of President Warren "Normalcy" Harding's landslide Republican election victory in 1920. Getting $5 million for Liberia from the U.S. Treasury would not be easy. Was Garvey's talk of a $2 million construction loan for Liberia legitimate? King was not sure and so did not want to alienate the UNIA. In a letter to *The Crisis*, solicited by Du Bois, King hedged: "Liberia has been an independent country since 1847 and naturally it has never considered the surrender of its sovereignty to any nation or organization. On the other hand, Liberia has always regarded itself as the natural refuge and center for persons of Negro descent the world over."[25] But the Liberian president's delicate balancing act was threatened by Garvey's incendiary oratory. In late April, King told F. W. Ellegor, a top UNIA officer, that "he objected to Garvey's method of telling the white people just what he is going to do, and that while he, as a Liberian would like to see the Negroes own Africa, he would be a fool to tell them so openly."[26]

While Garvey's confidence in his Liberia project knew no bounds, some in the UNIA began to express doubt. Ellegor, for instance, had traveled to Washington in April specifically to tell the Liberian president "not to say anything for or against Garvey's Liberian loan, as it would cause a panic and a run on Garvey's office, and probably his life, if the poor people who subscribed [to the loan] found out that the Liberian government was not behind it, as was the general impression among all of Garvey's followers." King, still unsure about the fate of the U.S. government loan, agreed, though he noted that "since his arrival in Washington the representatives of British, French and American Governments persistently asked [him] whether he endorsed [the UNIA's Liberian plans] or not."[27]

On August 3, Harding set aside his isolationism and revived the party of Lincoln's paternalist sympathies for downtrodden blacks. He urged Congress to approve the Liberian loan. Garvey understood the import of the president's message. The very next day he dispatched a letter congratulating King on the news but also pleading with him to ignore "certain misrepresentations as to the political aims of this association [i.e., the UNIA] toward Liberia."[28]

Garvey's case began to suffer additional setbacks. In October, the radical Harlem paper *The Crusader*, a UNIA foe, ran an editorial headlined "Figures Never Lie, But Liars Do Figure" by W. A. Domingo, a Jamaican immigrant and longtime acquaintance of Garvey. Domingo alleged that little of the $144,000 raised for the construction loan had gone to Liberia; rather, it had been wasted or diverted to the Black Star Line and *Negro World*, the UNIA newspaper. Both duplicity and incompetence were at work, Domingo asserted, adding that a $4,400 sawmill destined for Africa still sat in a Hoboken warehouse.

Several months later *The Crusader* printed a series of scathing articles accompanied by incriminating UNIA documents. The author was Crichlow, who alleged that everyone involved in Garvey's scheme, American and Liberian, was corrupt and incompetent. "[T]he vaporings of the 'Negro World' notwithstanding," he wrote, "[the UNIA] is doing next to nothing in the furtherance of its Liberian construction and African redemption program."[29]

For all his inflammatory rhetoric about liberating the world's "four hundred million Negroes," Garvey's plans were for the most part not radical ones; indeed, he had first come to the United States to study with Booker T. Washington. He preached the gospel of success—both individual and racial. Garvey urged his followers to invest—for the race, of course, but also for their own personal financial futures—in steamship lines, construction bonds, and real estate. His speeches frequently followed the rhythms of a salesman's patter.

But Attorney General A. Mitchell Palmer and J. Edgar Hoover, his ambitious young protégé at the Bureau of Investigation, heard something different. They heard a black man spewing a radical, anti-American ideology and worried as millions of Negroes listened and applauded. Hoover, as one historian of early twentieth-century black America noted, was "hooked on a fixation" about Garvey and the UNIA, "which would before long become a vendetta."[30] Agents were assigned to the case, white ones at first, but that proved counterproductive in dealing with an organization that thrived on conspiracy theories. So Hoover reluctantly hired the Bureau's first black agents to infiltrate Garvey's inner circle, seeking evidence that would allow him to prosecute Garvey or, at the very least, deport him back to Jamaica.

He would find the evidence he needed. Bookkeeping at the UNIA was notoriously sloppy and there were many angry former employees still waiting to be paid and ready to talk to what they thought was another disgruntled Garveyite. The Black Star Line captain J. W. Jones, for one, spoke to an agent about tens of thousands of dollars, raised from investors for Liberian construction, diverted to pay the salaries of UNIA officials and fund their lavish travel junkets. Among the most damning pieces of evidence was the secret report Elie Garcia had sent to Garvey in the summer of 1920. "[Americo-

Liberians] are absolutely hostile to 'immigration' of American or West Indian Negroes; that is, if said Negroes show any tendency to take part in the political life of the Republic," he wrote, adding, "[s]tarving Liberia has no conditions at the present for any large number of persons."[31]

As Hubert Harrison, a former *Negro World* editor, later told government investigators, the Garcia memo clearly showed that Garvey knew "he had no base [in Liberia] to work from or on," even as he was telling investors—in speeches and prospectuses sent by U.S. mail, a key component in a federal indictment—just the opposite.[32] "All those who have not bought shares [in the Black Star Line are urged] to do so immediately," Garvey announced in a year's end sales pitch, "because between January 1 and December 31, 1921, it is expected that [the UNIA] . . . will have transported between five hundred thousand and one million civilized, industrious Negroes from this western hemisphere into the great Republic of Liberia."[33]

On January 12, 1922, Garvey was arrested by Hoover's agents in New York on charges of conspiracy and mail fraud. A month later, Garcia and two other UNIA officials were arrested on the same charges. It would take federal prosecutors nearly a year and a half to convict Garvey on the mail fraud charges; the UNIA head would not actually begin serving his five-year term at the Atlanta Federal Penitentiary until February 1925. In the meantime, the Garcia report would come back to haunt Garvey and the UNIA in other ways. Less than two weeks after Garvey's initial arrest, President King was at last handed a copy of the secret memo in which Garcia had denounced the Americo leadership as "degenerated and weak morally."[34]

For the increasingly suspicious King, Garvey's arrest and Garcia's report meant that he could disengage his country from the UNIA. He wasted no time dismantling the organization's operations in Liberia. He had Gabriel Johnson dismissed as mayor of Monrovia and replaced by Andrew Butler, the police chief who had grilled Garvey's envoy so rudely two years before. This latter appointment must have been especially gratifying to the president, who, like many of the

Americo "old guard," had always bristled at Johnson's "potentate" title, "stately [UNIA] robes," and $12,000 per annum salary, nearly five times that of the president's.[35]

The Americo elite remained divided, however. King represented the old mercantile elite, which envisioned the country yoked to a broader, transatlantic economy dominated by America. He led the ruling True Whig Party, whose core lay in settler-thick Monrovia and its environs. UNIA backers such as Johnson, meanwhile, had inherited Blyden's dream of a Liberia that was African before it was anything else. They were typically members of the opposition People's Party and lived in the upriver settlements that would benefit from immigration.

But all Liberians understood what Garvey did not: that wariness and secrecy were the keys to their country's geopolitics. Secretary of State Edwin Barclay did open up to Crichlow in the earlier days of the UNIA-Liberian relationship, and revealed a foundational aspect of the Liberian worldview. "It is not always advisable nor politic to openly expose our secret intentions . . . our secret thoughts," he said, in cautioning the UNIA to tone down its anti-imperialist rhetoric, lest it arouse the suspicions of Britain and France. "That is the way we do . . . or rather don't do [things] . . . in Liberia. We don't tell them [white imperialists] what we think; we only tell them what we like them to hear . . . what in fact, they like to hear."[36]

On November 27, 1922, the U.S. Senate ignored State Department lobbying and denied the Liberian loan, caving to pressure from midwestern isolationists who wondered how the government could find $5 million for Liberia and nothing for suffering farmers; from Southerners angry at the loan sponsor's other piece of legislation, an anti-lynching bill; and from assorted Republicans who saw no reason they should honor a pledge first made by the detested Woodrow Wilson administration.

King did not go scrambling back to the UNIA, as Garvey might have hoped, however. World War I had not fundamentally changed the dynamics of West African geopolitics, other than removing Germany from the picture. He still had to consider the reaction of London and Paris to Liberian actions, and both capitals had decided that Garvey was more than a mere irritant. In a speech in January 1920, he had promised war against Europe, saying that Europeans "talk about their aeroplanes . . . and about their machine guns. You just wait awhile! . . . In the next two years we are going to show them . . . [that] all their tanks and machine guns and aeroplanes will be like Santa Claus' toys to what we mean to put out."[37] Throughout western and southern Africa, British and French colonial officials barred UNIA agitators and deported local Garveyites.

Garvey's rhetoric was ultimately responsible for the Liberian elite's decision to distance itself from him and his organization. King patiently tried to explain this to UNIA officials. "Representatives of the Garvey Movement have visited me," he told a reporter for the *Baltimore Afro-American* in 1921, "and I have urged them to discard their political propaganda and the impossible talk about driving the white race out of Africa."[38] He was more specific in his discussions with U.S. State Department officials: "the danger existed . . . that . . . Foreign countries, particularly France and England, might become anxious with regard to the position of Liberia in connection with this movement [i.e., the UNIA]."[39]

Meanwhile, the feuding among the Garveyites in Monrovia and revelations that much of the loan money set aside for Liberian development had been stolen by association officials undid what remained of the UNIA's credibility among ordinary Liberians, many of whom had once believed in its battle cry of black solidarity, even as they hoped that its plans for Africa would bring much-needed jobs and economic development. As Johnson explained to UNIA delegates at the annual convention in August 1922, the organization was now "looked upon by many of the people there as a huge joke."[40]

Though it did tone down talk about the liberation of Africa, the UNIA did not give up its plans for Liberia. It sent a new delegation to Liberia at the end of 1923 to negotiate yet another settlement agreement with the authorities in Monrovia. The three members, including actress Henrietta Vinton Davis, famed for her Negro dialect renditions of Shakespeare, received the usual enthusiastic reception during an event organized by the local UNIA chapter, with ex-president Arthur Barclay and Chief Justice J. J. Dossen in attendance.

After putting off the meeting numerous times, King also received them, but his early ambivalence about the UNIA had turned to wariness. He went out of his way to deny reports that UNIA emigrants were not wanted and once again offered land for settlement and promises of full cooperation from his government. But he made it clear that the meeting was not official, but between private citizens only. As for the UNIA's plans, any emigrants would have to come as individuals, not in groups sponsored by outside organizations, and they would be scattered about the country. Liberia had to keep in mind, he said, its "[o]bligation to the Great Powers [i.e., Britain and France], and as such to the maintenance of the Independence of the Republic."[41] The always effervescent Davis did not seem to understand the import of King's terms. "The three of us went home," she reported later to UNIA officials, "feeling so happy that we had accomplished that for which we were sent."[42]

Garvey greeted the optimistic reports with his usual ebullience. In a May 1924 editorial in *Negro World* he once again called for African Americans to immigrate to Liberia. A month later, he announced plans for a new delegation, this time of technical experts who would start building the infrastructure in preparation for the arrival of the emigrant masses. Acting as if King's warnings against large emigrant expeditions were really for the consumption of officials in London and Paris, the UNIA began running ads announcing its plans for four colonies in Liberia, including detailed layouts for a settlement at Cape Palmas, provocatively close to the French frontier.

On June 20, 1924, Garvey's technical experts set out from New York Harbor, ten days after a dispatch by Abraham Butler in Monrovia had appeared in the pages of the anti-Garveyite *Baltimore Afro-American*. "We in Liberia are tired . . . of reading dumps of The Negro World in which appear articles misleading of the American Negro, which goes to give them an idea that they have been asked or would be welcomed in coming to Liberia," he complained, before offering to pay Garvey $10,000 if he could "produce a single letter from President King giving him the permission to land his immigrants in Liberia." His countrymen, the former police chief warned, would do everything it took to stem a "Garvey invasion," including armed resistance, bloodshed, even a "call on England and France for help."[43]

The UNIA thought that Butler could be ignored. The Reverend R. Van Richards, chaplain to the Liberian Senate, said to a mass gathering at Liberty Hall that summer that far more important personages than Butler supported its plans. "Do you think if the Liberian Government did not desire to help this movement to develop the country," he asked his audience, "[Chief Justice Dossen] would take any part in it?"[44] Garvey did not respond directly to the Butler piece; instead, he praised the leader of the latest expedition, a civil engineer named William Wallace Strange. "We have found our Colonel George Washington Goethals, such a man as Colonel Roosevelt [i.e., President Theodore Roosevelt] found when he undertook the Panama Canal," Garvey told a cheering send-off crowd at Liberty Hall. "We have our Goethals who is going to lay the foundation of Africa's commercial and industrial development under the auspices of the Universal Negro Improvement Association."[45]

But Liberia had already turned emphatically against the UNIA. Liberians could not help but notice that the published outline for the Cape Palmas colony included not just churches, parks, and schools, but a courthouse and police station. This was, they felt, a sure sign that the UNIA intended to set up an alternative civil administration for its colonies, in direct violation not only of Liberian law but of the UNIA's promises that its intentions were strictly commercial and

industrial. Those who believed that UNIA money nevertheless outweighed potential infringements on national sovereignty were disabused of their faith in Garvey when officials from the U.S. Shipping
Board asked Liberian authorities to seize tens of thousands of dollars
of UNIA goods in the customs house at Cape Palmas. Garvey's check
to the vendor had bounced.

In late June, as Garvey's delegation steamed toward Europe, en
route to Monrovia, Secretary of State Edwin Barclay instructed the
local agent of the Elder Dempster shipping line that the passengers
would not be allowed to land and that the expenses of their return
voyage would be the company's responsibility. UNIA immigration to
Liberia finally and officially ended on July 3, when Barclay instructed
Ernest Lyon, Liberia's American consul, to meet with U.S. State Department officials and request that they "neither facilitate nor permit
the emigration under the auspices of the Universal Negro Improvement Association of Negroes from the United States with intent to
proceed to Liberia."[46] Lyon then went public, warning prospective
UNIA emigrants that the government of Liberia would not issue
them visas.

The Garveyites' initial response to the ban was conciliatory. They
cited "enemies of our race" for instigating trouble between the Liberian government and the UNIA. At the organization's annual convention in August 1924, the delegates, in an open letter to King, expressed
their official disbelief that "the head of a Negro State . . . could be
responsible for doing anything that would tend to dampen the spirit
of love that the people of the Universal Negro Improvement Association have for you and your country and the effort that they are making to assist in making your nation the pride of the race and a credit
to o[u]r civilization."[47] Chaplain Richards assured the delegates that
"[a]s soon as the Liberian government had been truly informed of the
power, honesty and sincerity of the association, all would be well."[48]

Garvey himself blamed the U.S. government and his longtime
nemesis W.E.B. Du Bois for the failure of his Liberia plans. There
was likely some truth in the accusation. The United States had made

Du Bois its representative at King's second-term inauguration, the kind of subtle diplomatic message Liberian officialdom was so adept at recognizing. Du Bois, for his part, categorically denied that he had anything "to do at all with the relations of Garvey and the Republic of Liberia."[49] But because he had never been shy about denouncing Garvey, there is no reason to think he would have kept mum in Liberia, a country for which he felt great affection despite his dislike of the idea of emigration.

Garvey had projected his own assumptions about pan-African solidarity onto an Americo-Liberian elite most interested in its political and economic survival. It was true, the editors of the pro-government *Liberian News* noted a month after the visa ban was issued, that Liberia was premised on the idea of a haven for the oppressed black masses. But times had changed. "Our political position is between two powerful colonizing states of a race different to our own. Our experience in the past has been to lose territory after territory through these powerful neighbours under some flimsy pretext or other."[50] Liberia did not plan to be further reduced by the UNIA's unruly presence within its borders.

The dalliance with the UNIA thus prodded Liberia to think seriously about its position in the modern world, and what its purpose was a century after the first colonists had arrived. King pithily described the changes his nation had undergone, and what kind of future beckoned. "Liberians, standing alone and fighting their own national battles for the last hundred years, have developed . . . a *national* point of view," he explained in his annual message to the legislature in 1924. "They fully realise and are conscious of the fact that Liberia's immediate objective is toward *nationalism* and not *racialism*; the making of a nation and not a race."[51]

Making a nation required money, though, and Liberia, as always, had little of it. The UNIA was rejected on principle, yes, but also because the King administration believed it had found, after the failure of the

Harding and Garvey loans, a new benefactor. Harvey Firestone, Sr., among the last of the self-made autocrats of the American industrial revolution, came to Liberia to build the world's largest rubber plantation and thereby to reassert his control over the industry, which had grown exponentially after the advent of the automobile. It is not clear who within the Firestone organization first suggested Liberia, but the idea was an inspired one. *Hevea brasiliensis*, the most productive of latex-sapped trees, grew even more prolifically there than it did in Malaya, where the British cultivated it on a vast scale, as proven on a small plantation set up years before at Mount Barclay.

In June 1924, Firestone sent his personal secretary to meet with King. The two quickly reached an understanding: a ninety-nine-year lease for a million acres at the extremely low rent of six cents an acre, per year. (Outright purchase of land by foreigners was prohibited under the Liberian constitution.) There would be no taxes either, other than a 1 percent levy on exports, and that wouldn't start for six years. Firestone would also be granted a monopoly; no other foreigner could grow rubber in the country. In return, his company bowed to the Liberian elite's reflexive sovereignty concerns and racial anxieties. Local natives would be given preferential treatment in hiring and white staff would be limited to 1,500. Firestone's man left for Ohio, having been assured that, in Liberia, the government went along with what the president agreed to. Indeed, a few in the legislature had qualms— particularly about whether the long-term lease violated the spirit, if not the letter, of the constitution—but in the end it did what it always did when pressured by the president: it approved the deal.

Then came the cable from Akron, Ohio. Firestone was sending his envoy back and he wanted to know if the legislature would stay in session till the envoy arrived. He'd even pay their salaries. This provoked outrage; even King agreed that Firestone's offer was an affront to Liberian sovereignty, and so refused it. When he arrived in January 1925, Firestone's man explained why his boss had made the offer in the first place: he was worried about Liberia reneging, by cutting a better deal with European competitors, for instance. Firestone did not like leaving anything to chance; Liberia would have to take out a $5 million loan if it wanted him to invest in the country as well as grant his company oversight of the nation's finances. By accepting such a heavy obligation and intrusion into its affairs, Liberia would cede control of its treasury to Firestone, just as it had to the United States government earlier in the century. Firestone would also have the ability to veto any outside deal. As one U.S. State Department official noted to a company representative, with the loan, "Mr. Firestone could virtually be the Government."[52]

Though the tire maker's money would allow the country to pay off its many other debts, the Liberians' impulse was to say no, just as they had to Garvey, and for much the same reasons. As one newspaper editor put it, would taking the money represent "the bartering away of our sovereign rights 'for a mess of potage?'"[53] Particularly galling was that Liberia would have to pay for its own indenture, footing the salaries—amounting to tens of thousands of dollars annually—of the Firestone officials who would administer the country's finances. The handbills that began appearing on Monrovia's streets captured the prevailing sentiment: "American Occupation of Liberia Arranged by President King."[54] Both the cabinet and legislature rejected the loan. King, however, could not afford to be indignant. Firestone was threatening to pull out of Liberia and to take with him the protective embrace of the American government, which had been so critical to Liberia's defense against meddlesome European nations. U.S. Secretary of State Frank B. Kellogg read Monrovia a diplomat's riot act: "the Liberian government should fulfill the Planting Agreements in strict accord with its pledged word."[55]

With no other options, the Liberia legislature ratified both the lease and loan agreements in November and December of 1926. It secured two face-saving clauses. Firestone agreed to an arbitration process for disputes and, to assuage Liberian fears of a single corporation holding so much power, the rubber company spun off a wholly owned subsidiary to administer the loan. But few people on either side of the Atlantic were fooled. Three-quarters of a century after a band of free blacks and freed slaves had proudly declared their independence from one American institution, the American Colonization Society, their impoverished and indebted descendants had, out of necessity, capitulated to another. Liberia would remain a virtually wholly owned subsidiary of Harvey Firestone until its economic expansion after World War II, and the pan-African dreams of Blyden and Garvey would never again play a serious role in the nation of the Americo-Liberians.

EIGHT

The Slave Ring

According to the *Guinness Book of World Records*, the most fraudulent election in history was the 1927 presidential contest in Liberia, which saw Thomas J. R. Faulkner challenge the longtime incumbent, Charles D. B. King. King won the contest with roughly 235,000 votes to his opponent's 9,000. But it was the turnout, not the margin, that led to Liberia's dubious honor. There were only 15,000 eligible voters in the whole republic at the time. The additional votes represented real people but not real voters—they came from the country's natives, whose constitutionally invalid ballots were cast on their behalf by government-appointed paramount chiefs.

The outcome, if not the vote count, was predictable. King headed the True Whig Party, whose continuous rule also set a world record. Visiting Monrovia during election season a decade later, the novelist Graham Greene remarked, "the curious thing about a Liberian election campaign . . . is that, although the result is always a foregone conclusion, everyone behaves as if the votes and the speeches and the pamphlets matter."[1] Even the loser usually played his appointed role, campaigning fiercely, conceding graciously, and then accepting his sinecure in the new government.

But Faulkner was no ordinary candidate. His background is obscure, beyond his origins; he was born in North Carolina just after the Civil War and grew up on the Baltimore waterfront. By the time he emigrated in the early twentieth century, however, he had clearly learned his way around a business. He had also picked up enough electrical engineering to open a power plant, an ice cream parlor, a telephone exchange, and an ice factory, which were all, except for the power plant, the first of their kind in Liberia. Foreigners who met him were impressed, and compared him favorably with the rest of the Americo community; he was seen as an entrepreneurial Yankee— "fearless, eternally active, of powerful physique despite his sixty years," noted a visiting American sociologist—in a languid land.[2]

Faulkner's relentless energy may indeed have exhausted his compatriots, but it was his moral rectitude that really bothered them. A defender of native rights, he had been criticizing the True Whig leadership for years, his "zeal for reform," the admiring sociologist noted, "almost an obsession."[3] This zeal brought him back to his native Baltimore two years after the election. There, he gave an interview to the *Afro American*, the local black newspaper, in which he laid out exactly how King had stolen the election, charges he repeated in meetings with State Department officials in Washington.

A fraudulent election in the faraway black republic would not make headlines in America or lead to an official protest. But Faulkner had another, far more serious allegation against the King administration, one that would lead to the worst crisis in the history of U.S.-Liberian relations and arguably the greatest crisis the country had ever faced. This scandal would be highly publicized, outraging people around the world and shaming the Americo community. The Liberian government, Faulkner asserted, was implicated in a modern-day slave trade.

A more shocking allegation could hardly have been imagined. Liberia had not only been founded as a refuge for freed slaves from North America, but had dedicated itself in its early years, at great expense in money and blood, to eradicating the slave trade in West Africa. Liberian militia companies had laid siege to heavily defended barracoons of renegade European slavers up and down the Windward Coast in the waning days of the transatlantic slave trade. They had launched raids against the villages of chiefs who profited from the business, risking retaliation from tribes that outnumbered the settlers by dozens to one. Though struggling for survival themselves in an inhospitable land, they had taken in and assimilated thousands of recaptives. And when the founders sat down to write their constitution in 1847, they were explicit on the matter: "There shall be no slavery within this Republic. Nor shall any citizen of this Republic, or any person resident therein, deal in slaves, either within or without this Republic, directly or indirectly."[4] Later, legislators made participation in the slave trade a capital crime.

For decades, Liberia had weathered existential threats from abroad. Now the most significant threat to the Liberian experiment appeared to be from within. Faulkner's accusations against Liberian officialdom bespoke not only a nation in decline, but one that had lost its moral compass.

Fernando Pó, the destination for the "slaves" Liberian officials were allegedly trafficking in, is a smallish, boot-shaped island in the Gulf of Guinea, some 1,200 miles to Liberia's east.* Now known as Bioko and part of Equatorial Guinea, it had been Spain's only colony in sub-Saharan Africa since the late eighteenth century, a rugged, unexploited landscape of dormant volcanoes, deep jungle valleys, and nearly inaccessible coastline.

Then, at the turn of the twentieth century, came the cocoa boom. Spanish and Creole planters became desperate for labor. Devastated by the diseases the Spanish brought with them, the island's native population, known as the Bubi, had long since retreated to mountain fastnesses. Nearby mainland colonies offered no solution either, as British, French, and German colonial authorities were in search of laborers for their own plantations and public works. That left Liberia,

---

*Ironically, Britain used the island as a base for its anti-slave-trading patrols in the Gulf of Guinea in the early nineteenth century, during a hiatus in Spanish rule of the island.

whose chief export by the end of the nineteenth century was Liberian natives leased out by private Americo labor contractors, sometimes in collusion with local chiefs. Some served in King Leopold's army of conquest in the Congo; others on plantations in the Gold Coast or Nigeria; a few helped dig France's ill-fated canal in Panama. But the vast majority, tens of thousands over subsequent decades, were shipped off to plant and harvest cocoa on Fernando Pó.

By all accounts, conditions on the island were appalling—twelve-hour workdays, nights spent locked in crowded barracks, a few yams and dried fish for sustenance, and for those who stole, shirked, or protested, brutal punishment. There were even reports of overseers flogging men to death. Many others died of disease, malnutrition, or exhaustion before their contracts were up. The African American journalist George Schuyler, who investigated Faulkner's charges by visiting Liberia and Fernando Pó, described conditions on the island—albeit in a 1931 *roman à clef* entitled *Slaves Today*—in the bleakest of terms. "There was no amusement, no entertainment, no diversion. [The workers] went out at dawn and returned at sunset. They never seemed to get fully rested. Most of them became thin and gaunt, easy victims of any passing malady."[5] And those who survived and returned to Liberia often went unpaid; some planters supposedly held their money in trust for them, while others outright refused to pay them.

From Monrovia's perspective, the recruitment of Liberian natives presented two problems. First, it drained the country of the few surplus native laborers it had, that is, those not engaged in subsistence agriculture and thus available for work on local, Americo-owned plantations and government-run road-building projects. Second, the trade was unregulated, and therefore the government collected no taxes on it. To remedy both issues, the legislature issued a series of rules and laws to govern the traffic. In 1903, it required recruiters to pay a $250 licensing fee and a $5 tax on each laborer shipped, along with a $150 bond against their safe return, all of which, of course, gave Monrovia a direct interest in promoting recruitment and, with the bond, a motivation for turning a blind eye to working and living conditions on the island.

These did not improve after the Liberian government officially recognized the trade, but more politicians began to take notice of them. Citing the testimony of returning laborers and other witnesses, President Daniel Howard wrote in his annual message to the legislature in 1913 that "conditions were represented as tantamount to slavery . . . [many laborers] being unwillingly forced to work for longer periods than that which they contracted before leaving their homes." Howard then dispatched Assistant Secretary of State J. J. Sharp to investigate. His assessment of the problem—"conditions were not all that might have been desired"—was as understated as his solution was inadequate: "Justice and acceptable conditions could be immediately and permanently obtained if the Government [of Liberia] had a consular representative at these islands [plural; there were also lesser problems reported on the nearby Portuguese island of Sao Tomé]."[6] Nevertheless, Sharp's report laid the foundation for the 1914 labor agreement signed by Howard and the governor-general of Spanish Guinea, which made it illegal for laborers' contracts to exceed two years and put the laborers in the care of the consul, who would have broad powers to investigate abuses.

The laborers' new rights thus depended on the consul. At the time Faulkner went to Washington, the position was held by none other than the former UNIA chief potentate Gabriel Johnson, the man Garvey's envoys to Liberia had accused of fraud and mismanagement.* Johnson proved just as untrustworthy in his new post. When, in the wake of Faulkner's allegations, laborers' complaints surfaced in Liberian newspapers averring that the "Consul was never in the office," Johnson replied by saying that, as far as he knew, "this is the first time any labourer from Fernando Poo had made such a statement."[7] Meanwhile, the U.S. State Department would not get

---

*The rumor was that King, who was also Johnson's brother-in-law, had given him the lucrative post in Fernando Pó as a bribe to get him to leave the UNIA.

involved in the matter over working conditions. It was more interested in how thousands of Liberian natives had ended up on the
Spanish island in the first place.

Though the Liberian constitution seemed to have settled the question of slavery and slave trading within the nation's borders, there was
nevertheless an understanding between government officials and
tribal chiefs that the prohibitions were not absolute. It could not have
been any other way; domestic slavery was woven into the fabric of
West African life, where people did not define themselves so much as
autonomous individuals but through the sum of the relationships that
sustained them—family, village, clan, tribe. Children and adults were
regularly "pawned," to use the Western term, to pay debts between
families or cement alliances between clans. "So firmly entrenched in
the social economy of primitive Africans is this custom," wrote the
Nigerian sociologist Nnamdi Azikiwe in the early 1930s, "that most
of the existing domestic pawns [in West Africa] do not wish to be
freed, for if they were emancipated their bond to the Chief would be
destroyed, and they would lose the protection of tribe. This would
make them friendless outcasts and homeless individuals."[8]
    European colonizers and the Liberian government brought taxa-
tion to the region, changing the dynamic of servitude. In Liberia as
elsewhere, chiefs were recruited to collect the fees governments imposed on householders, including the infamous "hut tax." Because
natives often lacked the hard currency to pay this fee and others,
governments imposed corvées. The chiefs would then select men to
go off and labor for no pay and sometimes for long periods of time on
public works, typically road-building or porterage. Firestone, once he
arrived, simply paid chiefs for labor recruits. As W.E.B. Du Bois, who
visited Liberia in the 1920s, pointed out, "labor supply for modern
industry in Africa always tends to approximate slavery because it is
bound up with the clan organization of the tribes. In the African tribe

there is no free labor capable of entering into an individual labor contract. Only the tribal chief can assign members of the tribe to work."[9]

Du Bois had a soft spot for the Americo-Liberians, and his assessment presumed that the chiefs and government negotiated as equals—that the tribal authorities enjoyed the kind of independence promised to them by Liberian law. But when the district commissioner came to town—borne along on a hammock hoisted by natives and accompanied by a platoon of rifle-bearing, loot-seeking Frontier Force soldiers—it was clear who was in charge, as the Wedabo people of Maryland County learned, to their lasting regret.

In the early 1900s a feud began between the Wedabo and the Po River people, both Grebo-speaking clans. To bring their trade goods to the county seat at Harper, the Wedabo had to cross the Po River people's lands and pay transit fees, which led to disputes and the occasional killing of a Wedabo trader. When their leaders complained to the Americo governor of Maryland County, they were told, "You Wedabo people are damn fools. When you see people are killing you why don't you do something to them instead of always complaining?"[10] And so, in 1924, they did, murdering three Po River men. This time, the district commissioner summoned Wedabo leaders for a palaver on the local beach, where he fined their paramount chief, Tuweley Jeh, one hundred pounds sterling and detained sixty subchiefs until Jeh could return with the money, which he promptly did. Then the governor—who would be at the center of the international controversy stirred up by Faulkner's allegation—got involved.

Allen Yancy was not an impressive physical specimen. A black American visitor to Harper described him as "a small ferretlike individual, whose head, sloping violently backward, was capped by a pompadour." His personality, by all accounts, was equally unappealing; he was known for having a "Napoleonic complex," for talking "with the air of a proprietor" and "gesturing at the town of Harper

[Maryland's capital] after the manner of one referring to his private farm."[11] Indeed, Yancy ran the county as his own personal fiefdom.

Born in 1881, the son of a Georgia preacher who had immigrated to Liberia just after the Civil War, Yancy was raised in Harper and, like many settlers in the tiny outpost at the southern tip of Liberia, had one foot in the "civilized" world of the Americos and another in Grebo culture. He had learned their language as a boy and had married a native woman, with whom he had eight children. He avoided participating in the great Grebo War of 1910, even though he was a captain in the local militia. Some said his stance was principled; soldiers serving under him remember a speech about how it was a rich man's war and poor man's fight. Others claimed that, terrified of the prowess of Grebo warriors, he had fled. Whatever the case, his studied neutrality led to many opportunities; he earned money repairing and selling guns to the enemy.

For his actions Yancy was accused of treason after the war. He tried to abscond to the Gold Coast but was arrested, court-martialed, and sentenced to hang. By this point, however, he had made useful contacts with the influential Barclay clan—President Arthur Barclay had given him his first political appointment, as justice of the peace, in 1905—who made sure he never reached the gallows. Wily and unscrupulous, Yancy would ingratiate himself with powerful people in Monrovia throughout his career. Despite being accused of embezzling funds from the German-owned trading post he managed and then stealing the books to cover up his crime, he was appointed county attorney by Attorney General Edwin Barclay, Arthur's nephew, and then governor by newly inaugurated President King in 1920. When King was informed of new embezzlement charges against Yancy—this time he was accused of stealing from the government— King was reputed to have told the investigator, "What? my Yancy? Leave him alone."[12]

As governor in Harper, the little man with the "cold cunning [in] his tiny bright eyes,"[13] like many Liberian politicians, made little distinction between his public duties and private interests. "His bank account, automobiles, and concubines increased so rapidly," noted one foreign observer, that "he became known as 'the millionaire of Maryland County.'"[14] His actions were tolerated by Monrovia because he delivered; tax revenues had never been higher and public works projects moved ahead vigorously. As one pro-Yancy paper noted, "he had had the motor roads extended the greatest distance interiorward [sic] . . . than they had been anywhere else in the Republic. They were fairly good roads too."[15] The source of his success was his ruthless use of native labor. "He developed his private farms and built houses from timber felled by free native labor," noted one critic, "designating this as public work." As for the roads programs, "the excesses . . . extended to brutality, extortion, and general exploitation."[16] And, of course, Yancy had his hand in the shipping of laborers to Fernando Pó. As governor, he was given five pounds for each native delivered to the island, as well as control of the pay held in escrow for the laborers if they survived and returned to Liberia.

In 1924, when Yancy learned of the events on Wedabo Beach, he not only fined the paramount chief, Tuweley Jeh, but told him to get a lawyer, too. Yancy suggested his cousin, the Maryland senator and future Liberian president William V. S. Tubman. His services would cost Jeh another hundred pounds. When the Po River representatives went to Monrovia to present their grievances directly to King, the president summoned Jeh and fined him yet another hundred pounds and then had him held in the capital to assure payment. Jeh appealed to Yancy, who arranged a loan from his old German bosses, for a consideration, of course. If the tribal leaders wanted their chief back, they either had to pay the obligation in English pounds or native flesh—five hundred "boys," the Americo term for native males of any age—for shipment to Fernando Pó. Otherwise Jeh would rot in a government cell. And should the Wedabo fail to produce the men, Yancy would have the Frontier Force burn two of their towns to the ground.

Unable to come up with the money, the Wedabo handed the "boys" over. But no sooner was Jeh back in Harper that Yancy told him to produce five hundred more men, some for Fernando Pó and others for the plantations of the governor and his friends. When Jeh protested, Yancy unleashed the Frontier Force. As an investigator who interviewed local Wedabo tribesmen in the wake of Faulkner's revelations later noted, the "soldiers, who lived chiefly by plunder, being then more than nine years in arrears in pay, helped themselves to the town's cattle, fowl, and rice, while the commander imposed arbitrary fines as his share of the spoils."[17] A dozen elders were then taken hostage and "required to work on the private farms of government officials until the younger men for exportation returned from the bush and surrendered." The impact on the tribe was devastating. Six years later, the investigator still found men in short supply and women singing a lament:

> He [Yancy] caught our husbands and our brothers,
> Sail them to 'Nana Poo [Fernando Pó]
> And there they die!
> And there they die!
> Tell us,
> Yancy, why?
> Yancy, why?
> Wedabo women have no husbands,
> Yancy, why?
> Wedabo women have no brothers,
> Yancy, why?
> Mothers, fathers, sons have died,
> Waiting for the return.
> Yancy, why?[18]

Up the coast in Sinoe County, a similar scenario unfolded in 1927, but the presence of an honest official led to a different end.

Postmaster General Reginald Sherman happened to be in the county seat of Greenville—named, a century earlier, after the Mississippi town its founders hailed from—when the Frontier Force marched 250 laborers into the local barracoon. When Governor Samuel Ross asked Sherman to contact Monrovia for permission to send the men on a different ship than the one originally booked, the postmaster insisted on meeting with the men first. He was not pleased with what he heard. A flurry of radiograms flashed between Greenville and the capital; Sherman insisted that many of the men were not there voluntarily and Ross complained about outsiders who "create disturbances."[19]

Acting President Edwin Barclay—King was out of the country on official business—was outraged. So were the press and public, alerted by Sherman. Overruling Ross's pleas to ignore the matter, Barclay sided with Sherman (an old political ally) and issued an order that every laborer be interviewed and those who wished to return to their villages be allowed to do so. Then, without giving the requisite six months notice to Spanish authorities, he abrogated the 1914 labor agreement.

It was a decisive act and one that seemed to put the Liberian government on the side of human rights. Yet Barclay's motives lay elsewhere. For one, hoping to negotiate better terms, the King administration had already hinted to the Spanish that Firestone's arrival might require Liberia to suspend labor shipments to the island. For another, Barclay's edict simply ended the government's involvement in the trafficking, not the trafficking itself. Yancy and Ross—the latter now in partnership with E.G.W. King, the president's brother—signed their own deals with the planters of Fernando Pó. Indeed, the trafficking only escalated as the two began to vigorously compete against each other; Yancy and Ross shipped more than 2,400 men total to the island between late 1928 and the end of 1929. Nor was anyone punished for their involvement in the business, at least not initially. Ross remained as governor of Sinoe while Yancy not only survived the scandal but was elevated to the vice presidency by the

True Whigs, putting him in pole position for the presidency in 1932, when King would reach his term limit.*

But the Ross-Sherman confrontation did have one important repercussion: It provided Faulkner with the information to bring down the regime he loathed. In early June 1929, just weeks after he had met with officials in Washington, the U.S. minister to Liberia, William T. Francis, who had earlier raised the labor trafficking issue with his superiors in Washington, paid an official visit to the Executive Mansion in Monrovia, where he handed a note from Secretary of State Henry Stimson to President King.† "I am directed . . . to advise Your Excellency," it read, "that there have come to the attention of the Government of the United States . . . that existing conditions incident to the so-called 'export' of labor from Liberia to Fernando Po have resulted in the development of a system which seems hardly distinguishable from organized slave trade, and that in the enforcement of this system the services of the Liberian Frontier Force and the services and influence of certain high government officials are constantly and systematically used."[20] Stimson demanded a "rigorous investigation" and hinted that a failure to address the problem would "threaten grave consequences" for bilateral relations.[21]

Washington's concern no doubt surprised the King administration. After all, the United States had traditionally stayed out of Liberian affairs, except when it came to European encroachment and the nation's financial struggles. Some Liberians, however, soon came to believe that Firestone was behind the note. He was not only one of America's most powerful industrialists, but a personal friend of President Herbert Hoover, who was trying to sell his "dollar diplomacy" foreign policy as a "benevolent" private enterprise alternative to Eu-

---

*Under Liberian law of the day, the president could serve two terms only, the first for eight years and the second for four.
†Per an unwritten State Department rule of the era, Francis, like most ambassadors to the black republics of Haiti and Liberia, was African American.

ropean imperialism. The historian Ernest Jerome Yancy (Allen's son and so not the most reliable source) quoted an American advisor to the effect that "the chief power behind" Stimson's note was the "Rubber Company," which, along with the American government, was "planning to set up a white dictatorship in Liberia."[22] While conspiracy theories of this sort were not uncommon among more racially sensitive Americo-Liberians, it is also possible that Firestone saw Fernando Pó planters as competitors for scarce native labor and may have sought to deflect attention from his own questionable labor-recruiting practices; a young Harvard researcher named Raymond Buell had made precisely this claim in a widely read study, *The Native Problem in Africa*, published the year before. Whoever was behind it, the note had its intended effect. While offering a "categorical denial" of the allegations, King and Barclay immediately agreed with U.S. demands for a League of Nations inquiry.[23]

The two did not immediately and unreservedly open up the country to foreign inspectors, of course. Employing all their diplomatic skill, King and Barclay delayed for six months and finally achieved a compromise. There would not be similar investigations of the forced-labor practices in European colonies, which they had pushed for, but the League of Nations commission would include an American and a Liberian, and so likely only one, not three, British or French apologists for imperialism. King's condition that the American representative be "no . . . Garvey man" was the rare point both sides agreed on from the start.[24]

On April 8, 1930, the African American scholar Charles Johnson, former Liberian president and éminence grise Arthur Barclay (Edwin's uncle), and the British tropical disease expert Cuthbert Christy, who led the commission, began their investigation. They quickly decided that the only way to obtain the necessary evidence and testimony was to go into the hinterland, where the recruitment had occurred. But with the wet season looming, the seventy-five-year-old Barclay decided to remain in Monrovia; he would end up taking part only in the hearings there and the drafting of the final report.

Over the next few months, Christy and Johnson traveled together and separately to the near hinterland, around the administrative center of Kakata (some fifty miles from Monrovia), and then down to Yancy's Maryland County. It was, as expected, rough going. They were stalked by leopards and attacked by driver ants. Christy nearly died from a parasite; Johnson primarily remembered "the rains, the never-ceasing rains."[25] Still, they fulfilled their assignment with aplomb; Johnson, the diligent and bookish son of Virginia slaves and a product of the University of Chicago's esteemed graduate program in sociology, even saw the expedition as an opportunity for scholarly research. "It has to be confessed," he wrote later in a colorful and idiosyncratic history of Liberia he titled *Bitter Canaan*, "that there was curiosity about the interior less specifically related to the inquiry at hand—about the influence of European culture and ideas upon native life in successive stages back from the coast."[26]

Johnson recorded many details of native life. Entering a new village, he and Christy were often met by processions of drummers and dancers. "The natives beat these instruments in hectic rhythm for a period, then stopped and with fixed expressions repeated stretches of song," Johnson wrote. "This was interspersed with dance movements consisting of quick shuffles and stamps, climaxed with grotesque hip movements." Then the local chief would make an entrance. At Kakata, the chief was a man named Dado, "in a white gown, black felt Fedora hat, and country sandals . . . his wizened old face twisted into a cunning grin."[27]

Tales of humiliation, intimidation, extortion, and brutality typically followed these elaborate welcomes. "The journey, once begun," Johnson noted, "was soon crowded with the imperative clamor of natives voicing their fervent desire to find a way of peace with the new demands for hut taxes, government rice, road labor, carriers, plantation labor, export labor, customs charges, and head money."[28] For the investigators, the stories all started to sound the same: a district commissioner borne by natives would show up, surrounded by a company of Frontier Force soldiers. He would demand "chop" (food) and natives would be ousted from their huts to make room for the visitors. Then the official would meet the local headman and announce the quota—100 men, 200 men, usually more than the surrounding farms could offer. After a few days, the official and his men would leave town with the unlucky conscripts, who had to supply their own "chop" and tools.

The stories of resisters or tribes that could not meet the official's demands had terrible endings. The local chief and elders would often be arrested and taken hostage and villagers would be beaten until the corvée of men was produced. "The soldiers threw me down and began to beat me," a Maryland villager told Johnson and Christy, "[then] put my foot between two pieces of hardwood and . . . tied the ends of the stick together, the tighter the ropes were drawn, the more the stick pressed into my flesh. I suffered awfully from this cruel treatment, the scar of the sore cut into my flesh by one of the sticks is right on my foot and I can show it to any person."[29]

Natives who appealed to Monrovia only compounded their misery, the investigators learned. When the Grebo paramount chief Broh dispatched two messengers to report abuses directly to President King a year before Johnson and Christy arrived, he and several other chiefs were dragged by soldiers to Yancy's farm outside Harper, where the vice president threatened them. "[I]f I please I can put you into this Spanish ship in the harbor and carry *you* to Fernando Poo," he claimed, "[o]r I can only give you to the soldiers to carry you to the barracks . . . But I will tell the soldiers on their way going that they may shoot you with their guns and they shall tell me upon returning that Broh die while were [*sic*] going. I can simply write to the President that Paramount Chief Broh die by sickness and the President will say, 'All right, that is the will of God.' "[30]

After four months, the three commissioners had heard enough. They had sat through hundreds of witnesses—paramount chiefs, subchiefs, district commissioners, high government officials, and ordinary natives—and taken down more than 250 depositions. Singling out Yancy and Ross for opprobrium, the investigators concluded that Liberian officialdom had indeed engaged in forced labor and labor recruitment. But they said that the scheme stopped short of formal slave trading, as defined by the League of Nations' secretary-general's own 1924 memorandum on the subject, which, amended by the United Nations, remains in effect to this day. They also offered several recommendations to the government: allow more foreign investment; grant the chiefs expanded powers; have Americans administer the hinterland; outlaw pawning and other native forms of bondage; rein in the Frontier Force; and, of course, immediately stop all labor shipments abroad. The two foreign commissioners disagreed on what would have been the most decisive recommendation of all, with Johnson successfully fighting Christy's proposal that Liberia become a League of Nations Mandate, administered by white officials.

The report, officially handed over to the Liberian government in September 1930, had an immediate and profound impact on the Americo-Liberian community. Most seemed genuinely shocked by the report's revelations. Situated in Monrovia and a few coastal and upriver enclaves, they had little idea what went on among the natives and felt great shame and empathy when they learned about the scheme and their government's complicity in it. As the journalist and educator Albert Porte remarked of his upriver Crozierville community, "tears came to eyes of both men and women when it was outlined by the speakers that the administration had given support to a destructive policy—slave raiding, slave trading, and intimidation of the citizenry."[31]

Remorse led to action. King immediately banned both labor exports and domestic pawning. A nervous diplomatic corps grew concerned that the outrage among Liberian citizens would be directed at Monrovia's tiny white community; historically, the city's mobs could just as easily turn against foreign accusers as the Liberians accused. The British minister even talked of having a warship dispatched. In this case, it was the unnamed "highest officials" singled out in the report who were the objects of popular wrath. Led by Faulkner, the protesters who marched on the legislature to present a petition demanding the resignation of King and Yancy and others turned out to be "an orderly crowd." As a local journalist portrayed the scene, "[i]t was like a church meeting . . . The multitude wore a quiet but grimly determined expression. It meant business and nothing but business."[32]

Still, on the whole, the Americo-Liberian community was deeply divided over the report and its conclusions. Almost all agreed that King and Yancy had to go, but the scandal also revived old political fault lines between those who wanted Liberia to open itself up to the wider (white) world and those who distrusted that world and wanted to remain safely isolated from it.

On the other side from Faulker and his supporters were people like the editor of the *Liberian Patriot*, who wrote that the "autocratic and arrogant" King's worst transgression was accepting the findings and recommendations of the report without consulting the "representatives of the sovereign people of this Negro Government." "Remember that the white man is always a white man in his political and economic urge," thundered the legislator James Wiles, "his interest is held paramount and dominance of the weaker race and people is ever his objective."[33]

Even King and Yancy had their defenders, since many people in government owed their jobs and fortunes to them. But their only defense was to accuse Faulkner of revealing Liberian domestic matters to the world. It was not enough. King and Yancy had no choice but to resign, which they did in early December; Secretary of State Edwin Barclay was hastily sworn in as president. Some opposition legislators were not satisfied, and insisted that King and Yancy be criminally prosecuted and that the money and property Yancy had seized be given to the families of laborers whose sons, fathers, and husbands had died on the cocoa plantations of Fernando Pó.

But that never happened. Yancy lived on another eleven years, moving to Lagos, Nigeria, where he died in disgrace but still wealthy. King, who was never directly implicated in the scandal, was hired by

Firestone to be his in-country legal counsel. The former president
lived into the 1960s and even became a respected elder statesman,
serving as the Liberian ambassador to Washington in the late 1940s
and early 1950s. Lower-ranking officials involved in the trade, particularly those with connections to the families who ran Liberia, were
assigned to new posts, the usual "punishment" for corruption or abuse
of power. The Sinoe County governor Samuel Ross suffered the worst
fate. After the report, he tried to flee to Germany but died, in what
one scholar described as mysterious circumstances, in Monrovia. The
boat returning his body to his native Greenville then sank, taking his
young son with it.

Faulkner's energy never flagged. In 1931, he took on the political
establishment again, and was again thwarted—this time by Edwin
Barclay—in his quest for the presidency. Once again, he accused the
True Whigs of stuffing ballot boxes, which they had done, of course,
though less flagrantly than in 1927. His subsequent efforts to recruit
black Americans to invest in Liberia were even less successful than
Garvey's had been a decade before.

Aside from King's swift abolishment of the labor trade and pawning, the
Christy Commission's recommendations were not implemented. Just
a few weeks after King and Yancy resigned, Antoine Sottile, Liberia's
contracted, Italian-born minister to the League of Nations, delivered
a spirited reply to the commission's report. In a speech before the
League, he dismissed the Liberian crimes as the work of individuals,
not the government as a whole, and asked what European country
was not guilty of labor abuses in its own African colonies. At least, he
said, "My Government, which has been called a Government of niggers, a Government of savages, *has had the courage to place the matter
before an International Commission of Enquiry.*"[34] He raised the question that Monrovia's political classes had asked ever since the League
opened its investigation: Why hadn't the Spaniards, who had hired
and exploited the natives, faced the same scrutiny and opprobrium?

As for the commission's recommendation that administration of the Liberian hinterland be placed under foreign supervision at Liberia's expense, Sottile claimed such a dispensation would prove too costly for the poor nation. Though Liberia was still poor, the real issue, as always, was its desire to maintain its sovereignty. Only a few years later, a mass uprising on the Kru Coast, the last of the great native wars that the Americoes had been fighting on and off for more than a hundred years, seemed to prove the necessity of foreign involvement in the hinterland. The international press assumed that the war was one of vengeance. "Liberian Natives who testified before the League of Nations Commission which inquired into reports of slavery and economic conditions in the Negro Republic, have been visited by severe reprisals," an Associated Press dispatch from January 1932 reported. "Homes have been burned . . . and even whole villages of those who reported to the League . . . have been destroyed."[35]

But an investigation overseen by the British, French, and American ministers in Monrovia revealed that opportunism, not vengeance, accounted for Kru aggression. An Americo-Liberian, an "unprincipled adventurer" and Captain Cadell–like figure named John Stuart or Major Frank or Major Ford—he had a number of aliases—had been going up and down the coast telling the Kru that, as a result of their testimony to Christy and Johnson, "the white man was coming to take over the country, that the Liberian Frontier Force was to be disbanded, that they need pay no further taxes." While the foreign ministers never uncovered Stuart's aims, his effect was predictable. "These rumours were carried from village to village and, if not entirely believed, they at least had an unsettling effect."[36] Local America commissioners did not help the situation by responding to the Kru's noncompliance with characteristic obtuseness and brutality.

Whatever its cause, the conflict eventually abated, as did the League's efforts to impose white administrators on the country. European representatives blustered about sanctions and sending gunboats to Liberia if the nation did not comply with the report's recommendations. In reply, Liberian diplomats offered minor concessions and soothing talk of reform. The Liberians had perfected this diplomatic dance. They simply waited out their antagonists, well aware that Franklin Roosevelt's government would make sure nothing threatened their independence. The League soon turned to more pressing matters, such as Mussolini's unprovoked invasion of Ethiopia, Africa's only other black-governed country. Indeed, compared with that episode, one historian wrote of the Fernando Pó slave ring that "Liberia's experience with the League has an *opera bouffe* quality."[37]

President Barclay spent the 1930s coping with the ramifications of the Great Depression, which undermined demand for Liberian rubber and other tropical exports, and repairing his country's relations with the outside world—though he did this reluctantly, as he was increasingly drawn to anti-West politics. He had always been wary of white governments and businessmen and sympathetic to Blyden's hopes that Liberia would turn to Africa for its identity and its prosperity. Nevertheless, he would cast Liberia's fate with the allies in World War II. The United States secured a refueling point for transatlantic flights, and, in return, Barclay secured a promise from Washington that it would build a deepwater port in Monrovia. The posting of thousands of well-fed and confident African American troops in Liberia during the war would prove even more influential, as it convinced many in the Americo community that their country's future lay with the West.

Yet Barclay's most important wartime decision was his anointment, in 1943, of William Vacanarat Shadrach Tubman, the former Maryland lawyer and Yancy's cousin, as his successor in the Executive Mansion. Over the next quarter century, Tubman would do more to bring his country and its political class into the modern world than all his predecessors combined. Liberia's days of forced labor and Frontier Force abuses were in the past; a new era of business opportunity—and police repression—would soon begin.

NINE

The Original African Big Man

The celebrations began modestly enough. "A card . . . a friendly letter, a personal call, a friendly drink together—such were the beginning of the birthday activities," the journalist Albert Porte recalled years later. Family and close friends—the men in formal wear, the women in evening gowns—would then gather at the old Executive Mansion on November 29, usually around sundown. Most guests brought "a bottle of some kind," which, for those in the know, meant a bottle of the president's favorite Champagne.[1]

If the weather held, the party took place on the rooftop deck, as thousands of bats, denizens of the capital's ironwood trees, hungrily swooped for mosquitoes. If the weather was poor, the guests gathered below in the ornate but decaying Victorian ballroom. No one enjoyed the festivities more than the guest of honor himself. William Vacanarat Shadrach Tubman, the short, cigar-chomping president with the big watery eyes behind thick black spectacles, was known as a "bon vivant," "raconteur," and "backslapper" who was never more comfortable than when surrounded by admirers.

Less than a decade after his ascension to the presidency in 1944, Tubman's ambitions were already evident in his invite list. "The circle of friends and associates widened," noted Porte, one of the president's most vocal critics. Legislators, the diplomatic corps, and foreign businessmen all flocked to the old mansion on Broad Street in a "frenzy medley" to demonstrate their loyalty.[2] In 1953, the legislature even passed a bill to make the president's birthday a national holiday, though Tubman refused to sign it. By the end of the decade, the birthday festivities had become an expensive traveling circus, as each county sought to outdo the others. Government workers—down to the lowliest elementary schoolteacher—had half a month's salary withheld to pay for the increasingly lavish gifts. In 1960, Bassa presented Tubman with a Chrysler. Maryland County, Tubman's home, followed up a year later with a yacht, and in 1962, Sinoe bought him an airplane.

There was some dissent over the cost of these gifts—Sinoe County's entire annual budget in 1962 could not have been a hundred thousand dollars—and more over the levies. But the sycophantic press insisted that the generosity of Liberians toward their leader was spontaneous. "Why are celebrants so determined to express their appreciation in [a] very loud and concrete manner? Why are the Counties caught in the birthday swing to this dimension," the editors of *Liberian Star* enthused in 1965, in a special birthday supplement. "To name but few, it is because under President Tubman's leadership vast programmes have been successfully implemented for the overall development of the human, natural and economic resources of Liberia. He struck the rock and riches flowed thus transforming the face of the country."[3]

The problem soon became what to give a president-for-life who had everything. A monument, a cultural center, and a military academy—all with Tubman's name engraved on them—were erected in his honor. In 1969, the citizens of Bomi Hills announced the ultimate accolade: for the "old man's" seventy-sixth birthday two years hence, they would build a new county seat and name it Tubmanburg. "Every prominent citizen of the territory," the government-run *Daily Listener* noted, "will build a home [there]."[4] Was it a prediction or an order?

It didn't matter. Tubman would never see the Bomi Hills plan come to fruition. In July 1971, Liberia's president for twenty-seven years died in a London hospital following a prostate operation, with his head in the lap of his longtime bagman. "I went out of my head, I jumped in the street," Jimmy Barolle recalled in war-weary Monrovia a quarter century later. "There is a crazy black man running between the cars, people said, and a policeman [explained] . . . the man that died there, this is one of his boys."[5]

Barolle wasn't just grief-stricken; he was convinced that Tubman's death had not been accidental. "[Vice President] Tolbert paid the doctor . . . a *South African* doctor," he remembered. "Tolbert say he has been VP for 19 years, why couldn't this man give up to let [me] take over?"[6] In Monrovia in 1969, a different conspiracy theory was on the tongues of the city's elite, many of whom believed that nobody was responsible for Tubman's death but himself. A notorious womanizer, Tubman, the rumor mill had it, was not in London for prostate surgery but for monkey gland implants, a long-discredited faux virility treatment. Regardless of what happened in that London hospital, the only president most Liberians had ever known, who had presided over the country's greatest economic boom and whose imperious reign set an example that would be emulated by autocrats across the continent, was gone.

There is no controversy surrounding Tubman's birth. He was born in 1895, in a two-story, zinc-roofed house in the Maryland County seat of Harper, 250 miles from Monrovia and with no road to get there. His "pioneer" lineage was solid, though not exceptional. Neither free-born nor mulatto—Tubman would always pride himself on his dark complexion—his paternal grandparents were part of the second wave of emigrants, that of impoverished slaves freed specifically to go to Liberia. William and Sylvia Tubman—the former said to be a distant relative of the Underground Railroad conductor Harriet—had been manumitted by the will of Richard Tubman, a Georgia planter, and sailed to West Africa aboard the brig *Baltimore*, in 1837, along with forty other freedpersons.

The Tubman family prospered, despite William's death in 1847.
Sylvia raised three sons and saw them educated. One, Alexander, the
future president's father, would join Liberia's elite. He became a successful merchant and a capable politician, rising to the position of
Speaker of the Liberian House of Representatives. However, he was
first and foremost a Methodist minister, and made sure his children
feared both him and God. Religion permeated the family's life, as it
did the lives of most settlers, but Alexander headed a notably austere
household. William and his siblings read the Bible and prayed at four
o'clock every morning. Tobacco and alcohol were banned from the
Tubman residence—but so were mattresses, which Alexander believed would turn his children "soft and lazy."[7] Sundays, the only day
the Tubman children were allowed to wear shoes, were set aside for
church and Alexander's sermons. Like the rest of settler Liberia,
Harper completely shut down on the Sabbath; fifty years later a travel
writer marooned in relatively cosmopolitan Monrovia on a Sunday
would complain of a city "surrendered to zealous evangelical inactiv-
ity, the silence being disturbed only by the chanting of hymns and
the nostalgic quaver of harmoniums in mission halls."[8] William's reli-
giosity had a peculiar intensity to it; he developed a lifelong habit of
praying naked and alone at moments of turmoil or indecision. Nevertheless, neither as a boy nor as a man did this genuine piety ever seem
to interfere with his propensity for sensual indulgence. Like many
Liberian men of his generation, Tubman would not have a problem
reconciling deep Christian conviction with a disregard for the faith's
more restrictive proscriptions, such as its insistence on monogamy.

Tubman attended the Cape Palmas Seminary (there were virtually no public schools in Liberia until Tubman's own reign) through
his elementary and high school years. Run by Methodist missionaries, it was, like most settler institutions, from another world, an old-
fashioned American schoolhouse set down on the steamy, palm-fringed
coast of Africa. Pupils sat quietly behind their desks, learning their
Bible, Latin, and ancient history by rote. They learned little that was
modern or practical—little that might prove useful in business and

industry—a constant complaint of domestic and foreign pedagogical reformers then and since. And, of course, there was no thought to teach the pupils about African culture or the Grebo language spoken by the vast majority of Maryland's inhabitants.

Tubman was a competent student, though more as a result of what one teacher recognized as his "remarkable memory" and less because of any innate intellectual curiosity.[9] What his classmates remembered, however, was not Tubman in school but Tubman after school, sneaking past his father's bedroom door at night to attend Grebo dances or surrounded by friends and acolytes whom he was recruiting for some sort of mischief.

That Tubman would embark on a law career after graduating from high school in 1913 was all but inevitable. Other than the ministry, which he briefly contemplated, there was no other option for an ambitious Americo boy. Settlers and natives, who followed their lead, sued each other, not to mention foreigners, constantly. "I do not believe that any group in the world loves litigation more than [Liberians]," an American engineer, commissioned by Firestone to build a road on its Maryland rubber plantation, complained. "A fight between two of my laborers over a shovel would end up in one of their courts with twenty or thirty more of my men summoned as witnesses . . . The loss in man-hours was appalling."[10] Charles Johnson, the American sociologist dispatched to investigate the Fernando Pó scandal, counted no fewer than 100 lawyers in Monrovia, a city with fewer than 5,000 residents.

The law not only promised steady work, but was one of the best ways into Liberian political circles, which could prove even more profitable. Indeed, in the early twentieth century, with Liberia's vast natural resources still untouched and trade dominated by foreigners, a government position offered the only path to the columned manse and country plantation to which many if not most settlers aspired. And so Tubman apprenticed with a legal luminary in Harper and passed the bar in 1916, after which he quickly made a name for himself as an effective and empathetic advocate by taking on cases other lawyers would not, notably those involving poor and native clients.

Meanwhile Tubman began to rise through the ranks of the Maryland government at a pace that was possible only in a tiny society with few other qualified individuals, becoming a court recorder at twenty, a collector of internal revenues at twenty-one, and a county attorney at twenty-three. He was soon noticed by the Liberian elite. On a visit to Maryland in 1920, President-elect Charles King was said to be so impressed by Tubman's oratory at a Masonic banquet that he instructed local True Whig Party officials to keep an eye on him and "whenever there is a political opening for young Tubman, bring him forward and I will support him."[11] And so at twenty-eight, Tubman became the youngest senator in Liberian history and, despite his greenness, one of the nation's preeminent legislators. "Anyone who wants to see the best Liberian Senator . . . in action," an admiring colleague remarked, "need only to visit the Chamber during the Firestone concession bill debate and keep his eyes on the stocky, fast-walking and fast-talking Senator from Maryland County as he ambles about the floor. A word here and there, a casual political arm around a recalcitrant shoulder, a brief companionable colloquy with some old-timers, and the result was that the bill glided through the Senate as though it was a motion for Christmas adjournment."[12]

While King's endorsement launched Tubman's political career, it also nearly ended it. The Fernando Pó labor scandal that engulfed the government in the late 1920s compromised everyone associated with the administration. Tubman was doubly implicated, as one of King's protégés and as Allen Yancy's cousin. He had not helped his own cause when, out of family loyalty, he successfully defended Yancy against slave-trading charges before the Supreme Court. The national True Whig leadership, eager to demonstrate to a hostile and skeptical world that they planned to reform Liberia, in a rare decision withheld their endorsement for Tubman's reelection. But party leaders had misread the political mood in Maryland, where most of the

Americo electorate viewed the League's charges against Yancy as racist calumny. The "no Tubman, no senator" campaign in 1931 may have been the work of Tubman supporters, or it may have been spontaneous. Whatever the case, it was successful. Polls were virtually shut down throughout the county, denying the True Whig nominee votes and cutting Maryland's representation in the senate in half until Edwin Barclay, King's replacement, finally agreed to a special election three years later.

But Barclay and the newly elected Tubman soon clashed. While King and Tubman were modernizers who agreed on the necessity of attracting foreign investment, Barclay represented an older form of Liberian politics, one that was distrustful of white outsiders and determined to preserve the nation's sovereignty and the economic prerogatives of the Americo-Liberian elite. He was also steeped, as a member of a Barbadian clan, in West Indian economic radicalism and racialist ideology that were inimical to King and Tubman's vision. Almost ascetic in his personal life, Barclay was aloof and cerebral, an outsider in the glad-handing world of True Whig Party politics and a stark contrast to Tubman.

Thus when Barclay put Senator Tubman on the Supreme Court, much of the Monrovia political establishment understood it as an attempt to neutralize him. And when, in 1942, Barclay chose Tubman as his successor, many guessed that Barclay thought he could hold on to power by choosing a man who from his perspective was a buffoon and therefore could be manipulated. But Barclay would soon understand that there was a perceptive, ambitious mind behind Tubman's affable nature.

American observers of Liberia in the mid–twentieth century tended to compare its politics to the South's. It was, in certain respects, a fair analogy. The True Whigs did bear a resemblance to the pre–Civil Rights–era Democratic Party, in that both parties ran their nominees virtually unopposed. "The decisions are made in caucus, the elections are meaningless," a *New York Times* correspondent quoted a "knowl-edgeable Liberian" as saying.[13] But the comparison went only so far, not only because of matters of race and racism but because of the smallness of Liberia's political class. "To attain prominence in public life an ambitious young man had to depend either on being selected directly by the President of Liberia," wrote Clarence Simpson, Tub-man's chief rival for the presidency in the early 1940s, "or work his way up through the party machine."[14] And public office opened every door in Liberian life. "An individual enjoys a position of influence in a church, a business, a charitable organization, or a fraternal society," noted one American scholar, "because he holds, or has held, office in the Liberian government or the True Whig Party."[15]

Participation in Liberian politics was synonymous with party membership. As Simpson recalled, "I don't even know whether I ever joined the True Whig Party, but my membership in it was taken for granted ever since I was old enough to vote."[16] Even if one did not donate a few dollars, march in a parade, or put up a campaign poster, the convention the party held every four years was an inescapable part of national life. "During the early part of [convention] week, [the] Maryland County Brass Band kept things in the city [Monrovia] lively by their mighty serenades," was how one paper described the days leading up to Tubman's formal nomination for president. "But the whole thing culminated today in a vast demonstration of over two thousand people, accompanied by three brass bands, carrying ban-ners, representative of the several counties . . . [all] manifesting the mighty political force that the True Whig Party really is."[17]

It was a grand show, but ultimately meaningless. The real deci-sions were made long before the delegates arrived, in Monrovia's Masonic Lodge Number One, where both Barclay and Tubman were members. Like so much else in settler culture, masonry in Liberia was a nineteenth-century American artifact transplanted to Africa. As de Tocqueville famously recognized, antebellum America was an associative place, where a weak state, frontier conditions, and relative isolation led people to form voluntary organizations for every purpose. The Masons, Good Templars, Odd Fellows, and Elks all had lodges in Liberia, though because Liberia had few other institutions, they were even more central to national life than they were in America, providing insurance and undertaking services and, with their balls and banquets, the trappings of high society. And none among them was more prestigious or influential than the Masons.

The order had a long history in the black republic. "We know that a great many founders of our country were active members of the Craft," Tubman himself once pronounced, "and I consider . . . our Constitution is Masonry put into political form and practice."[18] The future chief justice James Pierre put the same notion in simpler terms when he addressed the order's annual convention in 1957: "Liberia has been rightly called a Masonic Country."[19] Liberian masonry was a mulatto enclave when such color distinctions mattered, before becoming a more inclusive but still exclusively America-Liberian institution by the turn of the twentieth century. By Tubman's time, "civilized" natives could join, but only if they had the right connections—if, in other words, they had been adopted by one of Liberia's leading settler families.

Foreigners and Liberians alike understood that the Masons ran the country. "All the big government decisions were made at the [Masons'] secret meetings," a member of Monrovia's elite recalled. "In court, the top lawyers would use Masonic signals to fix cases with the judges."[20] Every major America-Liberian settlement had its temple. Monrovia's was a battleship-size edifice constructed in severe neo-Federalist style that stood atop Snapper Hill, the highest point on Cape Mesurado. The building had a steel-framed eye, ten feet in diameter, on its roof, which gazed down upon the city below. Ordinary citizens, particularly uneducated natives, feared the place, likening what went on inside to the practices of the long-outlawed Leopard societies of the Liberian bush that sacrificed victims in secret rituals and devoured their hearts to, they believed, increase their power. "When I was boy, we stay[ed] far away [from Monrovia's temple] at night," one Liberian, an adolescent in the 1970s, recalled years later. "We know it was too much Kwi [Americo-Liberian] witch-craft there."[21]

Tubman was a True Whig and a Mason, but instead of carrying on the traditions of his distinguished forebears, he helped transform Liberia into a nation of the world. He sided, despite his provincial upbringing, with the King faction in Monrovia, which understood that Liberia's future prosperity lay with the new U.S.-led, postwar free trade order.* And he was aided by a booming world economy, rebuilding after depression and war, that needed Liberia's resources, which Tubman was only too happy to offer. An economic backwater when he came to power, Liberia by the end of his reign would be known as the "Switzerland of West Africa."

That the country's hinterland had some of the richest iron ore in the world had been known for a century or more. On his epic journey to Musardu in the 1860s, Benjamin Anderson came upon a deposit "so pure that the road leading through it was a polished metal pathway, smoothed over by the constant treading of travelers . . . [and] hardly treadable in the dries [when] it becomes so thoroughly heated."[22] European mining companies had reached similar conclusions in the 1930s and 1940s but were dissuaded from involving themselves in Liberia, not so much by its lack of infrastructure as by its suspicious and hermetic ruling caste. "What I feared most were not these costs [of building roads and railways], but the attitude of the Liberian government," a Dutch geologist remarked after the war. "They seemed to be of the opinion that the iron ore mining was a most lucrative business and that this was a beautiful opportunity to line one's purse." The Barclay administration, ever suspicious of white outsiders, put up obstacle after obstacle to a potential deal. "I am of the opinion," the miner

---

*Tubman also went with the idea, first proposed by the Franklin Roosevelt administration, of a Liberian ship registry, which allowed the world's maritime industry to take advantage of its lax shipping regulations, while simultaneously filling Liberian coffers with a steady source of revenue.

concluded, "that only an American enterprise will succeed, as only they can reckon with the collaboration of the Liberian authorities."[23]

Into the breach strode the entrepreneur Landsdell K. Christie, a charismatic forty-one-year-old who had been thrown out of West Point for disciplinary reasons and was heir to a Brooklyn garbage scow fortune. During the war, he served in the Belgian Congo, arranging the transport of ores, including secret shipments of uranium for the Manhattan Project. To get to the Congo, he often passed through the U.S. Army Air Corp's seaplane base at Fisherman's Lake, some fifty miles outside Monrovia, the key Allied transport hub in the South Atlantic.* It was here, an old friend and aide reminisced, that Christie decided his future lay not in New York's trash but in Africa's soil.

Just weeks before the Nazi surrender in Europe, Christie was in Monrovia, cash and concession agreement in hand. He understood the Liberian elite's suspicion of white outsiders, so he hired H. Lafayette Harmon, the capital's savviest political fixer. But it was Tubman's ambition that would make his enterprise a success. Tubman, who saw foreign investment as the best way to realize his big plans for the country (and for himself), eagerly reached an agreement with Christie that allowed the American to mine Liberia's iron ore and pay only 15 to 20 cents per ton to Tubman's government. Even Tubman's court biographer admitted a quarter century later that the deal was a poor one for Liberia; as he calculated, "at the end of forty years Liberia would have sold the best ore at Bomi Hills for a bare $8 million."[24]

The agreement was signed in Christie's lawyer's offices in New York by Treasury Secretary William Dennis, and when word of it reached Liberia, protesters took to the streets of Monrovia, furious at what many viewed as a clear case of bribery. The other interpretation in circulation was that the newly installed and still economically inexperienced Tubman was a twentieth-century Edmund Roye, the president who had been duped by London financiers in the 1870s. At

---

*In 1943, Franklin Roosevelt passed through Fisherman's Lake on his way to the Casablanca Conference, becoming the first sitting U.S. president to set foot on African soil.

the root of Liberian anger and distrust, however, was that Tubman had violated the spirit, if not the letter, of the constitution. No constitutional provisions were more zealously guarded than the reservation of citizenship for persons of African descent and the prohibition of land sales to foreigners. Tubman did not sell Christie land but the eighty-year lease he agreed to was a sale in all but name, as distasteful to contemporary Monrovia nationalists as the Firestone deal had been to their fathers. Tubman, the opposition press cried, was "selling the country."[25]

Tubman himself would admit only a couple of years later that the deal was an unfavorable one. He decided to renegotiate it, but made clear that this signaled a recalibration, not an abandonment, of his economic philosophy. Years later, in a 1955 campaign speech, he named the philosophy the "open door," and insisted that the country's traditional autarky—as well as the Monrovia elite's "narrow, selfish, contracted and strangulating policy . . . that we could develop our nation by our own might, resources and knowledge"—were obsolete. "I will never subscribe to such a supercilious, short sighted, contracted and phobic policy," he proclaimed, "that paralyzed industry and investment and kept the nation in poverty, suspicion, despair, commotion and turmoil."[26]

Among the old guard, the Christie deal and those that followed raised the old fears about loss of sovereignty and subjection to white outsiders, even though revenues from mining allowed Tubman to pay back the humiliating Firestone debt in 1951, years ahead of schedule. Any dissent would only have had the opposite of its intended effect, though. Tubman's fear of political opposition often determined his policy, so that when it came to business, he preferred outsiders because, as noncitizens, they were less of a political threat, their presence in the country depending on the good graces of the president. In the 1950s, he began handing out lucrative government contracts to foreign enterprises and the country's growing Lebanese expatriate community.

Meanwhile, the money poured in, a trickle at first and then, by

Liberian standards, a veritable flood. Between 1955 and 1964, foreigners invested more capital—over $300 million—in Liberia than
they did in its previous century of existence. The government's annual budget grew from a million dollars when Tubman took office in
1944 to more than $50 million in the late 1960s. Some of this new
money served useful ends: paved roads fanned out from the capital
(though the tarmac on the "principal highway" ended at Tubman's
country estate in Totota), and hundreds of primary and secondary
schools were built. But prestige projects claimed much of it. By the
early sixties, some $50 million had been spent on gleaming new pub-
lic buildings in Monrovia, including a new capitol, national bank
headquarters, city hall, and seaside Executive Mansion for the president. Twenty million dollars in the making, the "dream mansion," as
Liberians called it, featured "an atomic bomb shelter, an underground
swimming pool, a private chapel, a trophy room, a cinema and . . .
because of the uncertainty of the city's public utilities . . . its own
emergency power plant, water supply and sewage system." As a correspondent for *Time* described it in 1964, "Tubman's new home com-
bines the comfort of a garish four-star hotel with the appearance of a
department store the week before Christmas."[27]

Tubman was unapologetic. When his gadfly Albert Porte complained about the $150,000 price tag of the new presidential yacht,
which had been a birthday "gift" from the people of Maryland, Tubman characteristically shot back with a personal attack—Porte was
"a grumbler . . . [who] makes so little contribution to the resources
of the country that [he] should be ashamed to talk about public
expenditures"—and self-serving nationalist appeals: he noted how,
as a supreme justice in 1939, he was forced to hitch a ride on an American ship to get from Maryland to Monrovia. " 'Do you mean to tell
me,' " he recalled the captain asking him, " 'that your Government has
no means by which she can get' " officials to the seat of government
" 'except they are transported there by . . . some foreign ships?' "[28]
The yacht was not intended for his personal pleasure, Tubman reasoned, but as a sign of Liberia's dignity.

Still, the president delivered, at least for those at the top of Liberian society. Liberia in the 1950s and early 1960s boasted the second-highest economic growth rate of any nation in the world, behind only Japan. While the primary cause was the postwar boom and the international automobile industry's insatiable appetite for Liberia's rust red iron ore and cheese wheels of latex, Tubman's economic policies did have a significant effect. Most of the profits went to foreigners, of course, but Monrovia's well-connected "big men" benefited as well, becoming the first truly rich people in the nation's history. While they were chauffeured in American sedans to desk jobs at foreign subsidiaries, their wives cruised the aisles at the White Rose Supermarket, lured by advertisements boasting "a fresh supply of goods from the U.S."[29] Their children, in crisp school uniforms, attended private academies, knowing that even mediocre grades would lead to a government scholarship to a U.S. university. As a Scottish shipping manager recalled, "The social life of expatriates and elites in Tubman's day was lovely—golf, picnics, and balls at the Ducor Hotel," itself a new, ten-story addition to the rising Monrovia skyline.[30]

But the new suburbs of Sinkor and Congotown, where the elite put up their marble villas overlooking the Atlantic, were not representative of Liberian life. In the words of the *New York Times* correspondent Helene Cooper, scion of one of the most pedigreed settler families, rich parents "raise[d] their perfect famil[ies], cosseted by well-paid servants, and protected from the ravages of West African squalor and poverty by central air-conditioning, strategically placed cocoanut trees, and a private water well."[31] The well-off had grown rich, but the poor remained poor.

Tubman liked to tell a story about a day his father escaped near-certain death. The event took place deep in the bush of Maryland County, in the 1870s, during yet another conflict with the Grebos over land, trade, and honor. The young Alexander was part of a contingent of militia sent to avenge the burning of the Americo settlement at Philadelphia, an event that had sent a stream of refugees, including the Barneses, Tubman's mother's family, into Harper. Outside the Grebo village of Wrukeh, they were ambushed. Alexander's brother William was slain, his body, in one settler historian's breathless account, "devoured . . . by tribesmen with cannibalistic tendencies."[32] Distraught, Alexander fell behind his retreating company. Alone in the bush, he heard a voice from behind a "bug-bug" hill, one of the towering termite mounds that dot the Liberian countryside. Alexander raised his gun only to realize that the voice was that of an old tribal acquaintance named Dyne Weah. Weah urged him to flee, saying that the warriors in pursuit would do to him what they had done to his brother.

So moved was Alexander by Weah's aid that he pledged himself and later his eldest son to Weah's family's care, to "see that they do not suffer in any way." Nearly one hundred years later, as President Tubman announced the beginning of a new era in settler-native relations, he recalled his father's words: "During your lifetime, I want you to do all you can to work for better understanding between the tribal people and the government, should ever an opportunity present itself."[33] It was an affecting story, and parts of it might have even been true. Tubman never failed to remind his audiences that it had a moral. Members of his family had fought and died in battles with the natives, he would say, so "[i]f I now declare a new day . . . letting the dead past bury its dead, I fail to see why anyone should linger and cling to the past."[34]

By the time Tubman got the opportunity to fulfill his father's wishes, open warfare between "civilized" and "tribal" was confined to history. The last native conflict occurred a dozen years before Tubman took office. But the old tensions still existed. Pliant chiefs had been co-opted and recalcitrant ones unseated, and when these tactics failed, Monrovia had sent in district commissioners. These were often unsavory characters from the lowest ranks of settler society, who viewed extorting the natives as their just compensation for a hardship posting. Attempts to assimilate the natives had failed. Natives adopted by Americo families or educated at mission schools might gain a seat at the foot of the settlers' table and, through intermarriage or concubinage, a place in their bedrooms. But the number of adopted natives was small, and efforts to incorporate the masses by administrative fiat had been largely fruitless. The result was that settlers and natives shared a territory that on maps read "Republic of Liberia," but little else.

Like his predecessors, Tubman arrived in office promising change; unlike his predecessors, he proceeded to enact meaningful reforms. He inaugurated "executive councils," adopting the tribal custom of palaver, whereby chiefs heard and resolved the complaints of their subjects. He traveled to every corner of the country, the dearth of roads requiring him, his secretary of information and cultural affairs later wrote in a paid *New York Times* supplement celebrating Tubman's efforts to modernize and democratize Liberia, to "risk . . . his life crossing swollen streams and rivers by means of swinging bridges made of wild vines or in frail dug-outs."[35] In 1954, tiring of hinterland travel, Tubman brought the chiefs to his home county of Maryland, launching the first in a series of National Unification Councils. During the 1955 council in Monrovia, he listed the accomplishments—schools, roads, health clinics—of his administration. There were more natives in government, he said, and less government in the lives of natives. "I can recall how at my first interior [executive] council you complained [that] . . . District Commissioners were unrestrained in their imposition of fines upon you and your people," he reminded the chiefs, "that for the most insignificant act your chiefs, wives and children were humiliated and imprisoned; that you were compelled to bury your manhood and bow down to them as though they were your masters and lords, instead of your public servants . . . Today those conditions do not exist anymore."[36]

Tubman called his efforts to bring twentieth-century civilization to the hinterland and to incorporate natives into Liberia's body politic his "Unification Policy." It culminated in the 1964 Unification Act, which finally put an end to the second-class citizenship of 98 percent of Liberia's population: the act reconfigured the hinterland territories as counties and granted their propertied residents suffrage.* Interestingly, it went into effect the same year Lyndon Johnson signed the Civil Rights Act, which buttressed and protected the citizenship of disenfranchised Southern blacks, including distant relations of Liberia's settler elite.

But having the vote and being a member of the vast majority of a nation's population did not naturally result in equality or access to power and wealth. For what really mattered in Tubman's Liberia was the same thing that had always mattered in Liberia: family. The elite in Monrovia called themselves the "honorables," a term as redolent of the antebellum South as the plantation houses settler elites once built for themselves on their up-country estates. The honorables possessed wealth and privilege and further set themselves apart through formal speech and etiquette. They possessed a noblesse oblige forged in high-church Protestantism and Masonic principle, which they honored just as their ancestors' masters in tidewater Virginia had once honored the chivalric code they lived by—that is to say, largely in the breach.

The honorables ran Liberia and, until Tubman's economic "open door," they owned most of it as well. They occupied almost all high government posts, monopolized the best-paying managerial positions set aside by foreign firms for Liberian nationals, and took the best land for themselves. The roads that Tubman built to connect the coast to the hinterland were not plied only by market women, baskets propped high on their heads. The honorables used them too, motoring to their rubber plantations, which they had carved out of native lands, not with the sword but with the help of Monrovia lawyers wielding pens and writs.

Natives hoping to get ahead in Tubman's Liberia, just like ambitious individuals among the settler middle and lower classes, had to

---

*Though largely ignored, the old financial restriction on voting still applied to the original coastal counties well into the 1970s.

secure the patronage of an honorable. "[A]s a native born I should stay in Monrovia," one high school student explained to an American anthropologist in the late 1950s, "and get acquainted with some of the Honorables of my country, in other words for me to be recognized more than a man who is not acquainted with the nobles in Monrovia. Today I find things easier with me in Monrovia than with some of my comrades who are newly coming into the city."[37]

For young Liberians, the student one sat next to in class mattered more than what one learned. But education was a relatively new means for Liberian natives and lower-class settlers to establish a connection with an honorable family. The tried and true methods were more intimate.

Taking in gifted native children as wards—Christianizing and "civilizing" them and granting them the all-important surname— had been a part of the settler ethos since the nineteenth century, and it was something many native parents sought for their children as well. Then there were the "country wives." A few open-minded honorables formally married natives; the father of Clarence Simpson, the man who challenged Tubman for the presidency in the 1940s, was a notable example. But many if not most honorable men established second households with native women on their plantations and farms up-country, an echo of the master-slave liaisons of the Old South that were at the root of some of the honorables' own family trees. As one anthropologist noted, "While the Christian ethic of marital fidelity is officially accepted, in practice fidelity on the part of the men is as little accepted among Americo-Liberians as among tribespeople."[38] Tubman himself was known for fathering children with at least a half dozen women, though most were of settler lineage.

The diplomat George Padmore, in recalling his own young adulthood in an upriver Americo settlement and his decision to marry President Barclay's secretary, understood that country wives indicated power and station. He wrote in his memoirs that "customs in

Liberia at the time [the late 1930s] were that [Americo] farmers married an educated [upper-class settler] lady mainly to maintain a prestige with the civilized community [but] he could likewise have as many native or farm wives as he might find financially possible to support." Such behavior was expected and accepted by virtually all Liberians, Americoes and natives alike. "Acquiring such farm women was considered a big gesture to the local tribe people, impressing them of one's leadership ability."[39]

Liberia was hardly the antebellum South, where masters chose or were compelled to deny their parental connection to the light-skinned slaves in their household. Moreover, the illegitimate children of settler men and native women were often treated as wards, as one American visitor observed in the early 1960s. "A woman of American origin but long naturalized and married to an Americo-Liberian, was the object of much criticism," he wrote, "because . . . she refused to take into her household any of her husband's outside children and in particular, a son of whom he was especially fond, whom he had legitimized, and whom he was educating at some expense. Her uncharitable behaviour was usually ascribed to the fact that she had been born a foreigner, and had never learned Liberian ways."[40] The honorable class was thus permeable. Wards, bastard offspring, and the legitimate offspring of formal settler-native marriages for the most part joined it. "Once you lived with the families," the native journalist and former ward James Wolo remarked years later, "there was the possibility that you can marry into the families and [then] you are a part of them."[41]

Those who could trace their lineage back to the country's beginnings still retained their status, however. "I can remember a period when you had first and second class Americoes," a Dutch aid worker who grew up in Liberia recalled, "when you had pure Congoes [a popular term for Americoes] and sort of Congoes. It was typical to see a Congo woman and Congo man and the man having other children who were also part of the family—as such, Congoes, but sort of second class

Congoes."*[42] Others spoke of a ceiling that kept half-castes and as-similated natives out of positions of real power in the government, the Whig Party, or the Masons. As the dissident journalist Tuan Wreh wrote just four years before the native coup in 1980, "[b]efore any Liberian can occupy a high position of trust and responsibility in government, his descent is usually investigated. The ruling clique continues to show hesitancy over whether a person of ethnic background should run for the Presidency and the Vice Presidency, or be appointed to the Cabinet and other high posts."[43]

Such investigations could turn up embarrassing secrets, even in the most prominent families. Traditionally, native wards, native wives, and mixed-ancestry children adopted settler names and manners, removing themselves as far as possible from village and tribe. In a Liberian notion borrowed from America, these half-castes and adoptees tried "passing" as "civilized." This deception was both easier and more difficult than it had been for the ancestors of some lighter-skinned honorables: Though skin tone among the settlers varied greatly and appearance alone was not a giveaway, Americo settlements were tiny, intimate places where neighbors took notice of the dirt under the fingernails of someone trying to bury his or her past.

By Tubman's time the term "honorable" had lost its rigidity. Where once even the most casual of visitors to Liberia could recognize the castes, now even anthropologists doing fieldwork in the country found it "difficult to assess" who was settler, who was tribal, and who was mixed.[44] Liberians had a better sense, but for them, the old distinctions no longer seemed to matter so much. For natives, "settler" and "civilized" were essentially synonymous. And for all but the haughtiest of settlers, often the women, lineage had come to matter less than lifestyle. Prejudice against those who had tribal blood flow-

---

*The term "Congo" was widely used across Liberia as a synonym for "Americo." Local Africans believed that the recaptive slaves brought to Liberia by the U.S. Navy in the nineteenth century and since incorporated into the bottom ranks of the Americoes came from the Congo. Although once a subtle dig at the self-regard and pretenses of the settler class, the term lost its pejorative connotations over the years and even the most illustrious of "honorables" began to use the term.

ing in their veins was now expressed subtly, if at all. "Prejudice against the assimilated?" recalled Eugene Cooper, a member of one of Liberia's most prestigious clans. "Not in my experience but deep down there might have been."[45] The changing attitudes toward the assimilated natives represented a second, though less fully realized, step in the Liberian elite's evolution toward greater inclusiveness, the first being the gradual disappearance of the color line between blacks and mulattoes in the post-Roye era of the late nineteenth century.

Tubman himself was of two minds about the honorables. His Unification Policy was premised on the idea that the old Monrovia settler elite had to cede a measure of its power to the native majority or, at least, to its "civilized" cohort. Tubman saw that Africa was changing around Liberia; the anticolonial "winds of change" that the British prime minister Harold Macmillan spoke of to an unheeding South African parliament in 1960 were blowing through Monrovia as well. No longer, Tubman understood, could Liberia stake its legitimacy in its status as Africa's only black-run republic. The natives were getting restless. Just three years earlier, the defiant Kwame Nkrumah had led the nearby Gold Coast (renamed Ghana) out of the British Empire, the first black-ruled, sub-Saharan colony to liberate itself from European rule. Tubman detested Nkrumah's socialist ideas, his rhetoric of Third World solidarity, and his efforts to forge a unified African polity ruled from Accra. He tried to position himself within the new Organization of African Unity as the continent's "elder statesman," steering the dozens of new leaders away from what he saw as Nkrumah's dangerous fantasies. Yet at home, he lectured his countrymen that "Americo-Liberianism must be forgotten."[46]

But it was to be a selective forgetting. Tubman understood the demographics of Liberia as well as any member of the settler community, and knew that making possible the full equality of the natives would quickly bring an end to Americo privilege and rule. Despite his strong early record on native matters, Tubman did little in the end to challenge the Americoes' stranglehold on government, resisting even symbolic changes. He would not amend the constitution's opening

line—"We the people of the republic of Liberian were originally inhabitants of the United States of North America." Matilda Newport
Day celebrations, honoring the mythic pioneer woman who turned
back an early native assault on Monrovia, would proceed as scheduled. "If the defenders of the Commonwealth had lost the day in the
Battle of Fort Hill there would have been no Liberia," Tubman insisted. "A day dedicated to her would appear to be most appropriate."[47] According to Wreh, he "closed his ears to [native] pleas" for a
reconsideration of official Liberian history.[48] If any native leader
talked of writing a history of Liberia that celebrated the roots of Liberia's masses, Tubman chastised him for raising the specter of "trib-
alism," a force that was roiling many new African states. And if any
native leader said it was time for a new political dispensation in which
the natives who made up more than 95 percent of the population
would rule the country, Tubman went beyond mere scolding.

Didwho Twe had been a thorn in the side of every Liberian administration since that of Charles King in the 1920s. A chief's son, a full-
blooded Kru with the tribal cicatrix on his forehead to prove it, Twe
had been born in 1879 and raised in Monrovia, on the sandy flats of
Bushrod Island, in a neighborhood that would be razed and flooded—
with little effort to find the displaced inhabitants new housing—to
build Monrovia's first deep water port early in Tubman's reign.

Twe must have been exceptional as a youth, since at every stage
in his early life there was an adult, usually foreign, eager to hoist him
up another rung. After an American missionary at the exclusive Patsy
Barclay Private School in Monrovia took Twe under his wings, the
boy was sent to Cuttington College, an Episcopalian institution deep
in the interior where bright native teens and settler offspring com-
mingled in classes dedicated to agriculture and industry. At the age
of fifteen, Twe was sent to America, where he would remain for the
next sixteen years, first as a student at St. John's Academy in Ver-
mont, and later at Columbia and Harvard, where he wrote articles for

various periodicals, including one for the *American Journal of Psychology*. An adventurer by nature, he hitchhiked across the nation and befriended a host of luminaries, including Mark Twain, who at the time was attempting to expose the atrocities being committed in King Leopold's Congo. What the young Kru man might have told Twain about the Americoes' treatment of Liberian natives is not known.

In 1910, Twe returned to Liberia. One of the best-educated men in a republic desperate for skilled and worldly diplomats, he was appointed to the commission tasked with settling the long-standing boundary dispute between Liberia and the British colony of Sierra Leone. Twe could have then taken the conventional route of the assimilated, "civilized" native. And in some ways he did. When invited to deliver a speech commemorating Matilda Newport Day to assembled dignitaries in Monrovia, he offered up the familiar paeans to pioneer fortitude. He credited the speech with securing him a seat in the national legislature, though later admitted that the sentiments it expressed "went against his conviction."[49] His private life followed a similar path. He set himself up as a rubber planter in the hinterland, most likely on lands seized from native farmers, and married a well-connected settler woman. The former Araminta Dent had been, in fact, Tubman's first wife.

Twe filled the John the Baptist role typical of early twentieth-century African nationalism. Instead of trying to overthrow an oppressive foreign regime, he sought to find a place for himself and those natives like him in the existing order. He spoke often about the need for the Americo regime to do more to "civilize" and uplift Liberia's "tribals," and to place them in positions of power, yet this was not a radical view at the time. But once in the legislature, perhaps thinking he was now safe from persecution, Twe became an outspoken critic of the government and, in 1929, delivered a speech that helped expose the Fernando Pó slavery ring. This critique would soon become acceptable but was not yet so. He was expelled from the True Whigs and the legislature within a matter of days, a year before King would be forced to resign in the wake of the scathing League of Nations report.

The incoming Barclay administration was no less forgiving of Twe. Faced with an uprising among the Kru, the new president called Twe and other dissident Kru leaders into his office, accusing them of soliciting foreign assistance. "I will burn down the whole Kru Coast," Twe recalled him thundering, "if you don't stop talking about 'white man,' 'white man.'" Twe tried to protest but, he later said, was cut off by Barclay, who sneered, "[y]ou damned civilized natives who ought to be leading your people are misleading them."[50] It was only a matter of time before the government issued an arrest warrant. Twe fled to Sierra Leone, where he confirmed Barclay's worst fears by seeking arms from Europe for a war against the Americoes. "Six machine guns and five hundred rifles with sufficient ammunition" are needed, he wrote an English friend. "This is now the only obstacle in the way to free a million people from oppression."[51]

Twe's return to Monrovia in 1936 proved anticlimactic, however. Unwelcome in Freetown—as one British official remarked at the time, "[I]f he disappeared, no one would be the worse off"—Twe probably had little choice but to return to his homeland, and Barclay told him he could stay if he refrained from political activity.[52] Twe did not heed these terms, and continued his largely ineffective fight for native rights. In 1951, he hazarded a run for the presidency. He tried to start a new political organization, the United People's Party, but Tubman's factotums in the electoral commission would not register it, so he revived the dormant Reformation Party, garnering the support of his fellow "civilized Kru." He accused the Tubman administration of ineptitude and corruption, but his real complaint was about another long-standing feature of Liberian politics: the right of a president to succeed himself, which had nearly set off a civil war during Edmund Roye's presidency in the 1870s and again when the True Whig Party mobilized its forces behind the amendment of 1951 that wrote perpetual succession into the constitution.

Tubman should not have feared Twe. The postwar boom was already beginning to be felt, making Tubman a popular incumbent. And, of course, the True Whigs had not lost an election for nearly seventy-five years. "Handsome full-color photographs of the President are on display almost everywhere," noted a *New Yorker* correspondent. "There is a President Tubman cigar and a Bobor [a native title of respect] Shad beer, and during the campaign seventeen thousand pocket mirrors with his features in relief on the back, and thousands of red-white-and-blue neckties bearing his portrait, were sold."[53]

The True Whigs hired goons to break up Reformation Party meetings, confiscated funds and equipment, and arrested party officials. In public, Tubman cynically bemoaned these acts, ordering his subordinates to let Twe continue to campaign and even offering the beleaguered candidate police protection. Tubman was also willing to overlook Twe's appeal to the native constituency, usually a cardinal sin in Liberian politics. What elicited the wrath of the Tubman regime was Twe's insistence that international observers oversee the election and tally the votes. For Tubman and the settler elite, still recovering from the League of Nations inquiry, Twe's demand was an affront. In a radio broadcast to the nation Tubman was apoplectic, accusing Twe and his running mate, Thorgues Sie, whom Tubman called "my inept ex-schoolmate," of treachery and sedition. "[W]hen Mr. Twe and Mr. Thorgues Sie and their few followers, undertook to invite international intervention in the domestic affairs of this nation," the president said, "they became violators of the Criminal Statutes of this Republic and had in reason and conscience to be made to answer for their crimes."[54]

At the last minute, Tubman and the Whigs had Twe's name removed from the ballot on a technicality: the Reformation Party was allegedly late in registering its candidates. Charges of sedition were then brought against Twe and eighty-six of his followers. Twe fled into the bush and, with the help of Kru oarsmen, across the Mano River into Sierra Leonean exile once again. He did not return to Liberia until 1960, when Tubman pardoned the paralyzed octogenarian and allowed him to die in Monrovia the following year. Twe got off relatively easily.

·

The crowd at Centennial Pavilion on the evening of June 22, 1955, was comprised of legislators, Supreme Court justices, cabinet secretaries, and most of Liberia's diplomatic corps. Tubman sat at the head table, directly in front of the bandstand. He had commissioned the monument eight years earlier to commemorate one hundred years of Liberian independence; the building was decorated with the symbols of settler hegemony, including a forty-foot tower out front with statues of a native woman and Matilda Newport hoisting Liberia's Lone Star flags. Inside the great hall, a row of ebony pedestals lined the walls, topped with busts of pioneer heroes and the token tribal: King Peter, the "good" native leader who, back in 1822, had sold the land on which the pavilion was situated to the settlers and was then ignominiously dethroned by his own people.

The crowd was there to celebrate the legislature's formal declaration of Tubman's presidential victory. After the ceremony, short films were shown, including one of the president's recent trip to Jamaica. As often happened during the wet season, the power failed. During a second outage, Inspector James Bestman, Tubman's chief security officer, noticed a pistol raised behind Tubman's back. He grabbed for it, a shot rang out, and the bullet ricocheted off a concrete beam, wounding Congressman Daniel Derricks. Two more shots were fired, the third striking another bodyguard in the hand before cracking the mirrored ceiling above Tubman's head. As a correspondent for *Time* magazine reported, chaos ensued. "Women in evening gowns fled, leaving their high-heeled shoes behind. Men broke for the exits, leaving not only their top hats but, in many cases, on this hot night, their tail coats. President Tubman, unhurt and dignified as ever, did not flee."[55]

Bestman and the other bodyguards eventually wrestled Paul Dunbar, a former police marksman, to the floor. Attorney General Joseph Garber and other officials impatiently grilled the would-be assassin at one of the banquet tables. "The question was put to me," Dunbar recalled later at trial, " 'Who sent you to assassinate the president?'" Nobody, he replied, "because I did not go there to assassinate the president." That was not what his interrogators wanted to hear. They ordered soldiers who had rushed into the hall after the shooting to drag him away. "I was then carried between the Executive [i.e., Centennial] Pavilion and the [old Executive] Mansion where I was thrown down by some soldiers with one of them having his boot on my throat and when I was brought back to the table I had to consent to everything they asked me." He was to confess to being part of a conspiracy involving some of the most powerful people in the republic, including the ex-president and Tubman predecessor Edwin Barclay, to kill the president and to overthrow the government.[56]

The shooting followed an election that had pitted Tubman against a breakaway group of True Whig officials and ex–cabinet members, led by the former interior secretary and close presidential confidante Samuel Coleman, who had quit the party a year before. Coleman had a history of antagonizing presidents. His revelations about King's involvement in the Fernando Pó slave ring persuaded the legislature to push for impeachment in 1930. Three years later, he fell out of favor with Barclay as well, and was forced to give up chairmanship of the True Whig Party after being convicted in a conspiracy to assassinate Barclay, a conviction overturned by the Supreme Court, which cited "gross irregularities" on the part of the lower court as well as "flagrant disregard of the law governing trials."[57] The newly appointed associate justice William V. S. Tubman had written the decision.

The reasons for Coleman's break from Tubman are not clear, but Tubman took it personally. In a speech in which he offered his understanding of the motives behind the assassination attempt, the president leveled what he considered the gravest political charge against his former friend: ingratitude. Despite Coleman's demonstrated incompetence, Tubman said he had repeatedly offered him opportunities to redeem himself. The so-called conspirators, for their part, called themselves the Independent True Whig Party. Recruiting an aged Barclay as their standard-bearer, they campaigned on a standard reformist platform: anti-poverty, anti-corruption, and anti–governmental incompetence. But as was always true in Liberia, policy and personality overlapped. It was said that Coleman and

Barclay harbored resentments against Tubman—Coleman for being overlooked as secretary of state and Barclay for being snubbed by Tubman at various state events. Their public stance was that Tubman was a dictator who had to be stopped in order to save the republic. "I saw totalitarian methods of administration being adopted in public business and social relations," Barclay announced in his nomination acceptance speech. "I saw the principles of democracy being debased to immoral mob-rule, and the spiritual morale of the people undermined by fear and terror of the President's Gestapo."[58]

The comparison with Nazi Germany, an instance of the characteristic hyperbole of Liberian political discourse, may have been a gross exaggeration, but it was not an outright fiction. By the mid-1950s, Tubman oversaw a network of informers and secret police, including the Orwellian "Public Relations Officers," or, as the locals referred to them, PROs. The PROs intimidated opponents, stifled dissent, and kept Tubman apprised of the actions and thoughts of the opposition. Inefficient and unimaginative, Tubman's security forces relied on brutality to get things done. In the months leading up to the 1955 elections, they cracked down on an increasingly marginalized but still highly vocal opposition press. The journalist Tuan Wreh was arrested and found guilty of contempt by an obedient legislature for writing a piece called "Inside Politics: Why You Should Not Vote for Tubman." The Liberian elite observed legal niceties; Tubman's thugs in the army did not. "I was escorted to the houses . . . of army officers to collect their toilet . . . These I emptied in the lavatory of the Executive Mansion staff," Tuan recalled in a trenchant history of the Tubman administration, published five years after the president's death. "Before a curious crowd that morning, I was forced to put both my hands (with emphasis on the right hand) in the toilet pails to mass the excreta and stir the urine . . . I was then told to inhale the nasty scent and splatter faeces on my cheeks and forehead."[59] He was later beaten by NCOs and enlisted men.

Tubman, a master of the art of resentment politics, portrayed himself as an outsider who challenged the Monrovia settler elite and stood up for ordinary Liberians against the reactionary "old guard" of the ITWP. He claimed that they opposed the Open Door Policy because it challenged their economic preeminence and their right to make insider deals and charge customers whatever they pleased. But what really infuriated them, Tubman insisted, was his more inclusive native policies. "Those outmoded pseudo-politicians declared that the administration was giving the country away to the native man," he charged, "and was promoting a group of people who had no political or social background and no claim to prominence."[60] And Tubman always returned to the theme of personal ingratitude. He claimed to have advanced their careers, given their children scholarships to study abroad, and even increased Barclay's pension severalfold—still, they had turned on him. The leaders of the ITWP were ingrates and backstabbers, "cringingly receiving salary and enjoying other emoluments of the . . . present administration."[61]

Similar to Barclay's Gestapo charges, Tubman's vitriol carried a truth within it. Foreign corporations and an influx of Lebanese traders—resented in Liberia and in West Africa more generally for usurping hinterland commerce and the import-export trade—were challenging the settler oligarchy, even as the latter made small fortunes renting out buildings and land, since foreigners could not own property. Many elite families, including the Barclays and Colemans, did indeed see their political influence wane under Tubman. This was not a result of the president actively recruiting native talent for his administration, however, but rather of his promotion of people on the margins of the honorables' society. These men, Tubman knew, would be loyal.

The campaign reached its nadir when each camp began to accuse the other of attempting to murder its candidates. At one point Coleman claimed that Tubman "had supplied jeeps to certain individuals who had strict instructions from him to run over Mr. Barclay who is in the habit of walking in the streets at night."[62] For his part, the president asserted that Barclay had devised a plot to bomb his favorite haunt, the Saturday Afternoon Club. Even more bizarre was the "witch doctor" affair. Tubman claimed that one V. S. Onemegba, a

Nigerian shaman, had been hired by the Barclay camp to kill him and other government officials with "witchcraft." Tubman insisted his allegations were true but refused to prosecute Barclay "for the reason that the Liberian Government would not permit itself to go on record as believing in or giving credence to witchcraft."[63]

In the end, the True Whigs machine politics prevailed. Through intimidation and ballot box manipulation, Tubman won by 244,873 votes to 1,182, a 99 percent margin that the reelected president unapologetically attributed to his administration's "outstanding success."* According to Tubman, the conspiracy that sent Dunbar to the Centennial Pavilion was born at that moment. "The entire plot was founded," Tubman explained to the legislature in his official report on the assassination attempt, "on no legitimate principle but the inordinate ambition and determination of that little group of wilful [sic] men of about ten in number, to gain power by force." Tubman explained that, in the wake of their election loss, Barclay, Coleman, and the leadership of the ITWP "became enraged because the people of the country had persistently and incontrovertibly expressed their vote . . . [for] the present administration, while in the meantime condemning them [the ITWP] . . . for their conduct as well as their vicious, malicious and false propaganda during the campaign."[64]

By mid-June, the "cabal" was allegedly meeting at Coleman's house in Monrovia and at his upriver farm in Clay-Ashland, where they planned not only to assassinate Tubman and other top leaders but to burn down the government arsenal and stir up "insurrection and incit[e] rebellion against the authority of the Government," though few details on these latter plans were forthcoming in the report.[65] The conspirators then recruited Dunbar, a friend of the Coleman family, to kill the president at the pavilion. Witnesses were

---

*It's likely that the editors of the *Guinness Book of World Records* chose the 96 percent margin of Charles King's victory over Thomas Faulkner in 1927 instead of Tubman's 99 percent margin because far more of the native population was enfranchised by 1955. Conjuring votes out of thin air may indeed represent a higher level of corruption than claiming that just about every vote was cast for one candidate.

brought forward to say that Coleman had removed his family from Monrovia to his farm, which had been "turned into a fortress" the morning of the planned assassination. Others said they had seen the ITWP lawyer S. Raymond Horace "wandering through the Centennial Memorial Pavilion" the afternoon of the shooting, "watching officials at work on the seating arrangements."[66]

In his forced confession hours after the shooting, Dunbar filled in the rest of the story. That evening, Horace had driven him out to the Coleman farm, where he was given the details of the assassination plan and a .38-caliber revolver, before being driven back to the city. Under the cover of darkness, Dunbar entered the pavilion, edged his way to within a few feet of Tubman during the movie screening, and raised the pistol. The morning after the shooting and Dunbar's "confession," the police and military raced out to Coleman's farm, having already begun to round up twenty-eight opposition party members as suspects in the "conspiracy." The officer in charge knocked on Coleman's door, warrant in hand, only to be met by a shout of "I will give these bitches hell" and a volley of machine-gun fire from Coleman and his eldest son, John.[67]

The official report was not entirely favorable to the government. It criticized security forces for going to the farm "with little or no plan of attack." An army captain and a police private were killed in the initial skirmish, and five others wounded. When the Colemans shot out the tires of their vehicles, "not one of which had been tactically kept out of gun range," the "besieging force" was faced with a decision: walk the twenty-five miles back to Monrovia for reinforcements—they were either out of radio contact or had no radios to begin with—or flush out the defenders. They chose to set fire to the barricaded farmhouse. It worked, but "during the excitement and confusion," the two escaped, "unscathed and fully armed." It took four and a half days to track the Coleman men down, though they were hiding just a few miles away, on a sugar cane farm. "Hopeless though their position was," the report concluded, "they again opened fire on the advancing force but were shot down."[68]

Tubman was avenged but his wrath was not yet assuaged. He had Coleman's younger son personally deliver the decomposing bodies to an army base in Monrovia, where they were put on public display. "Thousands of Monrovians came to see the horrible spectacle," according to Wreh. And even after they were finally turned over to the family for burial, the journalist insists, Tubman made sure that no embalmer would touch the bodies, no grave diggers would put them in the ground, no clergymen would give the rites, and few mourners would attend the funeral. Wreh concluded that it was "an act of barbarism unequalled in Liberian history."[69]

The trial, held in the fall of 1955, was a foregone conclusion, though every formality was followed. After being convicted by the circuit court on charges of treason, Dunbar and seven of his co-conspirators were sentenced to be hanged, a verdict upheld two years later by the Supreme Court. But critics of the regime were not satisfied and pointed to the many holes in the government's version of the events. How could a marksman miss his target from six feet away, Wreh wanted to know. Indeed, why had he even bothered to get so close? Dunbar's initial confession had clearly been coerced; later, in the safer confines of the court, he had stated that he was in the pavilion that night simply to take shelter from the pouring rain and that, as an ex-policeman, he always carried a loaded revolver with him. Curious to see what was going on, he had taken about fifteen paces into the hall when a guard noticed his gun and grabbed for it. In the tussle, the gun went off. It was all an unfortunate accident.

What did that mean for the conspiracy? If what Dunbar said was true, there had been none. But even assuming that his presence at the pavilion had not been as innocent as he claimed, there was only one living witness who could credibly tie Dunbar to the ITWP leadership. Yet Soko Brown, a co-conspirator who became a state's witness in exchange for immunity, had always been on the fringes of the ITWP inner circle. He was the only one of the conspirators who had not been rounded up by police and paraded to jail in his underwear on the night of the assassination.

The consensus among Liberians, then and since, is that there was no conspiracy, nor any assassination attempt. It is generally accepted that Tubman used the incident and the convictions to crack down on what little opposition to him remained. In a typically Liberian gesture of official magnanimity, he eventually granted all of the convicted conspirators, including Dunbar, a full presidential pardon. They all then issued public letters of apology and contrition, thereby achieving the harmony so valued in the tight-knit world of Americo-Liberian politics.

Tubman never again faced a remotely serious challenge to his authority. In 1959, his opponent was a church organist named W. O. Davies-Bright, who declared in his official platform, "not being particularly opposed to the continuation in office, of President Tubman, this venture of mine . . . is purely sportsmanlike, and is in response to the ardent desire of Dr. Tubman for fair and friendly competition."[70] The ballot symbol Davies-Bright chose to represent himself to illiterate voters was a sheep. He would receive 55 votes, including Tubman's.

Even so, Tubman grew increasingly paranoid of subversion from abroad. His loathing of Kwame Nkrumah never abated, and as the Cold War intensified in Africa, he saw Soviet agents behind every ironwood tree and their alleged Liberian collaborators in university classrooms, newspaper offices, labor union halls, and diplomatic missions. Communist plots were unearthed on a regular basis, among students at the University of Liberia in 1962 and striking rubber workers at the Firestone plantation in 1966, for instance. Tubman's hand-picked ambassador to Kenya in 1968 was accused of being a Communist and of treason, but his actual transgression, like that of Coleman, had been disloyalty and ingratitude to the president. In court, the government's evidence against Ambassador Henry Fahnbulleh consisted of, among other exhibits, a pin he'd received from Mao Zedong, Chinese books he kept in his study, and the official portrait of William Tubman he failed to hang on his office wall.

In his more lucid moments, Tubman recognized that the real threat to his presidency, perhaps even to the Americo-Liberian regime itself, lay not in conspiracies inspired by foreign nations but in forces he himself had unleashed. For all his repressive policies, Tubman, with revenues from the Open Door Policy, built the schools that introduced thousands of young natives, mixed-heritage Liberians, and poor settlers to the wider world. In an interview with a *Time* reporter in 1969, he admitted that the hundreds of students his government had sent to be educated at American colleges would be difficult to control once they returned. "I'm committing political suicide," he said, half-jokingly. "These boys will come back experts, and I know nothing but the Bible."[71] What he did not acknowledge or perceive is that these students would also come back radicalized by their experiences on American college campuses, and that their ideology, not their expertise, would be the foundation of their challenge to the ruling class. He also did not foresee, dying in his London hospital bed, that it would be a barely literate master sergeant from the farthest corner of the Liberian hinterland, not an educated young Liberian, who would end a century of True Whig rule, and in the most violent way imaginable. In the end, the Americo-Liberian regime did not commit "political suicide." It was murdered.

TEN

Father and Son

At some point in the middle of the twentieth century, a young Grebo boy from rural Maryland County got it into his head to move to the big city. It was a common ambition at the time. Tubman's economic and educational policies had helped spread the dream of the original settlers, that of prosperity. The world, hungry for automobiles, came to Liberia, which possessed the iron ore they were made from and the rubber they rode on. Tiny zinc-roofed schoolhouses cropped up across the hinterland, filling young heads with modern ideas and modern desires—a new Liberia, a well-paying desk job.

Joseph Samson came from a poor native family, one of nine siblings. But he had two things going for him. He was a quick study and his mother was related to a paramount chief, who also happened to be a key figure in the local True Whig Party machine. In 1955, the chief died and President William Tubman came to Harper, Maryland's seaside hub, to pay his respects.

Samson did everything he could to catch the president's attention, writing him a letter and hanging around his compound. Tubman ignored him but an advisor, an accountant named Thomas Ireland, hired the boy to run errands, and was soon impressed by his diligence. They talked. Samson told the older man of his ambitions; Ireland offered to bring him to Monrovia, on the presidential yacht no less, and make him part of the Ireland family.

Not all Americo families who took in wards endeavored to "civilize" them. Some wards were treated like "menials," one nineteenth-century African American diplomat noted, kept from school, forced do perform "domestic chores" from morning till night.[1] That was not Samson's fate exactly, though the tensions inherent in a system that thrust persons of such different backgrounds and status into the same family soon became evident. Mrs. Ireland did not take to the boy, especially when he ignored her orders to leave class and do chores. She called him "frisky."[2] The situation became unbearable for Samson, who soon got himself adopted by an even more powerful member of the settler elite—Joseph Chesson, American-trained lawyer, diplomat, and future attorney general.

This adoption would prove fateful. For the next quarter century, the tortured, oedipal relationship between the two men—each, eventually, would be accused of ordering the other's execution—would contribute to the end of the ancien régime, and the violent unraveling of the polity the Americo-Liberians had ruled for 133 years.

Family was everything among the incestuous Liberian elite, not just as sentiment or homily, but as a practical matter. Scholarships to foreign universities, legal apprenticeships, recommendations, promotions, the favor of the True Whig Party, if one was politically inclined—none of it could be achieved without the right family name or the sponsorship of a powerful patriarch. Tubman, for one, was related to no fewer than two congressmen, three ambassadors, four members of his own cabinet, and the chief justice of the Supreme Court.

Nobody absorbed this lesson of Liberian life better than aspiring young natives of the Tubman era. "Even if you went to Harvard and came back," Jimmy Wiles, son of one of the more successful wards, noted years later, "you couldn't get a top government job unless you came from a respected settler family."[3] Wiles's recollection elided an important fact: "Respected settler family" status was fluid in Liberia. High society and government ministry corner offices belonged to the "honorables," blood descendants of immigrants from North America and the West Indies, but wards routinely took on their adoptive families' names. Joseph Samson went a step further, officially changing his name to Joseph Chesson III.

The clever young Grebo saw his opportunities clearly, and took them. He particularly impressed Chesson's wife, Mamie, who helped win him a scholarship to the Booker Washington Agricultural and Industrial Institute in up-country Kakata, the nation's leading vocational school, where he earned a bookkeeping degree.* She also gave him money to go to America—in Liberia, having been "abroad" always meant having been to America, and was a coveted status marker—and attend North Carolina College (now North Carolina Central University), a historically black college, which, in the late 1960s, was just beginning to integrate. He worked in the school cafeteria to pay his living expenses, earned a law degree, and then returned to Liberia.

Over the next decade, Chesson enjoyed a measure of success. He rose to mid-level positions in various ministries, practiced law in the Grebo backcountry of Grand Gedeh County, and, in 1977, secured from the local True Whig establishment approval to run for senator, guaranteeing his victory. It was a predictable trajectory for an American-educated lawyer and ward of one of the most powerful men in Liberia, yet almost unthinkable prior to the Tubman era. Then, just a month into office, Chesson's fortunes unexpectedly and dramatically reversed. He fell out of favor with his political benefactors and was impeached.

Recalling the incident years later, Chesson offered a convoluted explanation for his downfall that had to do with his representation of

---

*While the biological sons of the elite usually attended Liberia College in Monrovia, BWI had an illustrious heritage of its own, having been founded in 1929 by the American Colonization Society and various other American missionary and philanthropic organizations. In the tradition of its namesake, it aimed to provide a more practical education for talented and aspiring natives and poorer settler youth. Still, noted a leading Liberianist, in 1969, "BWI lacks prestige among the Americo-Liberian families . . . A diploma from BWI carries no political influence . . ."

an individual in a private court matter while he was a senator. From his perspective, his error did not rise to the level of an impeachable offense. But his past belligerence—disobeying his first foster mother and, later, the Senate president pro-tempore Frank Tolbert, whose calls to stand in prayer he refused to abide (he preferred kneeling), citing his "constitutional rights"—hints at what may have been the real cause. He harbored resentments against the settler class that had taken him in but always reminded him of his place. "You think Frank Tolbert['s] son will be treated like that?" he wondered three decades later. "None of their [settlers'] children could be treated like that. But because my father was not among them . . . so they treated me anyhow and I didn't like it."[4]

While Chesson was pursuing traditional markers of success in Liberia, others of his generation and background were charting a radical course for themselves and their country. Tubman's expansion of the education system changed the face of Liberia. A handful of students attended Liberia College in 1951; seventeen years later, the country boasted 1,300 college students at several institutions. Scholarships to the United States, once the prerogative of only the wealthiest and best-connected settler families, were increasingly offered to promising native sons and daughters. There, like Chesson, they acquired the skills and knowledge they expected would lead to careers, political power, and membership in Liberian high society. Yet after returning to Liberia, many were disappointed by the dearth of jobs and the reluctance of the entrenched elite to admit them into their class.

Their disappointment often found an outlet in the African American civil rights struggle—educated Liberians, native and settler alike, had always followed American politics as if it were their own, which in a sense it was. The fight by American blacks for simple human dignity and equal rights reverberated among idealistic young natives and settlers, the former chafing at a century of second-class status, the latter identifying with a movement to uplift people that were, albeit distantly, family.

The liberation of Africa from European colonial rule had a similar impact on ambitious Liberian youth. Natives in Liberia found inspiration in their brethren taking power for themselves across the continent, even if, as in the bloody Congo, the outcome warned against their idealism. At the same time, some of the more reactionary elements among the settler elite began to argue that only stronger ties with Europe would secure Liberia's survival, even though it had long been a point of pride among the elite that they had maintained sovereignty in the face of European imperialist encroachment. Thus Liberians, especially educated youth denied opportunities because of their lineage, began to see a century of settler hegemony and a century of European rule in Africa as indistinguishable from each other.

The death of Tubman in London in the summer of 1971 carried the promise of change. "Uncle Shad" had ushered in an era of unprecedented prosperity and progress, but one that included the repression of labor unions and of political dissenters. Tubman, with his Unification Plan, acknowledged that power might one day devolve from settler to native, but if there was to be a transition, it would be on his timetable. Anybody who thought differently, as the native journalist Tuan Wreh learned, might find themselves bloodied and humiliated, cleaning the toilets of the Executive Mansion with his bare hands.

Upon Tubman's death, William Tolbert, Jr., the second son of a moderately successful rice and coffee farmer from the up-country settlement of Bensonville, assumed the office.* Educated at Liberia College rather than abroad, Tolbert served for years in the house and senate and, as a minister, became president of the World Baptist Alliance. Nevertheless, he was not seen as a major figure in Liberian politics. Viewed as a political factotum throughout his long vice

---

*As the Tolbert family, which included two other political brothers, rose in status, the town's name was changed to Bentol, reverting back to Bensonville after the 1980 coup.

presidency, Tolbert was not expected to last long as Tubman's successor. Challengers quickly appeared, including the urbane, Harvard-educated Secretary of State Joseph Grimes and the powerful Speaker of the House Richard Henries, but Tolbert proved a surprisingly canny politician, brushing away all challenges and consolidating his grip on the True Whig Party machine. A wooden speaker without the flair of his predecessor, the paunchy and balding Tolbert unexpectedly displayed a common touch once in office.

Tolbert understood the changing political climate, better than other True Whig stalwarts, that for educated native and settler youth, Tubman's Liberia had not been merely a frustrating place but an embarrassing one, with its slavish Americanism and stuffy formalism. So Tolbert immediately moved to distance Monrovia from Washington, voting with the nonaligned bloc at the United Nations, allowing the Soviet Union to set up an embassy in the country, and transferring diplomatic relations from Taiwan to Beijing. He set up a commission to strip triumphant Americo-Liberianism from the nation's symbols of sovereignty (though it ended up recommending few changes) and curtailed official reenactments of the native massacre on Matilda Newport Day. In a move that no contemporary account or recollection of the man leaves out, he showed up at his first formal inauguration not in the tailcoat and top hat favored by the "old man," but in a safari suit, the preferred garb of the continent's new native rulers.

The outfit was mostly for show, as were many of his initiatives, such as the anti-poverty "mats to mattresses" campaign, the patriotic "higher heights" and "total involvement" appeals, and the anti-corruption "rally time" campaign. But Tolbert did offer one real change: he eased the political repression of the Tubman years. In one of his first acts as president, he dismissed from the security ministry the thousands of paid informants known as Public Relations Officers. He also relaxed press restrictions and made it clear that pointing out the government's shortcomings would no longer land a dissident in Belle Yella, the country's infamous jungle prison.

To the country's political establishment, Tolbert's headlong rush to reform seemed too hasty. They derisively called him "Speedy," and the nickname stuck. Even his wife suggested he "slow down and relax a bit."[5] But for the country's restive and increasingly radicalized younger generation, he was not moving fast enough.

Though it would spark a revolution, the Movement for Justice in Africa (MOJA) had modest origins. On March 21, 1973, a group of students and professors at the University of Liberia, along with a few outsiders, met in the school's auditorium. The United Nations had declared the date "International Day for the Elimination of Racial Discrimination" in white-ruled Rhodesia and South Africa. Despite Liberia's official opposition to apartheid and his own leftward lurch, Tolbert departed from the policy of other African nations and pursued one akin to what the Reagan administration would later call "constructive engagement." In 1975, the president's own brother would host the South African prime minister, John Vorster, at his private home in Bentol.* Liberia was also a notorious depot for transshipping goods from the boycotted white republic. MOJA was determined to put an end to this activity. But their agenda notably did not include a challenge to the True Whigs' monopoly on power.

MOJA's appeals for African solidarity did not win it many followers and it soon shifted focus to domestic concerns. It began working with church groups to block a bill legalizing gambling in Liberia and helped the aging investigative journalist Albert Porte fight off a $250,000 libel suit brought by Stephen Tolbert, the president's younger brother, whom Porte had accused, in a pamphlet titled "Gobbling Business," of using his position as finance minister to line his own pockets.† MOJA also spun off Susukuu, a grassroots cooperative

---

*Stephen Tolbert, who had business ties with South Africa, later said, despite intense criticism, that his only regret was putting a white-bound, rather than black-bound, Bible on Vorster's nightstand.
†The case would die with the plaintiff when Stephen Tolbert was killed in a small plane crash over the Atlantic in April 1975.

development group, which, in the words of its chief founder, "help[ed] poor people to improve their own living standards, to help them help themselves."*[6] In this effort, MOJA self-consciously donned the mantle of its inspirational forebear, Edward Blyden, in an attempt to bring together African communal traditions and progressive Western thought on individual freedoms and governance. But the action that would prove most fateful for the country was MOJA's creation of a night school in Monrovia, known as the Barracks Union, which offered classes on reading, writing, and politics to the much-abused native rank and file of the Army of Liberia, including a barely literate but ambitious master sergeant named Samuel Doe.

More reformist than radical—even President Tolbert was a member for a time—MOJA had no explicit political ambitions, at least not at first. That was not the case with its main rival, the Progressive Alliance of Liberia (PAL). Founded two years after MOJA by Liberian students in the United States, PAL from the beginning espoused "black power" and the fashionable *ujamaa*, or "African socialism," of Tanzania's Julius Nyerere.[†] Both ideologies again owed much to Blyden, in the case of the black power movement, with Marcus Garvey serving as a historical intermediary.

The two groups also differed institutionally. While both were led by well-educated natives, wards, and alienated settler youth, MOJA's founders came from academia and PAL's from politics. In fact, PAL was the brainchild of Gabriel Bacchus Matthews, a City University of New York graduate who served as Liberia's vice consul in the United States, until his falling out with the foreign minister, allegedly over charges of embezzlement. Matthews made PAL the vehicle of his own political ambitions, relocating the organization from New York to Monrovia in 1978.

---

*The name Susukuu is a combination of two Kru words: *Susu*, meaning a traditional savings and loan society, and *Kuu*, referring to an agricultural work group.
†In Swahili, *ujamaa* meant "extended family."

It was to MOJA and especially PAL that the disenchanted Chesson turned after the True Whigs ousted him from the Senate in 1978. Recalling that time decades later, his anger was still palpable. "They [the True Whigs] expelled me but, nationally, I was going to expel them from politics."[7] The similarly aggrieved Matthews—a ward of President Tolbert—welcomed the younger Chesson into the organization's ranks and quickly dispatched him to win the release of party activists jailed in Grand Cape Mount County. Chesson had found a new home, politically speaking. But his switch to the radical opposition cost him his literal one. When Joseph Chesson, Sr., Liberia's attorney general and an administration hard-liner, learned of his ward's apostasy, he banished him from the family compound in the upscale suburb of Sinkor. Chesson, Jr., immediately dropped his adopted name.

For generations ambitious wards had taken on the names of the "honorables" who adopted them. But the radicals of late-1970s Liberia viewed these monikers with the same contempt their counterparts in America directed at "slave names." Thus, rather than reverting to Joseph Samson, the disowned ward of Joseph Chesson, Sr., did what many other assimilated natives opted to do: He reclaimed his tribal heritage. Going forward, he would be known as Chea Cheapoo.

For all their efforts to identify with the working poor of Monrovia and the illiterate tribal peasantry of the hinterland, both MOJA and PAL remained elitist operations. With the exception of the people touched by MOJA's Susukuu outreach programs, most Liberians were barely aware of the organizations' existence. As for the power brokers in Monrovia—and, for that matter, the angry and frustrated younger generation—few believed that MOJA and PAL would bring about real change. Ironically, there was only one precedent in Liberian history of an opposition group effecting change: when the True Whigs themselves had emerged in the 1870s and 1880s to usurp power from Monrovia merchants and forge a new, more color-inclusive elite. More typically, serious challengers were co-opted or repressed, depending on the whims of the president and the interests of the "honorables." There was no reason to think that MOJA and PAL would be any different, that their leaders would not join their enemies or surrender. There was also no reason to think they could make inroads with the long-suffering and disenfranchised native poor, who represented 95 percent of the population.

In fact, it would not be the activism of MOJA and PAL that would ultimately spark the political awakening of the natives and bring down the True Whig establishment. It would be something far more prosaic: a bag of rice or, more precisely, the price people had to pay for it.

It did not take long for the early colonists of North America to realize that the riverine coasts of South Carolina and Georgia made for ideal rice-growing country. But growing rice on a commercial scale requires sophisticated hydraulics and expert knowledge of the grain's complex growing cycle. So colonists from temperate Britain turned to their slaves, especially those from the Windward Coast, where the growing and preparation of rice were centuries-old practices. Slaves from what would become Liberia helped make possible the most lucrative southern crop, after tobacco, of the colonial era.

Ironically, the black settlers who came to Liberia a century later—largely from the tobacco country of the Chesapeake—knew little about growing rice. Rice, though, would soon become the foundation of the ordinary settler's diet, as it already was of the native's— palm oil with a little dried fish or meat and a few vegetables, a handful of the searing grains of paradise pepper that first lured European explorers to the region, and mounds upon mounds of rice. But rather than learn how to grow it themselves, the Americoes simply bought it from the natives, which freed them to focus on trade. By the early twentieth century, however, the demand for rice outstripped supply, forcing Liberia to import it, which only added to the nation's debt. Firestone's arrival in the 1920s exacerbated the rice shortage, as natives were lured or forced from their jungle fields to the company's rubber plantations. The Tubman years were characterized by Liberia's iron mines, not its rice fields, and by the spread of roads to the interior, which precipitated a land grab by Americoes. Communal native lands dedicated to rice production now belonged to well-connected absentee landlords, who preferred to grow rubber and sell it to Firestone.

Meanwhile, Liberians of all classes began to develop a taste for the imported, polished product over the coarser native variety. By Tolbert's day, roughly one-fourth of the nation's 200,000 tons of annual rice consumption came from abroad, most of it from the United States. So critical was rice to the Liberian diet that the government imposed strict price controls. No one could charge any more or less than $22 American for a 100-pound sack. Yet the government offered little help to the 137,000 small farmers trying to grow rice for profit on small plots that averaged two and a half acres. Like many other African nations, Liberia placed a higher premium on social peace in the capital than economic development in the countryside. The results were predictable: a steady flow of impoverished peasants swelled Monrovia's slums and the ranks of the unemployed expanded.

The new urban poor, forced out of rice growing, still needed it for sustenance. Thus, when the agriculture minister Florence Chenoweth suggested amid the general inflation of 1979 to raise the price of a sack to $30, there was an uproar. The government reasoned that raising the price would put more money in the hands of the remaining peasant farmers, encouraging them to grow more and meet the president's goal of an end to imports by 1980.

The activists of MOJA and PAL were unconvinced. Liberia's largest importers of rice were companies controlled by the Tolbert family. In fact, for all of the president's earnest speeches about government reform, there was a sense that, with regard to corruption, the country was moving backwards, even from the notoriously lax standards of the Tubman years. "Up to here, okay," the "old man" had been fond of saying, pointing to his wrist, then, tracing a line to his shoulder, he added, "up to there, no."[8]

Meanwhile, the 1970s were punctuated by a series of economic shocks that brought the industrialized West's great post–World War II boom to a halt. As a supplier of raw materials to one of the hardest-hit sectors—automobile manufacturing—Liberia's economy went into a tailspin. For the poor, this meant real suffering. For the rising generation of educated natives and wards, it meant frustration. "A lot of these indigenous people were coming back home [from their schooling abroad] and demanding their piece . . . of the action," noted Archie Bernard, the radicalized scion of one of Liberia's wealthiest families. "'We're supposed to be part of this, too,' they said. 'That is why the 'old man' [Tubman] told us to go to school. So where is my opportunity?'"[9]

Young Liberians who had encountered Marxism and the idea of Third World solidarity at Western universities in the 1960s and 1970s had found their cause. "If you read *Das Kapital,* it gets to be hypnotic," Bernard added, years later, about his own youthful enthusiasms. "You see young people, their minds get to have a yearning . . . to relieve all this pent-up frustration. At the end of the day, the young man is highly educated and can't get a job. So he gets this thing, this radical ideology. You listen to a person who is articulate and you can almost be hypnotized by it."[10] Matthews, Cheapoo, and their fellow travelers had learned a blueprint for revolution, even if their understanding of Marxism was often muddled. Recognizing Africa's long tradition of petty entrepreneurialism and witnesses to the incredible abundance of American capitalism during their student years, they had little interest in centralized, Soviet-style economies, though many praised the peasant-based socialism of Mao's China. Still, the abysmal results of the government's price fixing had created, in their minds, the proper conditions for revolution. Now it was a matter of forming the vanguard that would lead the masses out of their lowly state.

On March 28, 1979, Matthews went, as part of a "people's delegation" that included three other PAL officials, to visit his foster father,

Tolbert, at the Executive Mansion. The meeting began cordially enough, with Matthews stating that PAL could offer a subsidy to rice farmers, who would get more for their crop while consumers would keep paying the well-established $22 per bag price. But Matthews's calculations greatly underestimated the cost of the program. He assumed that the subsidies would run to $19,500 annually, while in actuality the farmers would need 150 times that.

Tolbert did not bother to quibble over the numbers and rejected the idea. He was more concerned with PAL's plans for a "mass demonstration." The right to assemble was written into the Liberian constitution and PAL had tried to go through official channels to get a permit, but Tolbert, fearing a reaction from party hard-liners, was wary of any actions that might foster antagonism and divisiveness. "[N]o such disruptive activities will be countenanced," Tolbert informed Matthews, "neither will the Government make a determination on national issues in an atmosphere of emotionalism . . . [nor] accept alibis for the promotion of lawlessness and the defiance of constituted authority."[11]

Prominent clergymen, MOJA leaders, and even Albert Porte, éminence grise of Liberian dissident politics, advised the PAL against the protest, and Matthews backed down. But his retreat, coming just hours before the Saturday afternoon march, was too late. As PAL leaders tried to disperse the 2,000 protesters massed in front of the organization's offices on Randall Street, security forces "stormed" the building. A group of demonstrators broke away and headed for the Executive Mansion, where they were met by water cannons, tear gas, and live fire, in the air at first, and then, after several policemen were injured, directly at the protesters. All hell broke loose, as the demonstrators were joined, and soon overtaken, by thousands of young men and boys from Monrovia's slums in the worst rioting in the country's history.

Tolbert summoned some of the more moderate leaders of the opposition, including the political science professor and MOJA cofounder Amos Sawyer, to the heavily guarded Executive Mansion.

"You see what you all have done?" Tolbert scolded. "You all happy now?"[12] Sawyer's sympathies were fully on the side of rioters, who he would later describe as a people "parched by the wretchedness of poverty, dazzled by the endless possibilities available to the affluent, languishing in the squalors of the city and the harshness and austerity of the rural village."[13] In Tolbert's presence, however, he proceeded cautiously, trying to point out that it was the police who opened fire first. But the president grew enraged and turned to his toughminded attorney general, who had been appointed to deal with the growing unrest in the country, and demanded a crackdown. Chesson ceremoniously drew a list of names from his pocket. Among those on it were Matthews, the Susukuu head Togba nah Tipoteh, and his now disinherited foster son, Chea Cheapoo. "There are warrants out for their arrest," Chesson informed Sawyer. "Tell them if they don't turn themselves in, they will be hunted down."[14]

It took three days and seven hundred troops from neighboring Guinea—Tolbert and Chesson did not trust Liberian soldiers to shoot their own countrymen—to suppress the rioting. Hundreds of businesses were looted and, by the official count, forty-one persons killed, though most suspected the actual total was several times that. In its official report, the Tolbert administration put the blame on professional agitators, foreign influences, and rioters hopped up on "dope and liquor."[15] Tolbert had forty arrested, charging Matthews, Cheapoo, and eleven others with treason, a capital offense.

But this being Liberia, the charges were soon dropped. Indeed, the government's actions after the riots followed time-honored custom. The offenders were imprisoned, brutalized, and humiliated, until they offered up apologies, like errant children, and were released. The apology Matthews wrote to Tolbert, which was published and distributed at government expense, was particularly abject. "Sir, permit me to express regrets on behalf of myself and my collaborators and to note the dilemma which we, young people, face," it began. "Your thoughts and actions, Sir, are based upon experience of things as they have been, as they are and, therefore, as they can possibly be. We, unfortunately, know only the present . . . [T]he costly lesson we have learned tells us that we are going nowhere for nothing unless we can rely on the experience and wisdom of men such as you."[16] Tolbert, clearly shaken, nevertheless played his designated part in the ritual, too. He lowered the price of rice, set up a commission to study the root causes of the riot—the recommendations of which he duly ignored—and eventually pardoned most of the men on Chesson's list, including Matthews and Cheapoo.

Tolbert had motives beyond merely quelling domestic unrest. His mind was on the upcoming annual meeting of the Organization of African Unity (now the African Union). As its head, he was expected to host its annual summit in 1979, an honor he had accepted four years earlier. Africa's strongmen of the 1960s and 1970s used the conference as a kind of potlatch to showcase their power and wealth, real or imagined. Tolbert wanted to show the world a united Liberia, and had reportedly freed the PAL dissidents from jail in return for assurances that they wouldn't make disturbances in front of the attending "VVIPs."

The president, determined to reassert Liberia's moral authority in a liberated continent that had seemingly passed it by, spared no expense. He had a vast bayfront hotel built on Monrovia's outskirts, connected to the capital by the country's only highway overpass. The government rented an aging ocean liner, the SS *America*, for the press and the overflow of staff; provided each of the continent's heads of state—fifty-one in all, not counting Rhodesia and South Africa—with a private beachside villa; and hoisted billboards depicting the attendees along the stretch of Tubman Boulevard from the airport to Monrovia, though six remained blank because coups and revolutions made it impossible to predict who from those nations would show up. The cost of the event lay somewhere between $100 million and $200 million, or between one- and two-thirds of the nation's GDP. Tolbert justified the spending as needed stimulus for a faltering economy, though everyone knew that much of it was consumed by graft and corruption.

Liberia's elite greatly enjoyed themselves, particularly at the casino aboard the *America*, while its ordinary citizens grumbled and the political opposition fumed. Looking back, the future president Ellen Johnson Sirleaf, then an official in the finance ministry but who would soon join the opposition, recalled, "to me, then, as to many others, it seemed unwise, if not downright dangerous, to be spending so much money hosting this exaggerated men's night out at a time when the Liberian economy was under such serious strain."[17]

The political system was under duress, too, and the True Whig leadership responded in the same manner that Tolbert had responded to the rice protests. When Sawyer decided to run as an independent for the Monrovia mayoralty, Foreign Minister Cecil Dennis, one of the supposed reformers in the party, called the MOJA activist to his home in the upscale neighborhood of Sinkor and tried to dissuade him. He made an argument that seems to have come out of the civil rights–era South, not Liberia: "You're being too pushy, slow down." He then warned Sawyer that Chesson and other True Whig hardliners wanted to throw the MOJA and PAL leaders back in jail. But Sawyer politely explained, "We've been waiting for 150 years," and returned to his campaign.[18] Tolbert, convinced that it was best for the country or in deference to men like Chesson, postponed the election, citing the need to reform the property requirement for voting, a law that had been ignored for years under Tubman as long as those unqualified voters cast their ballots for True Whigs.

With the OAU summit over, Matthews and the other dissidents transformed PAL into a formal political party, the Progressive People's Party, that would be ready to challenge the True Whigs for the mayoralty (the election had been rescheduled for June 1980), for the legislature in 1981, and for the presidency in 1983. As usual, Tolbert, who had gone on record that he would not run again, wavered; he had a judge block the PPP's formal registration on a technicality, then backed down when the party threatened another round of demonstrations.

Side-by-side interviews with Tolbert and Matthews in the February 18, 1980, edition of the British magazine *West Africa* revealed just how far apart the two men and the parties they represented were in the final months of the old regime. Whereas Tolbert offered up platitudes about Liberian democracy—"the fact that . . . a second political entity . . . has emerged only confirms our fundamental belief in . . . political freedom"—Matthews was adamant about his goals. "Our aim is to bring about revolutionary change wherever possible . . . with the Whig Party," he pronounced, "or in spite of the Whig Party."[19]

The True Whigs had no intention of working with Matthews or anyone else outside the party apparatus. Indeed, the harassment of opposition activists and leaders had already begun. On March 7, the PPP responded with a "midnight rally" outside the party's headquarters. But instead of speeches on democracy and the need for an end to one-party rule, Matthews unexpectedly called for a march on the Executive Mansion to meet with Tolbert and demand his immediate resignation. When it turned out that the president was at his up-country plantation, the PPP leader turned to his cheering supporters and called for a general strike, should Tolbert refuse to step down. Matthews's maximalist turn baffled even longtime observers of the Monrovia political scene; after all, the party had been allowed to register and hold rallies. MOJA officials tried to distance themselves from PAL, announcing that their politically immature rivals were engaged in "adventurism" that "discredited progressive work in Liberia."[20]

Tolbert called the PPP's demand a "diabolical and treasonable design" that would "enthrone anarchy and deprive the sovereign people of Liberia of their inalienable rights and cherished tradition of choosing their leaders through the electoral process." He suggested that the members of the political establishment, himself included, were personally at risk. "Their [the PPP's] action to convene [in] secret and carry out demonstrations by night in the streets and to converge near strategic government installations cannot in any way be construed as an attempt to dialogue with government," he insisted. "Mr. Matthews and his atrocious associates seemed determined to enter the premises of the Executives."[21] Tolbert had Matthews, Cheapoo, and the rest of the PPP leadership thrown in jail once again. Chesson, charging them with sedition and the capital offense of treason, set their trial for April 14.

It would never come to pass. The trial, the political infighting, the Tolbert administration, and Americo-Liberia itself would very soon be swept away by a more dangerous force than disgruntled young radicals. Distracted by the agitation of Matthews and the PPP, Tolbert, Chesson, and the rest of the True Whig Party oligarchs were unaware of developments in the barracks of the Barclay Training Center, half a mile up the beach from the Executive Mansion.

Few Liberians or foreigners took the Armed Forces of Liberia (AFL) seriously. The AFL was poorly trained and equipped, and its officer corps was known mostly for providing sinecures for the privileged sons of the Americo-Liberian elite. It was the army of a tiny, indebted country that had faced no external enemies since the close of the Scramble for Africa in the early twentieth century. The enlisted men were natives, usually recruited from the more isolated and least "civilized" ethnic groups of the interior—that is, those least likely to challenge the existing order. While some natives saw the army as an opportunity to better themselves, the reality was just the opposite. Soldiers were paid a pittance, housed in rank and leaky barracks, and their duties frequently involved petty chores for officers and other elites. It was not unusual to see a platoon of privates clipping hedges at a government minister's house or parking cars at a swank diplomatic reception at the Ducor Hotel.

Samuel Doe, the slim, sad-eyed sergeant who rose through the ranks under the old regime only to play a leading role in the coup, came from the smallish Krahn tribe of distant Grand Gedeh County, favored by recruiting officers for their martial traditions. In an interview five years after taking power, Doe recalled no particular ambition to join the army; his preference had been vocational training at the Booker T. Washington Institute and a career as an electrician.

But when promised a scholarship in 1969, either in his eighteenth or nineteenth year, he enlisted. Smart and willing to follow orders, his ascent was swift. By the late 1970s, he had been promoted to master sergeant, becoming the highest-ranking noncommissioned officer in the AFL. An impressed Tolbert put him in charge of transport for the OAU summit.

Doe remembered his experiences differently. His recollections are filled with perceived slights and insults: overlooked for a training course in the United States, forced to pay for his own education, and even denied leave to attend his high school graduation. At the Barracks Union night school he was taught by, among others, Amos Sawyer. He learned to read and write, and at the same time received a political education: Marxism, African nationalism, Third World liberation, and the bitter history of settler-native relations were all part of the curriculum. Doe either did not hear, or chose to ignore, his professor's caveat: that change must come peacefully, through the political process.

Much about the 1980 coup that ended the 133-year rule of the Americo-Liberian elite remains murky, even basic matters such as the number of participants and the identities of its leaders. Doe, the ranking member of the fifteen- (or sixteen- or seventeen-) man team that burst into the Executive Mansion in the early morning hours of April 12 and murdered the president in his pajamas, was quickly dubbed the mastermind. But there are many people, including Doe himself, who insist that he was a reluctant participant, only joining his fellow soldiers after the initial plans had been drawn up. The true ringleader, according to this version of events, was one Thomas Quiwonkpa, a popular NCO from the larger Gio tribe. Doe was recruited later because he was the highest-ranking enlisted man. If this is true, his emergence as head of the People's Redemption Council (PRC), the governing entity in the wake of the coup, was almost accidental. He was supposed to be a placeholder until new presidential elections, which Quiwonkpa expected to win, could be held.*

In any case, each man would have been motivated by a nagging sense of injustice, radical ideas propounded by MOJA and the PAL/PPP, the miserable living conditions of the men they led, the orders they received to shoot their countrymen during the rice riots, and the humiliation they felt at Tolbert's use of Guinean troops to finally restore order. Indeed, the planning of the coup is believed to have begun shortly after the rice riots.

But it was the events of March and April 1980, in the last scorching days of the dry season, that gave the conspirators a sense of urgency. Tolbert was lashing out against enemies real and imagined, including those at the barracks. Officers perceived as sympathetic to the radicals were being thrown in the brig. Rumors were circulating that True Whig hard-liners were finalizing coup plans of their own and that the CIA, upset by Tolbert's abandonment of Tubman's pro-American foreign policy, was involved in them. Most pressing was the rumor that Chesson planned to preempt the April 14 trial of Matthews, Cheapoo, and other jailed PPP leaders and have the men summarily executed.

The soldiers put their plans into action on the evening of April 11. To ensure that Tolbert, who usually slept at his well-fortified, upcountry compound, was at the mansion, they recruited his chauffeur to tip them off. The men gathered on the beach behind the mansion and broke into two groups; one would enter the residence and the other would provide backup in case troops loyal to Tolbert tried to intervene. Then, according to several accounts, the first group walked across the expansive mansion lawn and knocked on the front door.

It was all over in about an hour. Conspirators on Tolbert's household staff let the soldiers in. They raided the armory—the poorly armed men had only two rifles between them—gunned down the surprised

*After years during which the two men grew increasingly estranged over Doe's autocratic tendencies and his favoritism toward his fellow Krahn, Quiwonkpa would launch a rebellion from Sierra Leone in 1985. It failed, and Doe had Quiwonkpa hunted down and executed.

guards, and made their way to Tolbert's eighth-floor bedroom. Why Tolbert did not escape is unclear; the bedroom was connected to a basement tunnel that led to the beach via a secret elevator, though it may have been out of order. The president's wife, Victoria, later said she was woken from a fitful sleep by the sound of gunfire, but that her husband dismissed her fears. She also insisted that the men who broke into her bedroom were "virtually naked and horrifying[ly] masked . . . like the warriors . . . during Liberia's tribal wars," but no other account confirms this.[22] Tolbert, half dressed, pleaded for his life, even offering the soldiers a suitcase filled with American dollars he kept in his room. He then ran into the hallway, where he was shot and his throat was cut. According to Quiwonkpa, he was trying to make an escape. Mrs. Tolbert, perhaps trying to put her late husband in a better light, later claimed that he was rushing to check on his grandchildren, who were staying at the mansion that night.

Doe's presence and actions during these events have not been proven. Most witnesses place him with the troops outside the mansion. Quiwonkpa was particularly dismissive. "I swear to my God, Doe did not fire one shot at Tolbert," he told an interviewer in 1985, months before he would lead his own failed coup against Doe. "He was hiding in the flower bushes around the mansion when we went on to the eighth floor."[23] Doe himself would remain vague on the events of that night.

But all that matters is where Doe was the next morning: in the broadcast booth of the national radio station, announcing to the Liberian people that Tolbert was dead, the PRC was in power, and that a new day had dawned. He spoke in a country English that no Liberian had ever heard coming from the radio before. "Gone forever are the days of 'Who you know?' and 'Do you know who I am?'" he told listeners two days later in his first formal address as chairman of the PRC. "We now enter the time of 'What can you do?' This is the people's thing, our people's thing . . . Long live the People's Redemption Council! Long live the Republic of Liberia!"[24]

Liberians danced in the streets of Monrovia. "There is little doubt that Sergeant Doe is popular here," noted a *New York Times* reporter, who followed him on a triumphant tour of Monrovia's back alleys a few days later. "[He] was greeted by thousands who struggled to touch him. When he smiled the crowds roared and when he waved they cheered."[25]

Doe also became popular with the agitators and intellectuals who had fostered his political worldview. He understood that he and his men, many of them illiterate, could not run a government, so he had the old settler elite dismissed from their posts and the young radicals, sprung from jail, put in their place: Matthews at the foreign ministry; the Susukuu head, Tipoteh, at the planning bureau. And Chesson was replaced in the biggest office at the modernist, eight-story Justice Department building on Ashmun Street by his prodigal foster son, Chea Cheapoo.

The Americo-Liberian era had come to an end. The old guard had not just lost their jobs, but their status, their privileges, and their property. Survivors would later describe a world turned upside down. The former first lady Victoria Tolbert recalled a dark basement room at the Executive Mansion where she was imprisoned without food and water for days. Defense minister and Tolbert son-in-law M. Burleigh Holder remembered feeling his way through the jungle outskirts of the capital amid a ferocious downpour, futilely attempting to escape his pursuers. On the streets of Monrovia, drunken soldiers careened through the capital in stolen Lincolns and Chevrolets they did not know how to drive, breaking through the gates of Americo villas in the better parts of town. Anybody with light skin or a settler pedigree was taunted by crowds and then beaten by men in uniform. Elite women were raped.

The ruling Americo men were rounded up and thrown naked into cells at the Barclay Training Center, where just hours before, the radicals themselves had been held. Foreign Minister Cecil Dennis, the True Whig Party chairman, Clarence Parker, the senate leader and president's brother Frank Tolbert, and the white-haired Chesson, perhaps the most hated man in the republic, were charged with corruption, treason, violation of human rights, and anything else the PRC could think of, legitimate or not.

Within days, the men were paraded into a makeshift courtroom in front of a five-member military tribunal. The ex–finance minister J. T. Phillips displayed bruises from a recent pistol-whipping; Dennis had nothing on but a pair of jeans.

If the old Americo regime had hewn to the letter of the law while ignoring its spirit, the new did away with all pretenses.

"Mr. [Frank] Stewart," one of the judges demanded of the former budget director, "how many houses you got?"

"Four . . . but in 1957, the price of cement was very cheap, so my wife . . . and I . . . we used small loans from the bank, and for seven years we worked building the blocks we needed to construct . . ."

Another judge broke in, "Holy Christ, cut this short or we goin' to be sittin' here right through lunch."[26]

Cutting things short was exactly what Doe did, as Stewart and twelve other top Tolbert administration officials, including Chesson, were dragged to a Monrovia beach, lassoed to hastily erected telephone polls, and shot to death by members of the Armed Forces of Liberia on April 22, just ten days after the coup.

And Cheapoo? Most of the survivors from the old regime held him, as attorney general, responsible for both the kangaroo court and the executions that followed, including that of his foster father. They paint a portrait of a cruel, vindictive individual. Victoria Tolbert remembers that he tried to shake her down for a million-dollar ransom. The future president Ellen Johnson Sirleaf, then the minister of finance, spared from execution by her record of public outspokenness against the administration she served in, said he had her brother jailed because he had laughed at Cheapoo years before, after his impeachment. He put dozens of executives at state-owned corporations, both Liberian and foreign, under house arrest until their books could be checked, and he pushed hard for more trials of former government officials.

But Cheapoo always maintained his innocence, insisting that the soldiers, not civilians like him, were ultimately the ones in charge. In his lengthy 2008 testimony before the post-civil-war, South African–style Truth and Reconciliation Commission, he told of being at lunch at a Lebanese friend's restaurant downtown on the afternoon of April 22, only hearing about the executions a few hours later from a secretary in his office. Then, in a steady voice, he spoke to the commission of his late foster father. "Chesson helped me to be where I am, he fed me, he clothed me, advised me. I got to be a lawyer because I wanted to be like him . . . When I was in prison . . . he always sent people in the jail to ask about me and he put it that way for the soldiers to know that he had dealing with me [i.e., was looking out for me]. So I couldn't have gone to kill Papa Chesson . . . I didn't have any animosity against him . . . I didn't kill my father."[27]

Perhaps not literally. But the revolution Cheapoo and other young radicals midwifed during the "year of ferment" between the rice riot of April 1979 and the coup of April 1980 killed their fathers' Liberia.[28] And tragically, the coup and executions were but a prelude to the unspeakable horror just over the horizon. However corrupt, unjust, incompetent, and occasionally brutal the Americo regime had been across its 133-year reign, its crimes paled in comparison with the dictatorships, invasions, assassinations, civil wars, and anarchy that followed.

As for the people who built that regime—the ultimate survivors in a hostile world, who struggled from the very beginning to live up to the high ideals on which their great and worthy endeavor was founded, but who so often fell short—they would be scattered far and wide.

Epilogue

Just about every Americo with an overseas bank account, an American passport, or stateside connections fled the country after the coup. Ironically, many ended up in Virginia, Maryland, and New York, states their ancestors had left more than a century before, and for much the same reason: to escape persecution for the color—in this case, the light brown—of their skin.

The young radicals Doe put in charge of the nation's ministries saw the downfall of the old regime and the departure of its constituents as an opportunity for root-and-branch reform. Planning director Togba Nah Tipoteh, founder of the grassroots cooperative Susukuu, launched a long-overdue land reform program. Education minister Henry Boima Fahnbulleh, Jr., whose grandfather was the ambassador Tubman had sacked for wearing a Mao pin, ordered an Afrocentric revamping of the nation's schoolbooks. Amos Sawyer, the University of Liberia academic who had founded the Barracks Union night school that had radicalized Doe and his fellow coup makers, helped draw up a new constitution, which was eventually ratified in a national plebiscite. There were symbolic changes, too. The Pioneer Room at the Hotel Africa, where Tolbert had hosted the OAU meeting a year before, was renamed the Native Room, while Independence Day celebrations were moved to April 12, the day of the coup, though this latter change never really caught on.

But the post-coup alliance of radical intellectuals and barely literate soldiers soon unraveled. Within a couple of years most of the former had quit their posts, frustrated by the incompetence of the PRC
inner circle and its growing repressiveness and venality. They were
powerless, too, especially after the Reagan administration began lavishing military and foreign aid on Doe, whom it saw as a Cold War
ally. Doe reciprocated by ending Tolbert's nonaligned foreign policy
and giving the CIA the run of the country, which included use of its
main airfield to transship arms to the Reagan administration's favorite African "freedom fighter," Jonas Savimbi of Angola. There was no
small irony in this. For more than a century, Americo-Liberians had
looked upon their ancestral land as a paternal protector, a role America accepted with great reluctance. Now, with the Americoes gone,
the two countries grew closer than ever, revealing a fundamental truth
about U.S. attitudes toward its African stepchild: that America stood
by Liberia only when it was in its own self-interest to do so.

Meanwhile, Doe abandoned the sentiments that had pitted him
against the old regime. Photos from the period show the sinewy army
sergeant who favored fatigues even at diplomatic receptions becoming a jowly head of state with a taste for three-piece suits. He was Dr.
Doe now, having received an honorary degree from a South Korean
university. (South Korea's government wanted a development contract.) He abandoned his modest Monrovia apartment for the Executive Mansion while his wife, having confiscated Victoria Tolbert's
Mercedes-Benz, insisted on a police escort to the supermarket. The
garish national celebrations of his birthday recalled the Tubman era,
except that Doe had to pay for the parties himself. Indeed, he became obsessed with the old man, endlessly watching films of him in
the Executive Mansion movie theater late at night.

Like his idol, Doe had no intention of leaving office, except to be
buried. The 1985 elections meant to inaugurate the Second Republic
were remarkably similar to those that characterized the First: a thin
veneer of legitimacy on top of utter fraudulence. Just to be able to
run, Doe had to backdate his birth to meet the new constitutional

age requirement of thirty-five. During the election itself, he stopped the counting of votes when things started to go against him, and had the ballots trucked to a suite at the Hotel Africa, where his electoral commission announced the final tally: the president had retained his office by a convenient, runoff-avoiding margin of 50.9 percent. "Unheard of in the rest of Africa, where incumbent rulers normally claim victories of 95 to 100 percent," a blithe American Under-Secretary of State Chester Crocker told a U.S. Senate committee.[1]

A month later, after a failed putsch by his former co-conspirator and current rival for the army's allegiance, Thomas Quiwonkpa, Doe unleashed the dogs of civil war. Liberia's borders contain sixteen ethnic groups, not counting the Americoes. For 133 years the natives had quarreled among one another, forming alliances at times and generally scrambling for the leftovers from the settlers' table. Doe's policies had favored his fellow Krahn, throwing off this delicate balance. The other tribes began to direct their anger over the corruption, brutality, and favoritism of the regime not just at Doe but at the Krahn too. Quiwonkpa's coup attempt on November 12, 1985, resulted in both Doe and his tribe's growing even more isolated, as well as paranoid. Doe had the well-armed Krahn attack Quiwonkpa's Gio tribesmen and their ethnic cousins the Manos. The result was a bloodbath.

The Gio and the Manos became the first to rally to the banner raised on Christmas Eve, 1989, by a most unlikely savior: Charles McArthur Ghankay Taylor. "We didn't even have to act," Taylor recalled of the weeks that followed his tiny force's invasion across the Liberian border from Côte d'Ivoire. "People came to us and said: 'Give me a gun. How can I kill the man who killed my mother?'"[2]

Taylor was Liberia's recent history in the flesh. His father was an Americo judge. At his elite prep school outside Monrovia, he learned the national myths about Liberia as a tropical outpost of American democracy, Western civilization, and evangelical Protestantism. But like many of his generation, Taylor had no patience for the pieties of his homeland, and got himself expelled for organizing protests against the Americo establishment. His rebelliousness likely stemmed, at least in part, from his status as a half-breed. His mother was a Gola woman, and he knew that despite his father's high standing he would never truly be accepted as a member of the ruling caste. But Taylor was not an idealist or an ideologue. His only loyalty was to himself.

During the 1970s, the smart and ambitious Taylor moved up the ranks of the protest movement that opposed the True Whigs. He attended college in Waltham, Massachusetts, and, in 1979, organized a demonstration outside Liberia's mission in New York to protest a visit by Tolbert, who then challenged Taylor to a debate. By all accounts, the young protest leader won every point but one. When he demanded the keys to the mission, embassy officials had the NYPD throw him in jail.

Tolbert, however, refused to press charges and invited Taylor, whose father he of course knew, back to Liberia, perhaps impressed by his opportunism. Within the year, Tolbert was dead and Doe was in power. Taylor's powers of persuasion allowed him to not only survive the coup, but to thrive in the new order. He was hired to run the government's purchasing agency, a dream sinecure for any would-be embezzler, and greed got the better of him. Charged with stealing nearly a million dollars, in 1983 Taylor fled to America, where, per a request from Monrovia, U.S. authorities had him locked up in a Massachusetts prison to await extradition. But he escaped. After Taylor's rise as a warlord, sensational stories about the exploit started to circulate. Half myth and all Hollywood, these involved a girlfriend baking a key into a cake and a midnight shimmy down a rope made of sheets. Journalists who followed his career say it is more likely that he bribed some guards. Whatever the means, Taylor quickly fled to Mexico, eventually making his way back to West Africa, where he planned a very different kind of homecoming.

At the time, the region was still fractured along old imperial lines. A Nigerian-led bloc of Anglophone states that had largely made their peace with Doe competed for influence with a Francophone alliance headed by Côte d'Ivoire's president-for-life, Félix Houphouët-Boigny, who despised the murderer of his good friend William Tolbert and Tolbert's son, and his own son-in-law, Adolphus. Muammar Qaddafi entered the fray, too, after his bid to lead the Arab world had been rejected; Africa was the new object of his megalomania. He sent aid to rebel groups and regimes across the continent, including Taylor's. He even brought Taylor's tiny militia of disgruntled and exiled Gio and Mano men, recruited in Ivory Coast and Guinea, to Libya for training, hoping that it would topple Doe's pro-American government.

Liberians' hatred of the Doe regime sent thousands flocking to the banner of Taylor's National Patriotic Front of Liberia. By the summer of 1990, Taylor's forces were on the outskirts of Monrovia. But Nigeria had no intention of allowing Liberia to become a satellite of Houphouët-Boigny or, worse, Qaddafi. Under the aegis of the Economic Community of West African States (ECOWAS), a peacekeeping force known as ECOMOG—anti-Taylor in all but name—was dispatched to Liberia. At the same time, one of Taylor's own, the mercurial Prince Johnson, broke with him and occupied key parts of Monrovia.

Doe refused to surrender, convinced there was bad magic at work beyond the Executive Mansion's perimeter manned by his elite Israeli-trained Krahn commandoes. (Taylor had secured the support of the country's *zoes*, or shamans.) Guaranteed safe passage to America or Nigeria by ECOMOG, Doe finally gave in, only to fall into the hands of the semipsychotic Johnson. Video footage of the former dictator's dismemberment in front of the beer-swilling warlord can still be viewed on YouTube.

The next six years were the bloodiest in Liberian history. Taylor launched assault after assault on Johnson in Monrovia, paying for weapons with the nation's resources. His troops, including brigades of drug-addled child soldiers, fought for themselves rather than for Taylor or for a united Liberia; one late offensive was dubbed

"Operation Pay Yourself." Taylor's troops split along tribal lines and warred among themselves. Liberia's civilians were caught in the middle. About a million people, almost half the country, fled to surrounding states or ECOMOG-controlled Monrovia, which, despite Taylor's periodic assaults, was still safer than the war-torn countryside. These refugees lived in bombed-out office and government buildings. Smoke from their cooking fires wafted out of the grand Masonic Temple on Snapper Hill.

They were the lucky ones. The barbarity unleashed by the Liberian civil war beggars the imagination: teenagers forced to kill their parents to prove their allegiance to one side or another, pregnant women bayoneted by rebels betting on the sex of their fetus, once-respected elders ordered by soldiers young enough to be their grandchildren to "give me six feet," meaning dig their own graves.[3] Estimates of the death toll vary widely, but no figure is less than 100,000, out of a prewar population of 2.5 million. It is rare today to find a Liberian who has not personally witnessed a murder, often of a loved one.

The warlords responsible for this carnage encouraged it as part of their attempts to plunder the nation's timber and mineral resources. Some of them had been native wards of leading Americo families, with degrees from American universities and ministry portfolios on their résumés. All were terrified of Taylor. ECOWAS and regional leaders organized numerous peace conferences; President Jerry Rawlings of Ghana invited Liberian warlords to settle their differences on a yacht on Lake Volta. Liberian wits suggested his peace plan was to sink the boat.

Eventually, war-weariness, international pressure, and, most important, Taylor and ECOMOG's recognition that the impasse would not be resolved by force, led to a working peace agreement. A bolstered ECOMOG contingent arrived, the general disarmament of the country was set in motion, and warlords were permitted to compete in national elections, which had been a point of disagreement in previous proposals.

Taylor possessed the resources to win the 1997 election, as well as a trump card: a vote against him was a vote to restart the war. Like Captain Stockton, whose threat forced King Peter to cede the land at Cape Mesurado 156 years before, Taylor had a gun to Liberia's head. "He kill my ma, he kill my pa, I'm gonna vote for him," was the chant that went up from crowds wherever he spoke.[4] He won 75 percent of the vote in an internationally monitored election, with Jimmy Carter asserting its fairness. At his inauguration, the self-declared, born-again Baptist Taylor vowed "not to be a wicked president."[5]

Taylor's tenure in the Executive Mansion was, like Doe's before him, corrupt, incompetent, and repressive. During his six years in power, the government remained insolvent, newspaper presses were routinely shut down, and the lights in Monrovia, which went out when the electrical grid was destroyed in one of Taylor's wartime assaults on the city, never came back on. While his henchmen stole with abandon and terrorized an already shaken citizenry, Taylor strove for hegemony over his own small corner of Africa. He revived his former alliance with the sociopathic Foday Sankoh and his Revolutionary United Front (RUF) rebels in neighboring Sierra Leone. Their preferred mode of persuasion was to cut off, quite literally, the hands raised against them, even those only casting a ballot. Taylor gave them guns and they supplied him with diamonds.

It took substantially less time for Taylor's regime to come undone than it had Doe's. The first to rebel were persecuted Mandingo refugees, members of one of the losing factions from the previous conflict, who launched an attack from Guinea in 1999. They styled themselves the Liberians United for Reconciliation and Democracy (LURD) and, like Taylor's NPFL before them, quickly swept across the country, only to be halted at Monrovia's gates. In 2003, they were joined by former Doe loyalists invading from Côte d'Ivoire, which, with Houphouët-Boigny dead ten years, was embroiled in a civil war of its own. LURD and the Movement for Democracy in Liberia (MODEL) attacked Monrovia in a pincer formation.

At the same time, the international community began to intervene in a serious way. In response to Taylor's support for the RUF, the

United Nations imposed an arms embargo on the country, though because Taylor did most of his business on the black market, this had little impact. Washington, long wary of Taylor for his Libyan connections, supported the UN's actions. Even a number of his allies in the region abandoned him, including the mercurial Qaddafi, now eager to appease the West. Then, in June, Taylor became the first sitting head of state to be indicted on charges of international war crimes. But not for his actions in Liberia—he was accused, rather, of abetting the horrific war crimes of his RUF allies in Sierra Leone.

Cheered by most Liberians in the country and abroad, the indictment by the International Criminal Court's Special Court for Sierra Leone only stiffened Taylor's resistance. The mass actions of Liberian women, under the leadership of the thirty-one-year-old activist and future Nobel Peace Prize laureate Leymah Gbowee, finally convinced him to attend peace talks in Ghana and sign a cease-fire agreement. Still, it was only when Nigeria offered Taylor asylum and Switzerland froze his bank account that he agreed to leave the country. Into the vacuum stepped 15,000 UN peacekeepers, the largest such mission undertaken to that date.

The years since Taylor's departure from Liberia have been happier for the country than they have been for its former president. The 2005 election and 2011 reelection of Ellen Johnson Sirleaf, a tough former finance minister and World Bank official, has brought economic competence to the Liberian government for the first time. Opposition figures—notably, the international soccer star George Weah and Winston Tubman, nephew of Old Man Tubman—have raised Johnson Sirleaf's past errors, including her work for Doe and her brief flirtation with Taylor's NPFL, and pointed at her current failings. Both have accused her followers of stealing votes, though there is little evidence to support these accusations. Johnson Sirleaf has also controversially opened Liberia to foreign investors, much as Tubman had done; at one point in her administration, a third of the country was leased for timber, mining, and agribusiness enterprises. Then as now, it is a sensitive point for Liberians. There have also been persistent rumors that the light-skinned Johnson Sirleaf is an Americo, or part Americo. In fact, she is three-quarters native, of Gola and Kru background. Her complexion comes from her maternal grandfather, a German trader.

The Liberian Iron Lady—Africa's first elected woman head of state—has had many unequivocal successes. She won international debt forgiveness for Liberia, launched a South African–style Truth and Reconciliation Commission, and raised Liberia's standing from 150th to 75th on Transparency International's corruption perceptions index. She has turned the lights back on in Monrovia. And, in 2011, she was co-awarded the Nobel Peace Prize with Gbowee and a Yemeni women's peace activist.*

For a time, Taylor dreamed of reclaiming the presidency, or at least his influence. From the old British governor's residence in seaside Calabar, he kept in touch with his many supporters in Liberia and was rumored to have ties to Weah's people, if not Weah himself. But Nigeria's president, Olusegun Obasanjo, made it known that as soon as Liberia had a government capable of making the request, he would extradite Taylor to Sierra Leone for the trial. Yet Sierra Leone feared that his presence could open old wounds and even lead to renewal of civil war. A complicated deal was struck. A branch of the Special Court would be established at the International Criminal Court in The Hague to try him and, assuming a guilty verdict, a prison cell would await him in Britain, Sierra Leone's former imperialist ruler.

When Taylor heard of the deal, he fled Calabar for the nearby Cameroon frontier, where his Range Rover, bearing diplomatic plates and packed with bags of U.S. hundred-dollar bills, was apprehended by suspicious Nigerian border guards on March 29, 2006. Three

---

*The prize did not come without controversy. Johnson Sirleaf was awarded the Nobel on the eve of her 2011 reelection, triggering cries from the opposition about foreign interference and favoritism.

months later, after pleading not guilty on all charges of arming the RUF, Taylor found himself in a jail cell in The Hague. His trial lasted nearly six years, ending with his conviction on April 26, 2012. A month later, the sixty-four-year-old Taylor was sentenced to fifty years in prison. Other than his family—his eldest son, "Chuckie," is currently serving a ninety-seven-year sentence in the United States for human rights violations he committed as his father's chief of security—and die-hard supporters, few have mourned Taylor's fate.

The society the Americo-Liberians created is no more. The Americoes themselves live on, though the number of people who can trace an unbroken ancestry to North American roots diminished considerably after World War II, as intermarriage among native and settler families became commonplace. Measuring their influence today is more difficult. "They are gone," a University of Liberia dean assured me in his bullet-pocked office in 1997, "and they are not coming back. The Liberian reality today is that no one group can dominate anymore."[6] The second part may be true, but Americoes have been overrepresented in every government since Doe's 1980 coup, including the current one. They still own an outsize portion of the country's lands and businesses, especially now that old property claims have been restored. This has led Liberian conspiracy theorists to conclude that the Americoes are still running things as they did under the first republic, except now from behind the scenes. Given Liberia's history of Masonic cabals and True Whig electoral manipulation, this view is not an unreasonable one. But it distorts the country's contemporary reality. In the wake of the great social upheavals and transformations of the late twentieth and early twenty-first centuries, the term "Americo" no longer serves as a synonym for "elite."

To the contemporary visitor, the Americoes' presence is spectral, though less haunting. Traveling outward from Monrovia on the poorly maintained roads that Tubman built in the 1950s and 1960s, one first comes across the split-levels and ranch homes the Americoes built in the capital's upscale suburbs, now occupied by native squatters. Deeper into the hinterland one can still see the odd plantation manse, overgrown by jungle. And, with an ear to history, the echoes of the early pioneers can still be heard: "It is a pleasant country . . . all things are plenty, the leaves are all green, the sufferings of slavery are nowhere to be seen, all men enjoying their rights and liberties under their own vine and fig-tree, with none to make them afraid."[7]

Though they may not have made it a reality, the Americoes enshrined that vision. Today, on the crumbling facades of government buildings, on every document submitted to a bureaucrat or judge, and on the frayed Liberian dollar bills stuffed in the pockets of roadside market women there appears the Great Seal of Liberia, depicting a silhouette of the *Elizabeth*, the ship that brought the first settlers to Africa in 1820, below the national motto: THE LOVE OF LIBERTY BROUGHT US HERE. Once the claim of a despised and exiled minority, it now belongs to every Liberian.

NOTES

Preface

1. Johnson Sirleaf, Ellen. *This Child Will Be Great: Memoir of a Remarkable Lady by Africa's First Woman President*. New York: HarperCollins, 2009: 84.
2. "Liberian Firing Squad Executes 13 Officials as Thousands Cheer," *New York Times*, April 23, 1980: A1+.
3. Letter from Peyton Skipwith to John Cocke, April 22, 1840. In Miller, Randall M. (ed.), *Dear Master: Letters of a Slave Family*. Athens: University of Georgia Press, 1990: 75.

1. The Black *Mayflower*

1. Coker, Daniel. *Journal of Daniel Coker*. Baltimore: Edward J. Coale, 1820: 10.
2. Ibid.
3. "A Counter-Memorial proposed to be submitted to Congress in behalf of the free people of colour of the District of Columbia," *National Intelligencer*, December 30, 1816.
4. *Sermon Delivered Extempore in the African Bethel Church in the City of Baltimore on the 21st January, 1816* (n.p.), 1816.
5. Jefferson, Thomas. *Notes on the State of Virginia*. New York: Library of America, 1993 (originally published 1787): 270.
6. Alexander, Archibald. *A History of Colonization on the Western Coast of Africa*. Freeport, NY: Books for the Libraries Press, 1971 (originally published 1849): 81–82.
7. Quarles, Benjamin. *Black Abolitionists*. New York: Oxford University Press, 1969: 4.
8. Grimke, Charlotte Forten. "Personal Recollections of Whittier," *The New England Magazine*, volume 8 (March 1893–August 1893): 468.

9. "A Voice from Philadelphia, January 1817." In Garrison, William Lloyd, *Thoughts on African Colonization* (preface by William Loren Katz). New York: Arno Press, 1969 (originally published 1832): part 1, page 9.

10. Ibid.

11. Litwack, Leon. *North of Slavery: The Negro in the Free States, 1790–1860*. Chicago: University of Chicago Press, 1961: 25.

12. Ashmun, Jehudi (ed.). *Memoir of the Life and Character of the Rev. Samuel Bacon*. Freeport, NY: Books for Libraries Press, 1971 (reprint, original 1822): 249.

13. Coker. *Journal*: 19.

14. Ibid.

15. Ibid.: 20.

16. Ibid.: 19.

17. "Letter from Nathaniel Peck to His Mother in Baltimore." In Coker, *Journal*: 45.

18. Ibid.: 46.

19. Ibid.: 24.

20. Alexander. *History of Colonization*: 120.

21. Ibid.: 123.

22. Ashmun. *Memoir of Samuel Bacon*: 267.

23. Alexander. *History of Colonization*: 122.

24. Ashmun. *Memoir of Samuel Bacon*: 264.

25. Letter from John Dix to Edward Trenchard, November 22, 1820. Reprinted in Huberich, Charles, *The Political and Legislative History of Liberia* (volume 1). New York: Central Book Company, 1947: 131.

26. Alexander. *History of Colonization*: 121.

27. Letter from John Dix to Edward Trenchard, November 22, 1820. Reprinted in Huberich, *Political and Legislative History*: 130.

28. Coker. *Journal*: 38.

29. Ibid.: 131.

30. Alexander. *History of Colonization*: 126.

31. Letter from Daniel Coker to Jeremiah Watts, April 3, 1820. Reprinted in Coker, *Journal*: 43.

32. Coker. *Journal*: 36.

33. Alexander. *History of Colonization*: 131.

34. "Inventory of the Church Archives of Virginia (Negro Baptist Churches in Richmond)." Richmond: Historical Records Survey of Virginia, June 1940.

35. Taylor, J. B. *Biography of Elder Lott Cary, Late Missionary to Africa*. Baltimore: Armstrong & Berry, 1837: 13.

36. Peck, Solomon (ed.). "History of the Missions of the Baptist General Convention." In *M. Spooner & H. J. Howland's History of American Missions to the Heathens*. Worcester, MA: Spooner & Howland, 1840: 444.

37. Taylor. *Biography of Lott Cary*: 34.

38. Ibid.: 29–30.
39. Ibid.

2. Original Sin

1. Quoted in Stockwell, S. *The Republic of Liberia: Its Geography, Climate, Soil, and Productions, with a History of Its Early Settlement.* New York: A. S. Barnes & Co., 1868: 10.
2. Williams, Samuel. "Four Years in Liberia: A Sketch of the Life of the Rev. Samuel Williams." In Moses, Wilson Jeremiah (ed.), *Liberian Dreams: Back-to-Africa Narratives from the 1850s.* University Park: Pennsylvania State University Press, 1998: 138.
3. Nesbit, William. "Four Months in Liberia: Or African Colonization Exposed," 1855. In Moses, *Liberian Dreams*: 95.
4. Ibid.: 116.
5. "Four Years in Liberia." In Moses, *Liberian Dreams*: 137–38.
6. Letter from Robert Stockton to the American Colonization Society, December 16, 1821. Reprinted in Huberich, Charles, *The Political and Legislative History of Liberia* (volume 1). New York: Central Book Company, 1947: 193.
7. Letter from Eli Ayres to the American Colonization Society, December 11, 1821. In Huberich, *Political and Legislative History*: 187.
8. Ibid.: 188.
9. Ibid.
10. Ibid.
11. Ibid.
12. Ibid.: 189.
13. Ibid.: 190.
14. Ibid.
15. Ibid.
16. Taylor, J. B. *Biography of Elder Lott Cary, Late Missionary to Africa.* Baltimore: Armstrong & Berry, 1837: 36–37.
17. Letter from Eli Ayres to E. B. Caldwell, August 23, 1822. In Huberich, *Political and Legislative History*: 209–10.
18. Henries, A. Doris Banks. *Heroes and Heroines of Liberia.* New York: Macmillan, 1962: 15.
19. *American Repository and Colonial Journal*, volume 2, number 5 (July 1826): 142.
20. Letter from Ayres to Caldwell, August 23, 1822. In Huberich, *Political and Legislative History*: 208–209.
21. Ibid.: 209–10.
22. Ibid.: 210.
23. Ibid.: 212.

24. Johnson, Charles. *Bitter Canaan: The Story of the Negro Republic*. New Brunswick, NJ: Transaction Books, 1987 (reprint of 1930 edition): 47.

25. Ashmun, Jehudi. Colonial Journal, August 31, 1822. In American Colonization Society, *The Annual Reports of the American Society for Colonizing the Free People of Colour of the United States* (volume VI, 1824). New York: Negro Universities Press, 1969: 30–31.

26. Ibid.: 31.

27. Ibid.

28. Ibid.

29. Gurley, Ralph Randolph. *Life of Jehudi Ashmun*. New York: Negro Universities Press, 1969 (reprint of 1835 edition): 127–28.

30. Ashmun. Colonial Journal, August 31, 1822. In ACS. *Annual Reports*, volume VI: 31.

31. Ashmun, Jehudi. "Memoir of the Sufferings, &c. of the American Colonists." In *African Repository*, volume 2, number 6 (August 1826): 178.

32. Ibid.: 178–79.

33. Ibid.: 182.

34. Ibid.: 183.

35. Ashmun. "Memoir of the Sufferings." In *African Repository*, volume 2, number 7 (September 1826): 215.

36. Ibid.: 216.

37. Report of Robert Spence to the Secretary of the Navy, June 27, 1823. In Huberich, *Political and Legislative History*: 287–88.

38. Ashmun, J. *History of the American Colony*: 40.

39. Ashmun. "Memoir of the Sufferings": 218.

40. Huberich. *Political and Legislative History*: 298.

41. Letter from Eli Ayres to American Colonization Society Board, February 18, 1824. In Huberich, *Political and Legislative History*: 221.

42. Ashmun. "Sketch of the Life of the Rev. Lott Cary." In Gurley, *Life of Jehudi Ashmun*: appendix page 150.

43. Ashmun, Jehudi. Colonial Journal, September 25, 1824. In Gurley, *Life of Jehudi Ashmun*: appendix pages 52–53.

44. Alexander, Archibald. *A History of Colonization on the Western Coast of Africa*. Freeport, NY: Books for the Libraries Press, 1971 (originally published 1849): 217–18.

45. Taylor. *Biography of Lott Cary*: 48–49.

46. Ashmun. "Sketch of the Life of the Rev. Lott Cary." In Gurley, *Life of Jehudi Ashmun*: appendix page 151.

47. Fitts, Leroy. *Lott Carey: First Black Missionary to Africa*. Valley Forge, PA: Judson Press, 1978: 56.

48. Taylor. *Biography of Lott Cary*: 94.

3. First Families and Fresh Graves

1. Washington, Augustus. "Liberia as It Is, 1854." In Moses, Wilson Jeremiah (ed.), *Liberian Dreams: Back-to-Africa Narratives from the 1850s*. University Park: Pennsylvania State University Press, 1998: 206.

2. Letter from Peyton Skipwith to John Hartwell Cocke, February 10, 1834. In Miller, Randall M. (ed.), *Dear Master: Letters of a Slave Family*. Athens: University of Georgia Press, 1990: 58–59.

3. Letter from Abraham Blackford to Mary B. Blackford, September 9, 1844. In Wiley, Bell I. (ed.), *Slaves No More: Letters from Liberia, 1833–1869*. Lexington: University Press of Kentucky, 1980: 21–22.

4. Letter from James C. Minor to John Minor, February 11, 1833. In Wiley, *Slaves No More*: 16.

5. Letter from Peyton Skipwith to John Hartwell Cocke, March 6, 1835. In Miller, *Dear Master*: 59.

6. Welch, Galbraith. *The Jet Lighthouse*. London: Museum Press, 1960: 193.

7. Burin, Eric. *Slavery and the Peculiar Solution: A History of the American Colonization Society*. Gainesville: University Press of Florida, 2005: 26, 148.

8. Ibid.: 148.

9. Clegg, Claude A. III. *The Price of Liberty: African Americans and the Making of Liberia*. Chapel Hill: University of North Carolina Press, 2004: 64.

10. "Latest from Liberia." In *African Repository and Colonial Journal*, volume 4, number 9 (November 1829): 282–83.

11. Letter from Virgil P. McParrhan to P. C. Cameron, May 29, 1848. In Wiley, *Slaves No More*: 261.

12. Letter from Ezekiel Skinner to American Colonization Board, January 17, 1837. In Huberich, Charles, *The Political and Legislative History of Liberia* (volume 1). New York: Central Book Company, 1947: 509.

13. Letter from A. D. Williams to the ACS Board. In Huberich, *Political and Legislative History*: 537.

14. Letter from William C. Burke to Ralph R. Gurley, March 6, 1857. In Wiley, *Slaves No More*: 196–97.

15. Letter from Jane Hawkins to the American Colonization Society, July 26, 1836. Papers of the American Colonization Society, Library of Congress.

16. "Latest from Liberia." In *African Repository*, volume 8, number 10 (December 1832): 298.

17. Letter from Washington W. McDonough to John McDonough, September 15, 1842. In Wiley, *Slaves No More*: 121–22.

18. Letter from Ezekiel Skinner to ACS Board, January 17, 1837. In Huberich, *Political and Legislative History*: 509.

19. Letter from George R. Ellis McDonough to John McDonough, March 25, 1847. In Ibid.: 145.

20. Letter from Diana Skipwith to Sally Cocke, August 24, 1837. In Miller, *Dear Master*. 1990: 87–88.

21. Letter from Peter Ross to Ralph R. Gurley, May 15, 1857. In Wiley, *Slaves No More*: 167.

22. Letter from Henry B. Stewart to William McLain, November 23, 1848. In Wiley, *Slaves No More*: 282.

23. Burin. *Slavery and the Peculiar Solution*: 148–49.

24. Ibid.

25. Letter from James P. Skipwith to John Hartwell Cocke, February 11, 1859. In Miller, *Dear Master*: 129.

26. Letter from J. W. Lugenbeel to William McLain, January 4, 1848. Papers of the ACS.

27. Letter from Lugenbeel to McLain, January 4, 1848. Papers of the ACS.

28. Letter from Captain J. I. Nicholson to U.S. Secretary of the Navy Mahlon Dickerson, January 8, 1837. In Huberich, *Political and Legislative History*: 512.

29. Letter from Moses Jackson to Eliott West, March 22, 1846. In Wiley, *Slaves No More*: 257.

30. Brooks, George E. Jr. A. A. (ed.). "Adee's Journal of a Visit to Liberia in 1827." *Liberian Studies Journal*, volume I, number 1 (1968): 66.

31. Letter from Diana Skipwith to Sally Cocke, August 24, 1837. In Miller, *Dear Master*: 87.

32. Letter from Diana Skipwith James to Sally Cocke, March 6, 1843. In Wiley, *Slaves No More*: 57.

33. Letter from George Jones to Ralph R. Gurley, October 11, 1856. In ibid.: 166.

34. Letter from Washington W. McDonough to John McDonough, October 19, 1842. In ibid.: 123.

35. Letter from Peyton Skipwith to John Cocke, May 20, 1839. In Miller, *Dear Master*: 70.

36. Brooks. "Adee's Journal": 60.

37. Letter from H. W. Ellis to William McLain, November 20, 1849. In Wiley, *Slaves No More*: 228.

38. ACS Minutes of the Board of Managers, January 1838. In Huberich, *Political and Legislative History*: 523.

39. "Extract from Eliza Hatter's Letter to Her Sister." In *African Repository*, volume 8, number 9 (November 1832): 280.

40. Johnson, Charles. *Bitter Canaan: The Story of the Negro Republic*. New Brunswick, NJ: Transaction Books, 1987 (reprint of 1930 edition): 73.

41. Letter from Peyton Skipwith to John Cocke, February 10, 1834. In Miller, *Dear Master*: 58.

42. Nesbit, William. "Four Months in Liberia: Or African Colonization Exposed," 1855. In Moses, Wilson Jeremiah (ed.), *Liberian Dreams: Back-to-Africa Narratives from the 1850s*. University Park: Pennsylvania State University Press, 1998: 90.

43. Letter from Matilda Skipwith Lomax to John Cocke, November 23, 1849. In Miller, *Dear Master*: 104.
44. Letter from Peyton Skipwith to John Cocke, April 22, 1840. In ibid.: 75.
45. Letter from Diana Skipwith James to Sally Cocke, March 6, 1843. In Wiley, *Slaves No More*: 57.
46. Letter from Alexander Hance to J.H.B. Latrobe, April 7, 1838. In ibid.: 218.
47. "Intelligence from Liberia." In *African Repository*, volume 5, number 4 (June 1829): 125.
48. Letter from James Skipwith to John Cocke, August 20, 1859. In Miller, *Dear Master*: 130.
49. Letter from Peyton Skipwith to John Cocke, April 27, 1836. In ibid.: 60–61.
50. Letter from Peyton Skipwith to John Cocke, January 30, 1838. In ibid.: 62.
51. Letter from Diana Skipwith to Sally Cocke, May 7, 1838. In ibid.: 89.
52. Letter from Peyton Skipwith to John Cocke, September 29, 1844. In ibid.: 80.
53. Letter from Richard Cannon to John Cocke, September 29, 1844. In Wiley, *Slaves No More*: 61.
54. Letter from James W. Wilson to William McLain, August 5, 1858. In ibid.: 245.
55. Letter from Abraham Blackford to Mary B. Blackford, February 14, 1846. In ibid.: 24.
56. Liberian Declaration of Independence, July 26, 1847. In Huberich, *Political and Legislative History*: 830–31.

4. Africa's Lone Star

1. Letter from Joseph Blake to Ralph R. Gurley, May 13, 1835. Papers of the American Colonization Society, Library of Congress.
2. Huberich, Charles. *The Political and Legislative History of Liberia* (volume 1). New York: Central Book Company, 1947: 403.
3. Clegg, Claude A. III. *The Price of Liberty: African Americans and the Making of Liberia*. Chapel Hill: University of North Carolina Press, 2004: 104.
4. Constitution for the African Settlement at———, 1820. In Huberich, *Political and Legislative History*: 146.
5. Report of the Board of Managers of the ACS, November 19, 1830. In ibid.: 398.
6. "Latest from Liberia." In *African Repository*, volume 8, number 10 (December 1832): 298.
7. Letter from Joseph Mechlin to Ralph Gurley, October 15, 1830. In Huberich, *Political and Legislative History*: 404.
8. Jones, Hannah Abeodu Bowen. "The Struggle for Political and Cultural Unification in Liberia, 1847–1930." Dissertation, Northwestern University, 1962: 136.
9. Roberts, Joseph Jenkins. First Inaugural, January 3, 1848. In Guannu, Joseph Saye (ed.), *The Inaugural Addresses of the Presidents of Liberia: From Joseph Jenkins*

Roberts to William Richard Tolbert, Jr., 1848–1976. Hicksville, NY: Exposition Press, 1980: 7–8.

10. Thomas, Charles W. *Adventures and Observations on the West Coast of Africa and Its Islands.* New York: Derby & Jackson, 1860: 156.

11. Ibid.

12. Johnston, Harry. *Liberia* (Volume 2). New York: Negro Universities Press, 1969 (reprint of 1906 edition): 149–50.

13. Blyden, Edward Wilmot. "Liberia as She Is; and the Present Duty of Her Citizens," July 27, 1857. In Lynch, Hollis R. (ed.), *Black Spokesman: Selected Published Writings of Edward Wilmot Blyden.* New York: Humanties Press, 1971: 64.

14. Letter from Sion Harris to William McLain, May 20, 1849. In Wiley, Bell I. (ed.), *Slaves No More: Letters from Liberia, 1833–1869.* Lexington: University Press of Kentucky, 1980: 227.

15. Syfert, Dwight N. "The Origins of Privilege: Liberian Merchants, 1822–1847." *Liberian Studies Journal,* volume VI, number 2 (1975): 116.

16. Ibid.: 122.

17. Letter from Francis Burns to Samuel Wilkeson, April 2, 1841. ACS Papers.

18. Shick, Tom. *Behold the Promised Land: A History of Afro-American Settler Society in Nineteenth-Century Liberia.* Baltimore: Johns Hopkins University Press, 1977: 40.

19. Letter from Joseph Denman to Joseph Roberts, October 6, 1841. Commerce Committee, U.S. House of Representatives. *On the African Slave Trade.* Washington: Gales and Seaton, 1843: 115

20. Skinner, Elliott P. *African Americans and U.S. Policy Toward Africa, 1850–1924: In Defense of Black Nationality.* Washington: Howard University Press, 1992: 115.

21. *African Repository,* volume 22, number 5 (May 1846): 159.

22. Letter from Peyton Skipwith to John Hartwell Cocke, June 25, 1846. In Miller, Randall M. (ed.), *Dear Master: Letters of a Slave Family.* Athens: University of Georgia Press, 1990: 82.

23. Letter from Joseph Roberts to Colonial Secretary (Sierra Leone) J. N. Lewis, October 7, 1841. In Commerce Committee, *On African Slave Trade.* 1843: 115.

24. Blyden, Edward Wilmot. "A Chapter in the History of Liberia," July 1892. In Lynch, *Black Spokesman:* 112.

25. Burrowes, Carl Patrick. "Black Christian Republicans: Delegates to the 1847 Liberian Constitutional Convention." *Liberian Studies Journal,* volume XIV, number 2 (1989): 80.

26. Extracts from the Journal of J. W. Lugenbeel. In Huberich, *Political and Legislative History:* 823, 825.

27. Ibid.: 823.

28. Message of Governor Roberts to Members of the Legislature, January 4, 1847. In ibid.: 809–10.

29. Extracts from Journal of Lugenbeel. In ibid.: 824.

30. Liberian Declaration of Independence, July 26, 1847. In ibid.: 828.

31. Constitution of the Republic of Liberia, 1848. In ibid.: 852–53.

32. Burrowes, Carl Patrick. "Textual Sources of the 1847 Liberian Constitution." *Liberian Studies Journal*, volume XXIII, number 1 (1998): 8.

33. Constitution of Liberia, 1848. In Huberich, *Political and Legislative History*: 863.

34. Liberian Declaration of Independence, July 26, 1847. In ibid.: 829.

35. Constitution of Liberia, 1848. In ibid.: 863.

36. Extracts from Journal of Lugenbeel. In ibid.: 825.

6. A Matter of Color

1. Blyden, Edward W. "An Address before the Maine State Colonization Society, Portland, Maine, June 26th, 1862." In Lynch, Hollis (ed.), *Black Spokesman: Selected Published Writings of Edward Wilmot Blyden*. New York: Humanities Press, 1971: 17.

2. Lynch, Hollis R. *Edward Wilmot Blyden: Pan-Negro Patriot, 1832–1912*. New York: Oxford University Press, 1967: 106.

3. Blyden. "An Address." In *Black Spokesman*: 15

4. Ibid.

5. Ibid.: 16.

6. Lynch, *Pan-Negro Patriot*: 6.

7. *African Repository*, volume 15, number 7 (1831): 260.

8. Washington, Augustus. "Liberia As It Is, 1854." In Moses, Wilson Jeremiah, *Liberian Dreams: Back-to-Africa Narratives from the 1850s*. University Park: Pennsylvania State University Press, 1998: 203.

9. Johnson, Michael P., and James L. Roark. *Black Masters: A Free Family of Color in the Old South*. New York: W. W. Norton, 1984: 225.

10. Clegg, Claude A. III. *The Price of Liberty: African Americans and the Making of Liberia*. Chapel Hill: University of North Carolina Press, 2004: 70.

11. Berlin, Ira. *Slaves Without Masters: The Free Negro in the Antebellum South*. New York: The New Press, 1974: 277.

12. Johnson and Roark. *Black Masters*: 215.

13. De Toqueville, Alexis. *Democracy in America*, volume 1 (translated by Henry Reeve). New York: Alfred A. Knopf, 1972: 389.

14. Lynch, *Pan-Negro Patriot*: 13.

15. Ibid.: 150.

16. Ibid.: 15.

17. Ibid.: 19.

18. Singler, John V. "Language in Liberia in the Nineteenth Century: The Settlers' Perspective." *Liberian Studies Journal*, volume VII, number 2 (1976–77): 77.

19. Lynch, *Pan-Negro Patriot*: 15.

20. Ibid.: 68.

21. Fairhead, James, Tim Geysbeek, Svend E. Holsoe, and Melissa Leach (eds.), *African-American Explorations in West Africa: Four Nineteenth-Century Diaries.* Bloomington: Indiana University Press, 2003: 26.

22. Jones, Hannah Abeodu Bowen. "The Struggle for Political and Cultural Unification in Liberia, 1847–1930." Dissertation, Northwestern University, 1962: 175–76.

23. Ibid.: 175.

24. Ibid.

25. Lynch, *Pan-Negro Patriot*: 151.

26. Ibid.: 141.

27. Blyden, Edward. "A Chapter in the History of Liberia." In Lynch, *Black Spokesman*: 100.

28. Jones, "Struggle for Political and Cultural Unification": 173.

29. Blyden, Edward. "A Chapter in the History of Liberia." In Lynch, *Black Spokesman*: 117.

30. Jones, "Struggle for Political and Cultural Unification": 172–73.

31. *African Repository*, volume 46, number 4 (1870): 121.

32. Holsoe, Svend E. "A Portrait of a Black Midwestern Family During the Early Nineteenth Century: Edward James Roye and His Parents." *Liberian Studies Journal*, volume III, number 1 (1970–71): 50.

33. Ibid.: 51.

34. Guannu, Joseph Saye. *The Inaugural Addresses of the Presidents of Liberia: From Joseph Jenkins Roberts to William Richard Tolbert, Jr., 1848–1976.* Hicksville, NY: Exposition Press, 1980: 78.

35. Ibid.: 76–77.

36. Lynch, *Pan-Negro Patriot*: 51.

37. Ibid.: 44.

38. Ibid.: 53.

39. Ibid.

40. *African Repository*, volume 46, number 4 (1870): 100–101.

41. *African Repository*, volume 49, number 6 (1873): 173.

42. Huberich, Charles Henry. *The Political and Legislative History of Liberia* (volume 2). New York: Central Book Company, 1947: 1133.

43. *African Repository*, volume 48, number 8 (1872): 255.

44. *African Repository*, volume 48, number 7 (1872): 221.

45. Shick, Tom. *Behold the Promised Land: A History of Afro-American Settler Society in Nineteenth-Century Liberia.* Baltimore: The Johns Hopkins University Press, 1977: 121.

46. Blyden, Edward. "Liberia as She Is; and the Present Duty of Her Citizens." In Lynch, *Black Spokesman*: 63.

47. Lynch, *Black Spokesman*: 141.

6. The African Banquet

1. Letter from John Seys, U.S. Vice Consular Agent, Monrovia to Lewis Cass, Sec'y of State, August 23, 1859, in Despatches of the United States Consulate in Monrovia, 1859–1906, Reel 2.

2. Letter from Consulate General of the U.S. in Monrovia J. H. Smyth, April 27, 1880, to John Hay, Asst. Sec'y of State, Despatches of the United States Consulate in Monrovia, 1859–1906, Reel 4.

3. Johnston, Harry. *Liberia* (volume 1). New York: Negro Universities Press, 1969 (reprint of 1906 edition): 402.

4. Syfert, Dwight N. "The Liberian Coasting Trade, 1822–1900" in *Journal of African History*, volume XVIII, number 2 (1977): 231.

5. Price, Robert William. "The Black Republic of Liberia, 1822–1912: A Ninety-Year Struggle for International Acceptance." PhD Dissertation, University of Illinois, Urbana-Champaign, 1980: 153.

6. Ibid.: 158–59.

7. Ibid.: 161.

8. Starr, Frederick. *Liberia: Description, History, Problems*. Chicago: S.N. (sine nomine, no name), 1913: 114.

9. McCoy to Secretary of State, February 1, 1893, number 52 in U.S. Department of State. Despatches from the United States Ministers to Liberia, 1863–1906, Microform M170-11.

10. Price, "Black Republic": 173–74.

11. Fairhead, James, Tim Geysbeek, Svend E. Holsoe, and Melissa Leach (eds). *African-American Explorations in West Africa: Four Nineteenth-Century Diaries*. Bloomington: Indiana University Press, 2003: 28.

12. Geysbeek, Tim. "The Anderson-D'Ollone Controversy of 1903–04: Race, Imperialism, and the Reconfiguration of the Liberia-Guinea Border." In *History in Africa*, volume 31 (2004): 201.

13. Ibid.

14. Ibid.: 203.

15. Ibid.

16. Ibid.: 206.

17. Ibid.: 203.

18. *Liberian Recorder*, August 29, 1903: 10.

19. Price, "Black Republic": 63.

20. *Liberia Recorder*, August 6, 1904: 5.

21. Starr, *Liberia*: 125.

22. Ibid.: 122.

23. Ibid.: 127–28.

24. Erhagbe, Edward O. "African-Americans and the Defense of African States Against European Imperial Conquest: Booker T. Washington's Diplomatic

Efforts to Guarantee Liberia's Independence, 1907–1911" in *African Studies Review*, volume 39, number 1 (April 1996): 57.

25. Ibid.

26. Starr, *Liberia*: 216.

27. Ibid.: 211.

28. Ibid.: 41.

29. Akpan, M. B. "The Liberian Economy in the Nineteenth Century: Government Finances." *Liberian Studies Journal*, volume VI, number 2 (1975): 153.

30. Quoted in Clegg, Claude A. "'A Splendid Type of Colored American': Charles Young and the Reorganization of the Liberian Frontier Force." In *International Journal of African Historical Studies*, volume 29, number 1 (1996): 53.

31. Rainey, Timothy A. "Buffalo Soldiers in Africa: The U.S. Army and the Liberian Frontier Force, 1912–1927—An Overview." *Liberian Studies Journal*, volume XXI, number 2 (1996): 217.

32. Clegg, "A Splendid Type": 66.

7. Conquering Hero

1. Cronon, E. David. *Black Moses: The Story of Marcus Garvey and the Universal Negro Improvement Association*. Madison: University of Wisconsin Press, 1969: 65.

2. Ibid.

3. "Reports of the Convention," August 4, 1920. In Hill, Robert A. (ed.), *The Marcus Garvey and Universal Negro Improvement Association Papers* (volume 2). Berkeley: University of California Press, 1983–2011: 529.

4. "Elie Garcia, UNIA Commissioner to Liberia, to Marcus Garvey and the UNIA," August 1920. In Hill, *Garvey Papers*: 662–63.

5. Ibid.: 663–64.

6. Ibid.: 663.

7. Ibid.: 667.

8. Ibid.

9. "Joseph L. Johnson to the U.S. Secretary of State," July 16, 1921. In Hill, *Garvey Papers*, 1983–2011 (volume 9): 89.

10. "Cyril A. Crichlow to Marcus Garvey," June 24, 1921. In Hill, *Garvey Papers*, 1983–2011 (volume 3): 485.

11. Ibid.: 486–87.

12. Ibid.: 487–88.

13. "Cyril A. Crichlow to the UNIA Executive Council," June 19, 1921. In Hill, *Garvey Papers*, 1983–2011 (volume 3): 478.

14. "Supplementary Report from Cyril A. Crichlow to Marcus Garvey," July 4, 1921. In Hill, *Garvey Papers*, 1983–2011 (volume 9): 56.

15. Ibid.: 55–56.

16. "Cyril A. Crichlow to the UNIA Executive Council," June 19, 1921. In Hill, *Garvey Papers*, 1983–2011 (volume 3): 485–90.

17. "Cyril Henry to O. M. Thompson," July 1, 1921. In Hill, *Garvey Papers*, 1983–2011 (volume 3): 503.

18. *African Repository*, volume 3, number 12 (December 1827): 301–302.

19. "Cyril A. Crichlow to the UNIA Executive Council," June 19, 1921. In Hill, *Garvey Papers*, 1983–2011 (volume 3): 488.

20. "Eliézer Cadet to *L'Essor*," June 10, 1919. In Hill, *Garvey Papers* (volume 1), 1983–2011: 418.

21. "Marcus Garvey to President C.D.B. King," August 4, 1921. In Hill, *Garvey Papers*, 1983–2011 (volume 3): 619.

22. "Alfred Hampton, Assistant Commissioner General, Bureau of Immigration, to J. Edgar Hoover," March 11, 1921. In Hill, *Garvey Papers*, 1983–2011 (volume 3): 254.

23. Du Bois, W.E.B. "Marcus Garvey." In *Crisis* 21 (January 1921): 112.

24. Du Bois, W.E.B. "Back to Africa." In *Century Magazine* 105 (February 1923): 547.

25. "Open Letter from C.D.B. King in the *Crisis*," June 1921. In Hill, Garvey Papers, 1983–2011 (volume 9): 51.

26. "Report by Special Agent P-138," May 18, 1921. In Hill, *Garvey Papers*, 1983–2011 (volume 3): 421.

27. Ibid.: 421–22.

28. "Marcus Garvey to President C.D.B. King," August 4, 1921. In Hill, *Garvey Papers*, 1983–2011 (volume 3): 619.

29. Crichlow, Cyril A. "What I Know About Liberia," in *The Crusader*, December 1921. In Hill, *Garvey Papers*, 1983–2011 (volume 9): 293.

30. Kornweibel, Theodore, Jr. *Seeing Red: Federal Campaigns against Black Militancy, 1919–1925*. Bloomington: Indiana University Press, 1998: 102.

31. "Elie Garcia, UNIA Commissioner to Liberia, to Marcus Garvey and the UNIA," August 1920. In Hill, *Garvey Papers*, 1983–2011 (volume 2): 667.

32. "Statement of Hubert H. Harrison," January 16, 1922. In Hill, *Garvey Papers*, 1983–2011 (volume 4): 425.

33. "Editorial Letter by Marcus Garvey," December 29, 1920. In Hill, *Garvey Papers*, 1983–2011 (volume 3): 114.

34. "Elie Garcia, UNIA Commissioner to Liberia, to Marcus Garvey and the UNIA," August 1920. In Hill, *Garvey Papers*, 1983–2011 (volume 2): 667.

35. Jacques-Garvey, Amy (ed.). *Philosophy and Opinions of Marcus Garvey* (volumes 1 and 2). New York: Atheneum, 1971: 366.

36. "Elie Garcia, UNIA Commissioner to Liberia, to Marcus Garvey and the UNIA," August 1920. In Hill, *Garvey Papers*, 1983–2011 (volume 2): 667.

37. "British Military Intelligence Report," January 7, 1920. In Hill, *Garvey Papers*, 1983–2011 (volume 2): 179.

38. "Article in the *Baltimore Afro-American*," July 15, 1921. In Hill, *Garvey Papers*, 1983–2011 (volume 9): 76.

39. "Memorandum by the Division of Western European Affairs, Department of State," April 8, 1921. In Hill, *Garvey Papers*, 1983–2011 (volume 3): 348.

40. "Opening Speech by Gabriel M. Johnson," August 1, 1922. In Hill, *Garvey Papers*, 1983–2011 (volume 4): 761.

41. Hill, *Garvey Papers*, 1983–2011 (volume 5): 591, note 5.

42. "Report of the UNIA Delegation to Liberia," August 27, 1924. In Hill, *Garvey Papers*, 1983–2011 (volume 5): 792.

43. "Article by Abraham H. Butler, Sr., in the *Baltimore Afro-American*," June 4, 1924. In Hill, *Garvey Papers*, 1983–2011 (volume 10): 177–78.

44. "Speech by Rev. R. Van Richards," June 29, 1924. In Hill, *Garvey Papers*, 1983–2011 (volume 10): 203.

45. "Article in the *Negro World*," June 14, 1924. In Hill, *Garvey Papers*, 1983–2011 (volume 10): 186.

46. "Edwin Barclay, Liberian Secretary of State, to Ernest S. Lyon, Consul General of Liberia, Baltimore," July 3, 1924. In Hill, *Garvey Papers*, 1983–2011 (volume 10): 204.

47. "UNIA to President C.D.B. King," August 3, 1924. In Hill, *Garvey Papers*, 1983–2011 (volume 10): 646.

48. "Convention Report," August 14, 1924. In Hill, *Garvey Papers*, 1983–2011 (volume 10): 737.

49. Hill, *Garvey Papers*, 1983–2011 (volume 10): 690, note 4.

50. "Enclosure: Article in the *Liberian News*," August 1924. In Hill, *Garvey Papers*, 1983–2011 (volume 10): 232.

51. Buell, Raymond. *Native Problem in Africa* (volume 2). New York: Macmillan, 1928: 733.

52. Knoll, Arthur J. "Harvey S. Firestone's Liberian Investment (1922–1932)." *Liberian Studies Journal*, volume XIV, number 1 (1989): 17.

53. *Liberian News*, May 1925: 4.

54. Chaudhuri, J. Pal. "British Reaction to the Firestone Investment in Liberia." *Liberian Studies Journal*, volume V, number 1 (1972–74): 40.

55. Knoll, "Firestone's Liberian Investment," 1989: 23.

8. The Slave Ring

1. Greene, Graham. *Journey Without Maps*. New York: Penguin Books, 1978 (1936): 238.

2. Johnson, Charles. *Bitter Canaan: The Story of the Negro Republic*. New Brunswick, NJ: Transaction Books, 1987 (reprint of 1948 edition): 161.

3. Ibid.

4. Liberian Constitution, 1847, Article 1, section 4. In Huberich, Charles Henry,

The Political and Legislative History of Liberia (volume 2). New York: Central Book Company, 1947: 853.

5. Schuyler, Charles. *Slaves Today: A Story of Liberia*. College Park, MD: McGrath Publishing Company, 1969 (1931): 170.

6. Azikiwe, Nnamdi. *Liberia in World Politics*. London: Arthur H. Stockwell, 1934: 170.

7. *Liberian Patriot*, January 3, 1931: 10.

8. Azikiwe, *Liberia in World Politics*: 182.

9. Du Bois, W. E. Burghardt. "Liberia, the League and the United States." *Foreign Affairs* 11:4 (July 1933): 687.

10. Sundiata Ibrahim. *Brothers and Strangers: Black Zion, Black Slavery, 1914–1940*. Durham, NC: Duke University Press, 2003: 83.

11. Johnson, *Bitter Canaan*, 1987: 163.

12. Ibid.: 165.

13. Ibid.: 163.

14. Ibid.: 165.

15. *National Echo*, June 1930: 3.

16. Johnson, *Bitter Canaan*: 165.

17. Ibid.: 9.

18. Buell, Raymond Leslie. "The Liberian Paradox." *The Virginia Quarterly Review* 7:2 (April 1931): 163–64.

19. Sundiata, *Brothers and Strangers*: 13.

20. "Appointment of the International Commission of Inquiry into the Existence of Slavery and Forced Labor in the Republic of Liberia, The Secretary of State to the Minister in Liberia (Francis)," June 5, 1929. In U.S. Department of State, *Papers Relating to the Foreign Relations of the United States, 1929*. Washington: Government Printing Office, 1944: 274.

21. "Appointment of the International Commission, The Chargé in Liberia (Wharton) to the Secretary of State," August 1, 1929. In Department of State, *Papers Relating to Foreign Relations, 1944*: 293.

22. Yancy, Ernest Jerome. *Historical Lights of Liberia's Yesterday and Today*. Xenia, OH: Alline Publishing, 1934: 289.

23. Johnson, *Bitter Canaan*: 176.

24. "Appointment of the International Commission, The Chargé in Liberia (Wharton) to the Secretary of State," August 1, 1929. In Department of State, *Papers Relating to Foreign Relations, 1944*: 293.

25. Ibid.: 215.

26. Ibid.: 199.

27. Ibid.: 201.

28. Ibid.: 199.

29. Ibid.: 183.

30. Ibid.: 181.

31. *Crozierville Observer*, October, 30, 1930: 1.

32. *African Watchman*, September and October, 1930: 2.

33. *Liberian Patriot*, November 15, 1930: 4.

34. "Statement Made by Dr. Juris Antoine Sottile, Discussion of the Report of the International Commission of Enquiry in Liberia Concerning Slavery and Forced Labour," January 22, 1931: 4. In Louis Grimes Papers, Part II, Roll 1.

35. Azikiwe, *Liberia in World Politics*: 288–89.

36. "Conditions on the Kru Coast, Report of the Investigation Conducted on the Authority of the Diplomatic Representatives of the British, French, and U.S.A. Governments," March 14–April 14, 1932: 2. In Louis Grimes Papers, Part III, Roll 1.

37. Sundiata, *Brothers and Strangers*: 151.

9. The Original African Big Man

1. "The Observence of President Tubman's Birthday in Liberia," October 1965 (unpublished manuscript): 2. In Albert Porte Papers, Microform Reel 1.

2. Ibid.

3. *Liberian Star*, November 26, 1965 (Special Birthday Supplement): xiv.

4. *Daily Listener*, September 4, 1969: 1.

5. Jimmy Barrolle, interview with author, March 10, 1997.

6. Ibid.

7. Smith, Robert A. *William V. S. Tubman: The Life and Work of an African Statesman*. Amsterdam: Van Ditmar, 1966: 31.

8. Lewis, Norman. "Our Far-Flung Correspondents: Tubman Bids Us Toil." In *The New Yorker* 33 (January 11, 1958): 98.

9. Greenwood, Ralph. "The Presidency of William V. S. Tubman, President of Liberia, 1944–1971." Dissertation, Northern Arizona University, 1993: 23.

10. Hogue, Dock. "Liberian Road." In *Atlantic Monthly*, May 1945: 65.

11. Henries, A. Doris Banks. *A Biography of President William V. S. Tubman*. London: Macmillan, 1967: 23.

12. Smith, Robert A. *William V. S. Tubman, 1895–1971: A Profile of an African President & Statesman*. Monrovia: Providence Publications, 1971: 31–32.

13. Mohr, Charles. "Tolbert Will Change Liberia: Question is 'How Much?'" In *New York Times*, November 9, 1971: 14.

14. Simpson, Clarence Lorenzo. *The Memoirs of C. L. Simpson*. London: Diplomatic Press and Publishing Company, 1961: 147.

15. Liebenow, J. Gus. *Liberia: The Evolution of Privilege*. Ithaca, NY: Cornell University Press, 1969: 85.

16. Simpson, *Memoirs*, 1961: 147.

17. *African Nationalist* (Liberia), January 9, 1943: 1.

18. Fraenkel, Merran. *Tribe and Class in Monrovia*. London: International African Institute and Oxford University Press, 1964: 193.

19. Hlophe, Stephen S. *Class, Ethnicity and Politics in Liberia: A Class Analysis of Power Struggles in the Tubman and Tolbert Administrations from 1944 to 1975.* Lanham, MD: University Press of America, 1979: 186.

20. Archie Bernard, interview with author, February 14, 1997.

21. Adolphus Kollie, interview with author, February 12, 1997.

22. Anderson, Benjamin. *Journeys to Musadu.* London: Frank Cass and Company, 1971 (1870): 83.

23. Farmer, Garland R. "About Landsdell Christie, the Liberian Iron Ore Industry and Some Related People and Events: Getting There." *Liberian Studies Journal,* volume XVI, number 1 (1991): 4.

24. Smith, Robert A. *We Are Obligated: An Interpretative Analysis of Twenty-Five Years of Progressive Leadership.* Hamburg: Hanseatische Druckanstalt, 1969: 131.

25. Ibid.

26. Greenwood, "Presidency of William V. S. Tubman": 95.

27. "Uncle Shad Forever?" *Time,* January 17, 1964: 27.

28. Porte, Albert. "Thinking about 'Unthinkable' Things: The Democratic Way," November 1967: 23–24. In Albert Porte Papers, Microform Reel 1.

29. *The Listener,* May 14–15, 1963: 4.

30. Arthur Cole, interview with author, March 3, 1997.

31. Cooper, Helene. *The House at Sugar Beach: A Memoir.* New York: Simon and Schuster, 2008: 9.

32. Henries, *Biography of William V. S. Tubman*: 6.

33. Smith, *William V. S. Tubman*: 18.

34. Townsend, E. Reginald, ed. *The Official Papers of William V. S. Tubman, President of the Republic of Liberia: Covering Addresses, Messages, Speeches, and Statements, 1960–1967.* London: Longmans Green, 1968: 189.

35. Townsend, E. Reginald. "Unification: Highways to Harmony." *New York Times,* November 27, 1966 (Advertising Supplement): K18, 31.

36. Tubman, William V. S., "To the Special Delegations of the Tribal People," January 22, 1955. In Townsend, E. Reginald, ed., *President Tubman of Liberia Speaks.* London: Consolidated Publications, 1959: 113.

37. Fraenkel, *Tribe and Class*: 201.

38. Ibid.: 170.

39. Padmore, George Arthur. *The Memoirs of Liberian Ambassador George Arthur Padmore.* Lewiston, ME: Edwin Mellen Press, 1996: 25–26.

40. Fraenkel, *Tribe and Class*: 115.

41. James Wolo, interview with author, February 22, 1997.

42. Bart Winteveen, interview with author, February 21, 1997.

43. Wreh, Tuan. *The Love of Liberty: The Rule of President William V. S. Tubman in Liberia, 1944–1971.* London: C. Hurst, 1976: 44.

44. Fraenkel, *Tribe and Class*: 35.

45. Eugene Cooper, interview with author, March 10, 1997.

46. "At the First National Executive Council of Chiefs," March 24, 1954. In Townsend, *Tubman Speaks*: 236.

47. Wreh, *Love of Liberty*: 44.

48. Ibid.

49. "Opposition Tenderized," *Time*, May 21, 1951: 31.

50. Sundiata, Ibrahim. *Brothers and Strangers: Black Zion, Black Slavery, 1914–1940*. Durham, NC: Duke University Press, 2003: 275.

51. "Twe, Didwho." In Dunn, D. Elwood, and Svend E. Holsoe. *Historical Dictionary of Liberia*. Metuchen, NJ: Scarecrow Press, 1985: 177.

52. Sundiata, *Brothers and Strangers*: 276.

53. Meeker, Oden, and Olivia Meeker, "Letter from Liberia," *The New Yorker*, November 29, 1952: 119–20.

54. "Broadcast on Didho Twe and the Reformation Party," May 1951. In Townsend, *Tubman Speaks*: 97.

55. "Shooting at Uncle Shad," *Time*, July 4, 1955: 26.

56. Wreh, *Love of Liberty*: 77.

57. Greenwood, "Presidency of William V. S. Tubman": 46–47.

58. Wreh, *Love of Liberty*: 60.

59. Ibid.: 92.

60. *Official Report of William V. S. Tubman, President of the Republic of Liberia, to the National Legislature in Extraordinary Session, Monrovia, on the Incident of the Assassination Attempt, June 22, 1955*. Monrovia: Government Printing Office, July 11, 1955: 7.

61. "To the Nation on the Assassination Attempt," November 8, 1955. In Townsend, *Tubman Speaks*: 139.

62. "Coleman Still Re-Crosses Mr. Onemegba," *The Listener*, January 30–31, 1955: 1.

63. *Official Report on the Incident of the Assassination Attempt*, July 11, 1955: 9.

64. Ibid.: 6.

65. *The Plot That Failed: The Story of the Attempted Assassination of President Tubman*. Monrovia: Liberian Information Service, 1959: 8.

66. Ibid.: 6.

67. *Official Report on the Incident of the Assassination Attempt*, July 11, 1955: 4.

68. *The Plot That Failed*: 8–9.

69. Wreh, *Love of Liberty*: 82.

70. "The Old Pro," *Time*, May 18, 1959: 30.

71. "Uncle Shad's Jubilee," *Time*, January 17, 1969: 20.

10. Father and Son

1. Walton, Hanes Jr., James Bernard Rosser, Jr., and Robert L. Stevenson (eds.). *Liberian Politics: The Portrait by African American Diplomat J. Milton Turner*. Lanham, MD: Lexington Books, 2002: 77.

2. Interview with Cllr. Chea Cheapoo in Truth and Reconciliation Commission Thematic and Institutional Hearings (transcribed for the author by T. Dickson Fully; available in audio form at the Special Court for Sierra Leone website: www.sc-sl.org), August 5, 2008: 3.

3. Jimmy Wiles, interview with author, February 15, 1997.

4. Interview with Cheapoo, Truth and Reconciliation Commission, August 5, 2008: 13.

5. Tolbert, Victoria Anna David. *Lifted Up: The Victoria Tolbert Story*. Minneapolis: Macalester Park Publishing, 1996: 102.

6. Togba-Nah Tipoteh, interview with author, March 6, 1997.

7. Interview with Cheapoo, Truth and Reconciliation Commission, August 5, 2008: 13.

8. Mohr, Charles. "Liberia Is Changing After the Tubman Era," *New York Times*, November 1, 1971: A14.

9. Archie Bernard, interview with author, February 14, 1997.

10. Ibid.

11. Boley, G. E. Saigbe. *Liberia: The Rise and Fall of the First Republic*. New York: Macmillan, 1983: 103.

12. Cooper, Helene. *The House at Sugar Beach: A Memoir*. New York: Simon and Schuster, 2008: 134.

13. Winfrey, Carey. "After Liberia's Costly Rioting, Great Soul-Searching," *New York Times*, May 30, 1979: A2.

14. Cooper. *House at Sugar Beach*: 135.

15. "An Official Account of the Civil Disturbances in Monrovia of April 14, 1979—What Happened." Monrovia: Ministry of State for Presidential Affairs, April 26, 1979: 1.

16. "Matthew Recants; Tolbert Replies." Monrovia [?]: MICAT Press, 1979: 4.

17. Johnson Sirleaf, Ellen. *This Child Will Be Great: Memoir of a Remarkable Lady by Africa's First Woman President*. New York: HarperCollins, 2009: 84.

18. Cooper. *House at Sugar Beach*: 131.

19. "Three Voices of Liberia: 'A Caring, Sharing Society,'" *West Africa*, February 18, 1980: 289, 293.

20. "Behind the Strike Call in Liberia," *West Africa*, April 7, 1980: 605.

21. Ibid.

22. Tolbert. *Lifted Up*: 138.

23. "Liberia: Quiwonkpa Breaks His Silence," *West Africa*, June 17, 1985: 1204.

24. "Doe's First Nationwide Broadcast, April 14, 1980." In Omonijo, Mobolade, *The Liberian Tragedy*. Ikeja, Nigeria: Sahel, 1990: 65.

25. Gutpe, Pranay B. "New Liberia Rulers Press Populist Line," *New York Times*, April 20, 1980: 7.

26. Cooper. *House at Sugar Beach*: 173–74.

27. Interview with Cheapoo, Truth and Reconciliation Commission, August 5, 2008: 30, 39.

28. Liebenow, J. Gus. *Liberia: The Quest for Democracy*. Bloomington: Indiana University Press, 1987: 171.

Epilogue

1. Johnson Sirleaf, Ellen. *This Child Will Be Great: Memoir of a Remarkable Lady by Africa's First Woman President*. New York: HarperCollins, 2009: 138.

2. Ellis, Stephen. *The Mask of Anarchy: The Destruction of Liberia and the Religious Dimension of an African Civil War*. New York: New York University Press, 1999: 78.

3. Cooper, Helene. *The House at Sugar Beach: A Memoir*. New York: Simon and Schuster, 2008: 255.

4. Author's journal, July 15, 1997.

5. Johnson Sirleaf. *This Child Will Be Great*: 221.

6. Al-Hassan Conteh, interview with author, March 4, 1997.

7. Peterson, Daniel H. *The Looking Glass: Being a True Report and Narrative of the Life, Travels, and Labors of the Rev. Daniel H. Peterson*. New York: Wright, Printer, 1854: 124.

ACKNOWLEDGMENTS

There is much accumulated interest on the debts I owe to those who played a role in the making of this book. First and foremost are the many Liberians who shared their time, their thoughts, and their voices. My visits coincided with some of the most traumatic episodes in their nation's history, with the end of its first civil war and the holding of a national election amid the tensions and destruction that war had left in its wake. They always remained gracious in spirit and generous with their time and energy.

I cannot speak highly enough of the courageous Liberian journalists who served as my guides, both figuratively and literally, helping me to understand the Liberian people and history in a way no written record can. They got me access to the people I needed to speak to and steered me around the many obstacles and dangers in a country emerging from war. In particular, I would like to thank James Dorbor and Henry Bestman. More generally, I would like to extend my gratitude to the many Liberians who sat down for interviews with me, often in the war-torn shells of their homes and workplaces. Many of the questions I asked them surely brought up painful memories. I want to thank Dickson Fully for transcribing Chea Cheapoo's testimony at the Liberian Truth and Reconciliation Commission.

I also send my heartfelt appreciation to those who made my stays in Liberia as comfortable and productive as they could be: the sisters of St. Teresa's Convent in Monrovia, the officials of the Firestone Natural Rubber Company, and especially Archie Bernard, who opened up his family's lovely Mamba Point house to me for a lengthy visit.

The non-Liberians who aided me in the country included the many NGO workers dedicating their lives to repairing a troubled land. In particular, I want to thank the folks at Médecins Sans Frontières and Save the Children, who allowed me to hitch rides with them up-country and provided me with safe and clean places to stay when I was there. No group, however, was more helpful than Friends of Liberia, an organization of still impassioned former Peace Corps workers, and its then director Jim Gray. Their decision to include me on their election monitoring team provided me an indispensable opportunity to further my research, even as it allowed me a chance to give something back to a country I had come to love. I also benefited immensely from the time I spent with my co-monitor Warren d'Azevedo, dean of Liberian anthropology. Back in the United States, I got helpful reminiscences about a long-lost Liberia from the Pepperbirds, expatriate alumni of the Firestone operations in Liberia.

Much of this book is based on historical sources. Sadly, Liberia's national archives were destroyed in the war. But through the dedicated efforts of the Indiana University Liberian Collections Project and its director Verlon Stone, much of its contents have been preserved and digitized in this country. Aside from d'Azevedo, scholars who aided my work include Al-Hassan Conteh, Elwood Dunn, and Svend Holsoe. I would also like to thank librarians and archivists at the Library of Congress and the Young Research Library at UCLA. The Liberian Studies Association and its publication, the *Liberian Studies Journal*, allowed me to keep up with the latest Liberian scholarship and developments.

This book would not have been possible without the support and guidance of my agent, Geri Thoma, and the editing staff at Hill and Wang: Dan Crissman, Thomas LeBien, and most especially Dan Gerstle. Without his editing skills and suggestions, this book would be a far wordier, and so far less worthy, read. I also extend thanks to the publicist, Brian Gittis. Other help in shaping the story came from my sister, Jill Ciment, and my dear friend and fellow historian Andrew Gyory, both of whom read and commented on lengthy excerpts of the manuscript.

Before signing off, I want to express my love to my wife, Irene, and the joys of our lives—Bibi and Bruno. I owe them many missed evenings and weekends. Lastly, I dedicate this book to my recently deceased mother, Gloria. Her love of life and learning has been an inspiration to me and to all of those who knew her.

INDEX

INDEX

Printed in the USA
CPSIA information can be obtained
at www.ICGtesting.com
LVHW090803150724
785511LV00004B/357